Kilnamanagh Castle and St Kevin's holy well

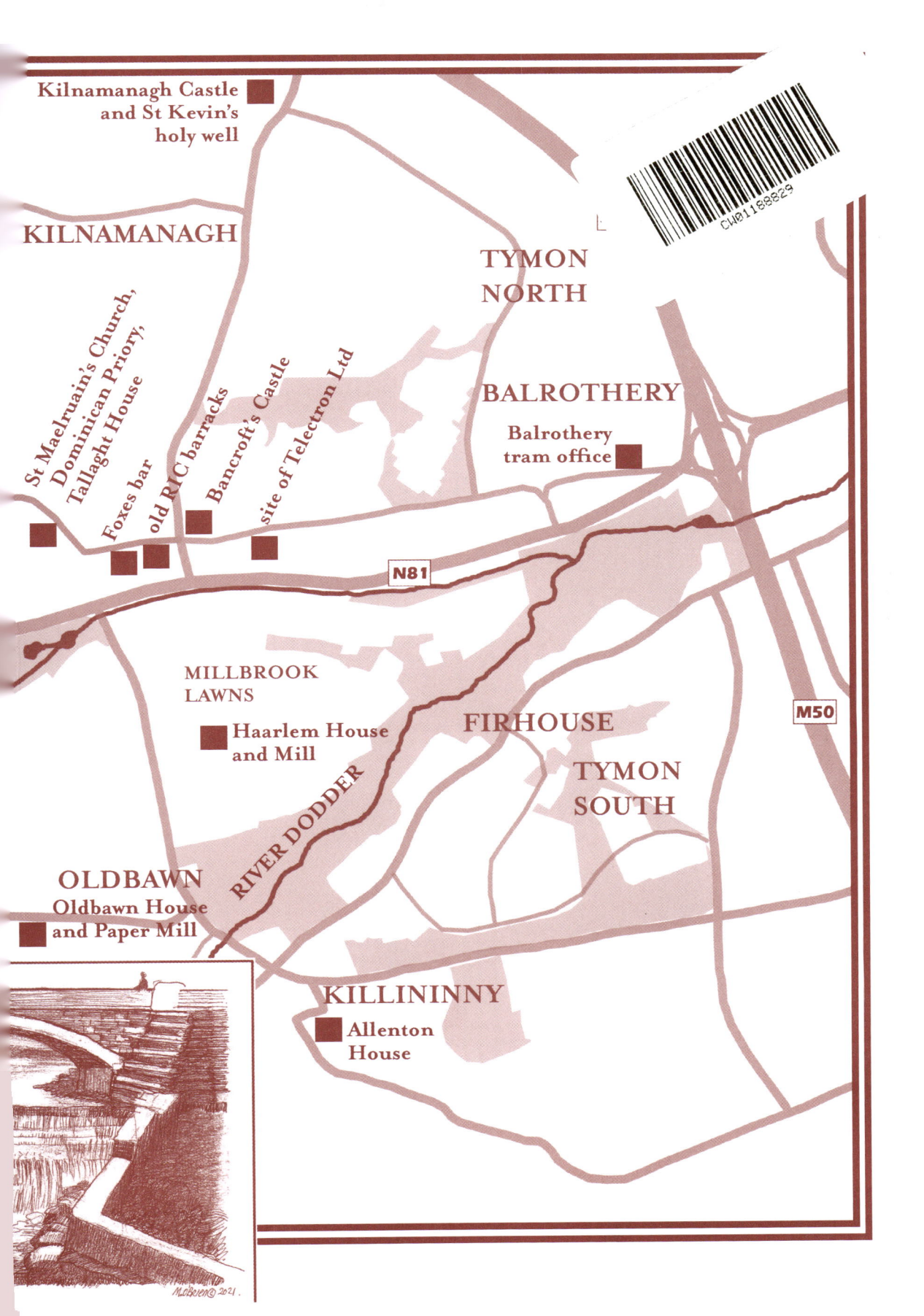

KILNAMANAGH

TYMON NORTH

BALROTHERY

Balrothery tram office

St Maelruain's Church, Dominican Priory, Tallaght House

Foxes bar

old RIC barracks

Bancroft's Castle

site of Telectron Ltd

N81

M50

MILLBROOK LAWNS

Haarlem House and Mill

FIRHOUSE

TYMON SOUTH

RIVER DODDER

OLDBAWN
Oldbawn House and Paper Mill

KILLININNY

Allenton House

A Ramble
— ABOUT —
TALLAGHT

First published 2023 by
The O'Brien Press Ltd,
12 Terenure Road East, Rathgar, Dublin 6, D06 HD27, Ireland.
Tel: +353 1 4923333; Fax: +353 1 4922777
E-mail: books@obrien.ie; Website: obrien.ie
The O'Brien Press is a member of Publishing Ireland.

ISBN: 978-1-78849-336-9

Copyright for text © Albert Perris 2023
The moral rights of the author have been asserted.
Copyright for typesetting, layout, editing, design © The O'Brien Press Ltd
Book designed by Emma Byrne

All rights reserved. No part of this publication may be reproduced or utilised in any form or by any eans, electronic or mechanical, including photocopying, recording or in any information storage and retrieval system, without permission in writing from the publisher.

6 5 4 3 2 1
26 25 24 23

Printed and bound by Hussar Books, Poland.
The paper in this book is produced using pulp from managed forests

Published in:

South Dublin County Council was pleased to support this publication under the South Dublin County Heritage Plan.

Picture credits
Michael O'Brien: pages 9, 39 (bottom left), 67, 123 (both), 134, 188 and 233; South Dublin Libraries: pages 10, 20, 28 (bottom), 31, 42, 43, 44 (both), 49, 62, 70, 82, 107 (all), 114, 121, 131, 133, 135, 136, 137 (Tomás Maher), 138, 141 (Joe Williams), 142, 149 (both), 154, 156 (Dimmock Collection), 158, 159 (both), 196 (Gerry Williams), 197 (top, bottom middle and bottom right), 197 (bottom left) (Gerry Williams), 199 (Helen O'Clery Gallagher), 201 (Deegan Photo), 203 (Deegan Photo) (left), 204 (Joe Williams), 212 (Patrick Healy) and 266 (both); National Library of Ireland: pages 12, 14, 28 (top), 95, 175 and 230; Royal Irish Academy: page 34; pages 35 (both) and 39 (top) courtesy of Dublin City Library and Archive; Brian MacCormaic: pages 38, 101, 103, 234, 242, 245, 257, 259, 260, 261, 262 (top) and 262 (bottom), 268; Royal College of Surgeons in Ireland: page 83 (both); Patrick Healy: pages 27 (both) and 113; Jeremy Harte, Bourne Hall Museum, Surrey, UK: page 111; John P Flanagan: pages 143, 236 and 239 (both); National Archives of Ireland: page 157 (both); Mary McGrath: pages 200 (both) and 203 (right); Ordnance Survey Ireland: page 231; Pete Smyth: pages 247, 249 (both) and 258; Albert Perris: page 270.
All efforts have been made to contact copyright holders; if, however, any infringement has inadvertently occurred, we request the owners of such copyright to contact the publishers.

A Ramble
ABOUT
TALLAGHT

HISTORY • PEOPLE • PLACES

Albert Perris

Illustrations by Michael O'Brien

To John Enjoy the Ramble. Remembering Shane at this Time Regards A Perris.

THE O'BRIEN PRESS
DUBLIN

Dedication

For Noeleen

Albert Perris is a researcher, writer and blogger, and the founder and author of the acclaimed blog 'A Ramble About Tallaght'. His articles there have to date received a quarter of a million hits. This is his second book relating to Tallaght. The first, *Since Adam Was a Boy: An Oral Folk History of Tallaght*, was published by TWS in 1999. Albert was born and lived in Tallaght for over 25 years.

He is happily married and now lives in County Kildare with his wife and their four children, his dog and their cat.

He remains active in the community and voluntary sector in Tallaght and South Dublin, and is a regular guest speaker at events and contributor to discussions there.

Contents

	Preface	page 7
Chapter 1	Genesis – Tallaght in Pre-History	11
Chapter 2	Christianity, Comets and Cholera	19
Chapter 3	Tallaght Castle and the Archiepiscopal Palace	48
Chapter 4	Tallaght House	69
Chapter 5	The Battle of Tallaght, 1867 – What the Dickens?	91
Chapter 6	The Big Houses	105
Chapter 7	Oldbawn Paper Mills	120
Chapter 8	Those Damned Inquisitors – The Dominicans in Tallaght	127
Chapter 9	On the Move – Planes, Trains and Automobiles	148
Chapter 10	Tallaght in Times of Strife	167
Chapter 11	Industry and Commerce	191
Chapter 12	The Best Laid Plans	228
Chapter 13	The Coming of Age of Tallaght New Town	252
	From a Settlement to a City – A Conclusion of Sorts	265
	Works Consulted and Bibliography	271

Acknowledgements

Amen. Sanus sit qui scripsit et cui scriptum est. Amen.
Amen. May he who has written and the one for whom it has been written be healthy. Amen.
From the *Stowe Missal*, probably, almost certainly, written in Tallaght in the ninth century!

I am particularly indebted to Isabel Kiernan Whelan; Niall Callery, Brendan Cullen, College Historian, Clongowes Wood College; Tomas Maher of Tallaght Historical Society; Father Donagh O'Shea OP of St Joseph's Retreat Centre, Tallaght village; Sharlene Ní Cinnéide, keeper of the graves in St Maelruain's Graveyard; Rosaleen Dwyer, Heritage Officer, South Dublin County Council; David Power and all the staff of South Dublin Libraries; John O'Neill, Castletymon Library; Michael Whelan, Irish Air Corp & Military Archives; Father Hugh Fenning OP (RIP); Liz Kennedy, TCC; Jeremy Harte, Curator, Bourne Hall Museum, Surrey, UK; 'Meath History Hub with Noel French', for information on the Fowler Family; Dr Lars B Nooij, PhD, Department of Early Irish Studies, Maynooth University; Rachel Smyth; Pete Smyth; Mairead Flanagan and the Flanagan Family; John Mullen; Brian MacCormaic and Paddy Cummins.

A particular thanks to John P DuLong, for sharing through private correspondence material from the Palmer family papers, relating to Tallaght House and Major Palmer's financial affairs and military services, from which I have liberally drawn. I am immensely grateful and appreciative of his generosity of spirit and assistance.

Royal College of Surgeons in Ireland (RCSI); National Archives; National Museum of Ireland; the National Library of Ireland; Tallaght Historical Society; South Dublin Libraries, for permission to reproduce selected images; Royal Irish Academy; Bourne Museum, Ewell, Surrey, UK;

Michael O'Brien for his vision and faith and all at O'Brien Press for their patience and pragmatism.

Preface

The little green prefabricated library on the Greenhills Road, close to where the old Tallaght Courthouse once stood, was a short-lived but important institution in Tallaght in the early 1980s. Important for me anyway. It was presided over by an ageing lady librarian with a stern face that probably belied a more gentle nature. I was ten years old. She was, perhaps, fifty. But she was aging. Of that I am now more certain than ever. As it transpires, we both were.

The gentle waft of plug tobacco, Sweet Virginia, drifting from the pipe in her hand, mingled with the smell of books and dust and sodden anoraks draped on the back of children's chairs pushed against electric storage heaters. Rainwater from the anorak sleeves dripped upon the floor. She rummaged through the little library tickets – green for children, royal blue for 'seniors'. She watched over her glasses – 'Sssh! No talking! No gum!'

She looked like the right person to ask! I held my frayed, rain-damp and crumpled green ticket in my hand. 'Can I help you, young man?' she whispered. 'I want to know how to cut a woman in half,' I whispered back. She gave me a stare, her eyes magnified behind her thin rimmed spectacles, suggesting she had been doing it herself for years. 'I want to do magic tricks.' At that moment I wanted to disappear. 'Like Harry Houdini,' I continued.

She briskly walked from behind the counter and took eight or ten steps that brought her, and me, halfway across the little library. 'There you go – bottom shelf. B for Bongo, Ali; C for Card Tricks; D for Daniels, Paul; H for Houdini, Harry.'

All I learned from the books in Tallaght Library that day was how to cut a deck of cards in half. I was crestfallen. I quickly tired of magic tricks when I came to the premature conclusion that there was no such thing as real magic. But I grew to love that little library.

Some years later, I was allowed to get a royal blue card, like my mother's – a senior card. Around this time, I picked up a brown and tattered paperback book covered in clear plastic. Within its pages were the memories of a very old man – memories of Tallaght; memories of Killinarden. The man in the book was nearly a hundred years old, and he had died 40 years earlier. Memories of Tallaght 140 years ago! When you are fourteen years old, 140 years is a very long time indeed, ten lifetimes ago.

The old man told stories of fellas getting hanged on the banks of the Dodder, of the Battle of Tallaght in 1867, of cock-fighting and of body snatchers – the 'sack-em-ups' – in the local graveyard. I knew, intimately, the banks of the Dodder. I knew Tallaght village. I knew my way around the graveyards. Reading that book transported me back in time.

Malachi Horan Remembers by Dr George Little has become something of a classic in Irish oral history. Nobody could have predicted it. Malachi, a very elderly small farmer from atop Killinarden Hill – poorly educated, untraveled, his sight failing – had something to say, which, as it turned out, thousands of people wanted to hear. Or read. At fourteen years old, I was one of them. Without even trying, I had discovered time travel.

Dr George Little was a poor historian. He lacked qualification, competence and experience to write a 'history' book. The book should have been a dust collector, but it ran to numerous editions. Its first edition is now a collector's item. It was a *local history* book, that appealed to many who had never even visited the locality. It was a book about life, related in lore and set in a community not dissimilar to many, indeed most, in Ireland. I have read it a dozen times. I have visited the headstones of some of the characters remembered by Malachi Horan. And I have paid my respects at his. The mortal remains of old Spooner of Killinarden Hill lie at peace in Tallaght Churchyard at St Maelruain's. If all dogs go to heaven, Spooner's old dog may have joined him there.

A Ramble About Tallaght, I hope, will inhabit the same space as *Malachi Horan Remembers*. It may take its place in the modest canon of local *history* of Tallaght publications. This is not an academic history, nor is it intended to be. I have studiously avoided the inclusion of footnotes and references, for fear that the presentation of such might lull the reader into a false sense of academia. This book is for the inquisitive citizen of Tallaght, interested in Tallaght and its people in times gone by.

In a sense, all of this work is of course based on the work of others. Sometimes that 'work' was a simple newspaper article from 1867. I have not evaluated the credibility, reliability, objectivity or veracity of sources. Indeed, in researching this book, I have often stumbled across inconsistency, apparent error or indeed politically biased accounts or reportage. But this book is for the layperson, not the academic, the scholar or the historian.

Between 1965 and 1975, the community of Tallaght experienced unprecedented development. But the following two decades was to be utterly transformative. Few places in Ireland, at that time, had undergone such a transition.

Born in Tallaght in 1972, my own development seemed to reflect the growing pains of the community I was born into. Innocence and potential was for a time eroded by cynicism and stasis. But fifty years on, as maturity approaches, it is time for reflection, time to take stock. What has made Tallaght what it is? Where did it come from? And what went before?

This book will have fulfilled its intended function if it finds its place on the bedside locker of a young Tallaght citizen and instils a sense of wonder, a sense of timelessness and a sense of place – when they look out at Tallaght Hill or Mount Pelia or Mount Seskin and know with confidence, that *I am of Tallaght*.

Albert Perris, 7 July 2023

Malachi Horan's cottage in Killinardan.

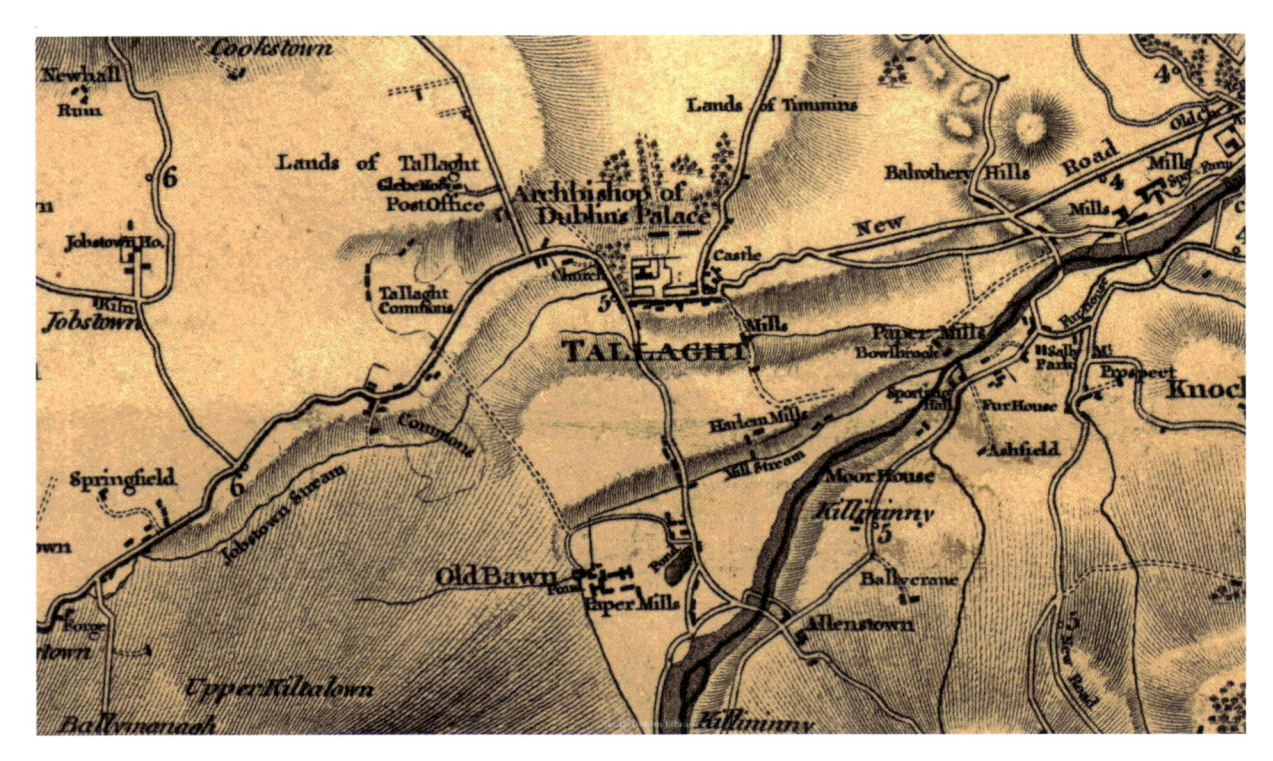

Tallaght and the surrounding area, from Taylor's map of the environs of Dublin, 1816.

CHAPTER 1

Genesis – Tallaght in Pre-History

In the Beginning – Tamhleacht Muintire Parthalon

Parthalon came, Parthalon died and his people were buried in Tallaght.

The myth of Parthalon, a foundation story of both Tallaght and Ireland, tells us that in *Anno Mundi* 2242 (2242 years after creation) a prince was banished from his father's kingdom in Greece, after attempting to overthrow his rule. He and his followers set sail and wound up in Ireland, in Ballyshannon of all places. Later his descendants settle on *Moy-Ealta-Edar*, 'the plain of the bird flocks of Edar (Howth)'.

Three hundred years after his arrival, the descendants of Parthalon and his people were wiped out by a great plague. In one week, all 9000 Parthalonians – 5000 men and 4000 women – died. They were buried in prominently marked graves in the hills around Tallaght or 'Tamh-Leacht' (*Tamh* is an epidemic pestilence and *Leacht* a plague monument).

The story of Parthalon has come to us from the *Lebor Laignech* (The Book of Leinster, c.1160) and the *Annála na gCeithre Máistrí* (the Annals of the Four Masters, compiled between 1632 and 1636 in the Franciscan friary in Donegal Town).

A Ramble About Tallaght

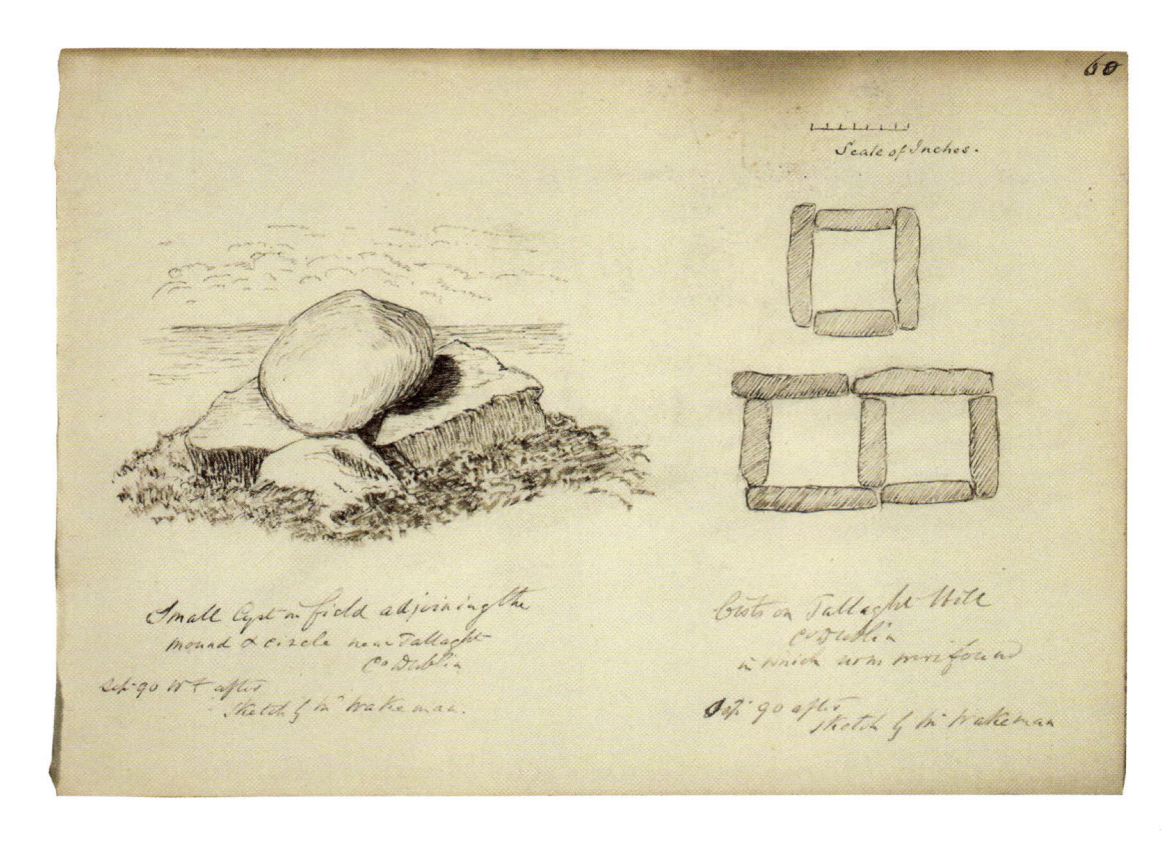

Drawing of a small cist found on Tallaght Hill.

The story of a prince attempting to displace his father, the King, and failing and fleeing, later to establish his own colony elsewhere, is not a unique one. That this new colony should then be wiped out by a plague or a pestilence – that it fails due to the wrath of nature or of the gods – is an appropriate and just end to this morality tale. Nothing great or enduring ever came from a son betraying his father, of one generation betraying the previous. In the myth or legend of Parthalon, we find the earliest story of Tallaght and the earliest story of Ireland entwined.

The story is also entwined with the Old Testament, starting as it does 'after the deluge', the great biblical cataclysm that set Noah's Ark on its voyage. Parthalon, we are told, arrived in Ireland 287 years after the biblical flood. As late as the nineteenth century, Irish scholars were debating the genealogy of Parthalon, descended as he must have been from Noah – the great man himself!

If nothing else, this detail helps us estimate an earliest date for the mythology of Parthalon, and to recognise that the tale was set within the Judaeo-Christian narrative. The 'Parthalonians', we are told, were among the first people to colonise Ireland 'after the Flood'. This must have seemed eminently sensible to the earliest generations of Christians in Ireland, explaining how people came to be in Ireland in the first place, and firmly placing Ireland and Tallaght in the biblical chronology of the Christian world. No doubt the story of the Parthalonians also helped Tallaght's first Christians understand why the place seemed to be so generously littered with ancient features – enclosures, raths, barrows and cists, passage graves and portal tombs.

The story of the Parthalonians is perhaps best now interpreted as a poetic transmission of an account of the earliest people arriving in Ireland, and of their ultimate demise. They came from far away, they lived on the island of Ireland, and they died of a pestilence. They were buried in accordance with their own established tradition, leaving indelible impressions on the landscape around Tallaght.

Passage tombs, such as those in Tallaght, are the most common type of megalithic monument in Europe. However, unlike many of their European contemporaries who favoured inhumation and buried their dead in similar tombs, Tallaght's earliest citizens were ordinarily cremated before their ashes were deposited, often in ornate vessels, in these cists and tombs.

Urns in Kiltalown

In June 1848, John Lentaigne of Tallaght House presented some curious finds to the Royal Irish Academy.

Peter Quin, a labourer on the lands of John Robinson of Kiltalown House, had been clearing furze near the top of the ridge of Tallaght Hill, close to the boundary of Killinarden. He was raking over the surface clay of a low mound when he found a quantity of broken stones, and under them a larger one. On trying to move the large stone with a crowbar, the thin slab broke into pieces, revealing a man-made chamber, a cavity or *kiswain* underneath. It was a small tomb, containing ancient skeletal remains and an urn, placed to the north of the remains. The urn was filled with a black sooty substance. Quin emptied the urn, not thinking its contents to be of any value. The black sooty substance drifted off in the gentle summer breeze.

A Ramble About Tallaght

Near the tomb, a number of other chambers were found, mostly empty and uncovered. All that remained in some were fragments of burnt bone. To the east of the *kiswain*, was discovered a great pit, about five foot deep with walled sides. It contained a great many fragments of burnt bone and ashes. It had clearly been used as a depository.

Another urn was found in the ground, close to the surface, very different in style to the one found in the tomb. The urns were decorated with zig-zag lines, likely made with a special tool or stamp. It was posited that the urns had been made on a wheel. One of the smaller urns contained broken fragments of a larger urn.

John Lentaigne was a noted collector and antiquarian, and recognised the importance of the finds. Local peasants or labourers would turn to him on occasion, presenting finds, no doubt hoping for a shilling or two in return for their ancient curios.

Fifty years after the find at Kiltalown, on the August bank holiday weekend of 1898, labourers were quarrying sand from a sandpit on Larry Dunne's land at Greenhills, when they made a similar discovery. On working a face of the sandpit, they came upon a vertical stone slab. As they removed more sand, the slab fell away, revealing an enclosed chamber lined with stones, a cist containing three earthen vessels, pieces of broken pottery and what appeared to be fragments of bone.

Urns in a stone cist found in the Tallaght area.

It was not the first time such antiquities had been found at this site. A few years earlier, similar vessels had been found by labourers working the pit. One of the vessels, intact, had been claimed and retained by Larry Dunne, as it had been found on his land. The labourers sold the other fragments of broken vessels and a couple of flint scrapers to a Mr Halbert, a dealer on High Street in Dublin.

On that bank holiday Monday, the men removed the contents of the cist, placing the three earthen vessels in a nosebag filled with straw. They made a parcel of other fragments of broken vessels, and another containing fragments of bone. On the morning of Tuesday, 2 August 1898, they made their way into the Dublin Museum of Art and Science, to try to sell their wares.

More recent excavations, in 1978, turned up similar finds in Glassamucky. Two burials were found during the removal of topsoil from a quarry there. One was a pit burial, containing a cinerary urn inverted over a cremation. The second burial came from a cist. A weaver's comb made of horn, believed to date from the Iron Age, was also found in this district. It is now in the National Museum.

In 1945, the family of the late Laurence Dunne of Greenhills gifted the intact prehistoric piece of pottery – a 'beautiful food vessel' – and several other pieces of ancient urns, found on his land, to the National Museum. The pieces date from the early Iron Age, and had been 'a source of anxiety' for the Museum for many decades.

Portal, passage, cist and wedge

Archaeological evidence of those who have lived and died in Tallaght dates back at least 5000 years. People have been burying their dead here since the Neolithic period.

In 1988, in Ballinascorney Upper, a Megalithic passage tomb, eight metres in diameter, was partially excavated. Two years earlier, parts of it had been displaced in the course of forestry work. The archaeologist Patrick Healy recorded that the 'monument consists of an incomplete circle of boulders with a hollow in the centre in which are four disconnected stones. It was probably a tomb with a burial chamber or cist in the middle and a kerb of boulders retaining either a cairn of stones or a tumulus of soil' (Archaeological Survey of Ireland). No finds were recovered during the excavation.

Stone circles, barrows, mounds, ring-ditches and cairns have all been found and recorded in the same neighbourhood.

Passage tombs have been found and recorded to the south of Tallaght at Montpelier Hill and Seahan Mountain, to the southwest at Knockanvinidee and to the west on Tallaght Hill and Saggart Hill. To the southeast in the distance, the Fairy Castle on Two Rock Mountain, a three-metre-high cairn measuring 27 metres in diameter, is believed to contain a Neolithic passage tomb. Portal tombs from the late Neolithic period have been recorded at Larch Hill and at Mount Venus (Rockbrook).

The prevalence of passage tombs across Europe has led to speculation that Irish passage tombs were a result of immigration or acculturation of people from overseas. Some of the oldest passage tombs in Europe can be found in Brittany, France, and they have similarities to those found in Ireland, in terms of structural design and artwork.

The remains of a wedge tomb, a comparatively rare type of megalithic tomb in the district, was discovered in Massy's Wood in Killakee in 1978. It dates from between 2400 and 2000 BC. Only two other such tombs had been recorded within a 10km radius – the 'giant's grave' at Ballyedmonduff (Glencullen), discovered around 1830; and Kilmashogue (within 3.3km of Killakee). Only one other wedge tomb is recorded within a 55km radius, that at Laughanstown. An excavation of the wedge tomb at Ballyedmonduff was undertaken by Rúaidhrí de Valera, son of Eamon, in the spring of 1945. Cremated human bone (a few pieces of rib and a lower molar tooth), a polished stone hammer, 27 flints and 150 pieces of pottery, some quite minute, were discovered.

In recent years, a long overdue and exciting archaeological appraisal of the tomb on Montpelier, at the Hell Fire Club, has been undertaken by Abarta Heritage. Artefacts dating to the Neolithic period have been discovered in the vicinity of the possible tombs on Montpelier Hill, indicating activity there from as early as 3500 BC. In 1986, Dr Stefan Bergh (now of University of Galway Archaeology Department) was visiting the Hell Fire Club when he found a chert scraper, a small prehistoric stone tool, approximately twenty metres northwest of the larger of the two tombs.

Evidence of ancient enclosures have been found in Killinarden, Whitestown, Ballymany and closer to Tallaght village, dating from various pre-Christian periods.

Under the tree at Spar

In 1973, a Middle-Bronze Age palstave axe was found at the rear of a house in Bancroft Estate, close to Tallaght village.

When the Village Green in Tallaght was being developed in 1990, due to its proximity to the ancient site of St Maelruain's Monastery, an archaeological appraisal of the site was required. Investigations there revealed the remains of a 'curving fosse' or enclosure. Traces of an inner bank of 2.6 metres were revealed. Within the enclosure, traces of iron slag, charcoal and animal bones were found. Radiocarbon dating of one of the bones indicates that it was relatively recent – around 680–90 AD. It strongly suggests human habitation in the immediate vicinity of what is now Tallaght village, before the foundation of St Maelruain's Monastery in 774 AD.

Taken together, the archaeological evidence suggests that for at least 3000 years before the Christian era, the lands at Tallaght were stomped by our ancestors. The town of Tallaght is situated within a prehistoric ritual landscape. All around it lie the remains of those who have lived here, and those who have died.

Tallaght in Celtic mythology

The neighbourhood of Tallaght features prominently in a number of critical texts of Irish mythology, most notably those relating to 'The Destruction of Dá Derga's Hostel' from the Ulster Cycle and the story of Tír na nÓg from the Fenian or Ossianic Cycle that follows it.

It is to the valley of Glenasmole that Oisín, son of Fionn McCumhaill, returns from Tír na nÓg after 300 years. Here he met a group of men building a road, who appeal to him to lift a large flagstone. Oisín obliges and, succeeding in lifting the stone, his saddle-girth breaks and he falls from his horse. On touching the ground, he loses his youth, ageing at once to become a blind old man.

The association of Fionn McCumhaill with the area is perhaps reflected in local placenames, such as Ballymorefin Hill and Seafin.

The tale of 'Togail Bruidne Dá Derga' (The Destruction of Dá Derga's Hostel) dates from at least the eleventh century, and describes Dá Derga's Hostel as one of the great houses of hospitality in ancient Ireland.

In the story, the court of a first-century Irish King, Conaire Mór, is recorded as visiting the great house. The court included sixty nobility, visitors, hostages, twenty-seven British nobles in exile, nineteen Saxons, three Picts and three royal druids. The hostel is filled with jugglers and poets, judges of the first rank, nine harpers and pipe players, three jesters, three charioteers, nine apprentices, swine-herds and janitors.

Nine guardsmen composed the King's military retinue, and were charged with the care of the hostages. The court included three cooks, drink-bearers, six cup-bearers, two table attendants and a steward.

It is generally accepted that the name Bohernabreena relates to the 'road to Bruiden'. When Eugene O'Curry of the Ordnance Survey visited the area in 1838 he found a number of connected mottes, mounds and cairns on 'the brink of Maureen's Brook', the source of the River Dodder. They had neither been opened nor named. The location of the mottes coincided with the location, in lore, of Dá Derga's Hostel. They are no longer visible.

While the academic assertion that Bother Na Breenam is the road to 'Bruidhean Dá Derga' has periodically been challenged, it has generally been accepted by those best qualified to contribute to the debate.

On 28 June 1788, fifty years before O'Curry visited the area for the Ordnance Survey and noted with interest the location of the moat at Maureen's Brook, the following appeared in Faulkner's Dublin Journal:

> Last week some labourers belonging to Mr Dogherty of Glenasmole were cutting turf when one of them discovered a gold crown at about four feet deep. It is about seven inches in diameter and weighs eleven ounces. It is perhaps the crown of some provincial king, before the introduction of Christianity. There are several figures raised on it but no such thing as a cross.

No doubt there are still ancient riches buried in them there hills, waiting to shed further light on the legends of Fionn and Tír na nÓg, on Conaire Mór and perhaps even the Parthalonians.

CHAPTER 2

Christianity, Comets and Cholera

At twelve noon on 12 June in the year of our Lord 1832, Patrick McDonald was at work in a field, digging a ditch in Bohernabreena, when he saw five strangers approaching at a distance from across the hills. The five men were barefooted and each carried a bale or bundle of turf under his arm. One of the figures was a balding, grey-haired man. The other four were stout and bareheaded. They approached McDonald and informed him they had been sent by the Catholic priest in Kilbride and told to deliver 'blessed turf' to local residents to protect their homesteads.

McDonald was advised that a 'comet' had dropped from heaven and that the town of New Ross, Co. Wexford, had been destroyed. The six men solemnly prayed over the sods of turf, saying seven *Paters*, seven *Marias*, a *Gloria Patria* and the *Apostles' Creed*. They instructed McDonald to burn a sod of the blessed turf on the threshold of his cabin (where he lived with his mother Nelly), and to make the sign of the cross with it on the door.

The men directed that once this was done, he should then take some turf and visit seven other houses within seven miles and request that those residents do the same thing. McDonald was asked to inform the residents he met of the urgency needed in protecting all homesteads in the district with the blessed turf.

A Ramble About Tallaght

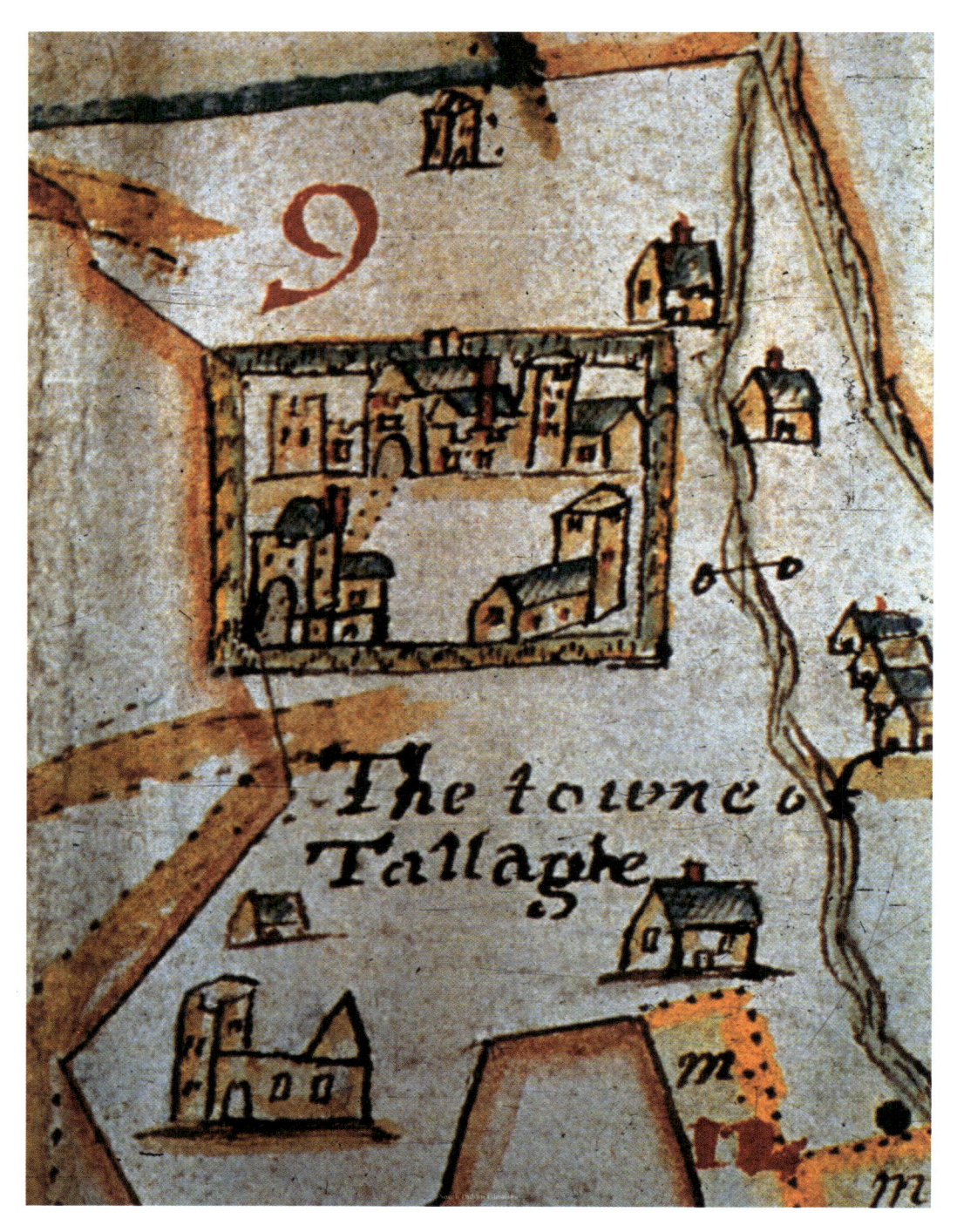

Map of Tallaght, 1654, by Robert Newcomen.

McDonald did as he was advised. Having protected his own home, he dutifully set off in the direction of the city to distribute the holy turf, requesting each man he met to likewise visit seven houses. He met with five or six labourers, with whom he shared his turf and instructions, before he arrived at Roundtown (Terenure), where he was taken into custody by the police. He made a sworn statement the following day, 13 June 1832, detailing the above account. He noted that the unnamed five men from Kilbride, all having visited seven houses, had returned in a homeward direction.

While Pat McDonald had been listening attentively to the five strangers in his field in Bohernabreena, in Ballymore Eustace the greatest confusion was sown among the townsfolk as a consequence of people running through the town carrying seven pieces of turf. At each house, they left a piece, with directions to burn the bit of turf at the door and say some prayers.

In nearby Rathcoole, hundreds of country people were seen running in all directions with pieces of peat turf in their hands. According to the Chief Constable at Rathcoole, 'the priests of every parish from Wexford to Tallaght were blamed as the originators of the report about the comet ... but on being asked by respectable persons whether this was true, [they] denied [it], and said it was all nonsense, that the people were really mad'.

Early Christianity in Tallaght

By 1832, the people of Tallaght had been devoutly Christian for over 1000 years. By the middle of the eighth century, the Christians of Tallaght had already concluded that the Irish Christian Church was losing its way and in need of reform. They found themselves at the heart of a reform movement, the *Céilí Dé* or 'Servants of God'. What became the monastery at Tallaght in the eighth century was by no means the first Christian centre in the district. Monastic foundations had been laid long before then, in Glenasmole by St Sanctán and in Kilnamanagh by St Eoghan. There may have been others.

Kilnamanagh – Cell manach Eascrach

Some 200 years before a monastery was established in Tallaght, early Christian monks established churches and abbeys in the area. In the first half of the sixth century, St Eoghan established one of the first such foundations – Cell manach Eascrach, or Kilnamanagh, a mile north of Tallaght.

St Eoghan (or *St Eugene* in Latin) is believed to have been born in Leinster. He was one of many young people, including Tiarnach of Clones and Cairbre of Coleraine, who were captured by pirates and brought to Britain. On gaining his freedom, he became a student at Candida Casa in Whithorn in Galloway, southern Scotland, founded by St Ninian. About 397, while the Roman legions still occupied Britain, St Ninian had established the first Christian mission north of Hadrian's Wall. He erected a small stone church, the Candida Casa or 'White House', which was Scotland's first Christian building. And this is where one of Tallaght's earliest monks had his schooling.

On returning to Ireland, St Eoghan came to Tallaght and founded his monastery at Kilnamanagh. He spent about fifteen years here training young priests, several of whom would go on to be bishops. Among his students at Kilnamanagh was his nephew Caoimhín – later St Kevin, who would go on to found his own monastery at Glendalough, Co. Wicklow.

According to legend, Eoghan had a vision, a divine command, to travel north. He obeyed the command with great reluctance and against the wishes of his monks. It has been suggested, however, that he was invited north to the See of Ardstraw, Co. Tyrone, because of his reputation for learning and sanctity. He went to Ardstraw about 540 and established his second foundation, for which he is best remembered.

His foundation at Kilnamanagh continued to flourish after his departure. Saint Eoghan died on the evening of 23 August, while his monks were chanting their evening office. He is buried somewhere in Ardstraw graveyard.

Born about 498, Caoimhín had been baptised by Cronan of Clondalkin. Like his predecessors, there is a great deal of ambiguity and uncertainty about much of his life. His date of death is recorded as sometime between 618 and 622. Early Christian litanies suggest he lived for up to

120 years, perhaps more indicative of the veneration bestowed upon him by those who came after than his physical longevity.

What is more certain is his association with Kilnamanagh in Tallaght and Glendalough, Co. Wicklow. What is equally certain is that within 100 years of his death, the cult or veneration of Caoimhín had become established. In addition to the 'Litany of Irish Saints', he is invoked in the Stowe Missal. By the time monks came to establish a monastery at Tallaght, the reputation of St Kevin and his early formation under Eoghan at Kilnamanagh was already widely known. Relics of Caoimhín were taken on tour, along with those of Cronan of Clondalkin.

The foundation at Kilnamanagh likely endured for many hundreds of years, but given its proximity to Tallaght, its importance was perhaps overtaken by that of St Mael Ruain from the early ninth century. The monastery at Kilnamanagh may have been sacked by Vikings when they raided Tallaght in 811. The monastery at Tallaght was rebuilt and Kilnamanagh was later the site of a medieval church, a subsidiary church of Tallaght.

By the mid-thirteenth century, Kilnamanagh was occupied by Sir John de Caucer. It is mentioned in a list of Wax Rent dated 1256–66 as subject to a rent of 2lb of wax. In 1306, Rolph de Rathdowne released a portion of land in Kilnamanagh to John le Ken and his heirs. In 1366, Richard Gyfford recovered the Manor of Kilnamanagh and a castle was constructed here as part of the Pale embattlements, part of which would endure into the twentieth century.

Remnants of an old monastic site and medieval church at Kilnamanagh could still be seen in 1837, by which time they had been incorporated into what had, several hundred years earlier, become Kilnamanagh Castle. Adjoining the ancient church had been a burial ground, believed to have been used for many generations, though by the 1770s it had long been forgotten.

From 1778, Kilnamanagh was occupied by the Farrell Family. Jane Farrell, a daughter of the house, married Laurence Steen, a gentleman from Co. Meath, in 1880. About 1778, Mr Farrell attempted to make a vegetable garden at the site and he found the plot to be full of long-decayed human remains. Indeed for the next 150 years, ancient human remains would frequently be upturned close to what had once been Cell manach Eascrach. Human bones were found here in 1778, in 1886, in 1944 and again in 1956, when a concrete path was being laid, leaving little doubt that this was indeed an ancient burial ground.

Pilgrims and progress

In addition to human bones found in this neighbourhood before its development, large quantities of ancient oyster shells had also been unearthed. In 1960, an old tree close to Kilnamanagh Castle fell, revealing a great mass of shells underneath. Oyster shells were an important part of the early monk's diet and indeed they have become a symbol of pilgrims travelling throughout Europe at that time. (In French, the scallop is called *coquille Saint Jacques* and in German *Jakobsmuscheln*, after St James.)

Later history of the site

In 1909, a young nephew of Mr and Mrs Steen, Ambrose Flood, found an old Irish pike head, seven inches by ten inches, in the ancient moat close to Kilnamanagh Castle. Their son Herbie inherited the property and lived there for some years. Herbie Steen's wife Angela, better known as 'Dolly', a nurse from Thurles, died from pleurisy in 1929, at 32 years of age. They were only married a year and Herbie was left with a baby daughter. He married Mary Bowen in 1934, but she too died young, after only eleven years of marriage.

The small Castle at Kilnamanagh was still held by Herbie Steen in 1944. There had once been a doorway from the Castle into the old church. The door was cased with oak, thickly studded with iron nails with thick heads, about three quarters of an inch square. Herbie Steen presented the old studded door to the National Museum.

In September 1958, Steen put his 203-acre farm at Kilnamanagh Castle up for auction. Much of the land had been in his mother's family since 1778. After disposing of Kilnamanagh Castle, he lived in 'The Bungalow' on the Greenhills Road. Herbie Steen died in August 1983, aged 91. It is a legacy from Herbie Steen that gifted the nation the last remaining remnants of a medieval church – Cell manach Eascrach, at Kilnamanagh.

In 1974, the land at Kilnamanagh was transformed into a modern residential housing scheme. In 1976, as winter gave way to spring, Kilnamanagh Castle was levelled by developers Brennan and McGowan, as the swinging scythe of unfettered development laid waste to Tallaght's ancient past. The old monastic site of Cell manach Eascrach and its later castle were swept away in the name of progress.

Two hundred years after Mr Farrell had unearthed ancient human remains close to Kilnamanagh Castle, the land was still offering up the secrets of its past. In 1975, a Mr Moore, a newly arrived resident in the new Kilnamanagh Estate, was digging in his back garden when he happened upon a yeomanry sword dating from 1790, made by Reid's of Parliament Street in Dublin – a testament to more recent history.

St Kevin's Well is the last remaining feature to give an indication that this was once a most important ecclesiastical foundation. It was retained in the middle of a compact residential street by the developers. This was not out of respect for the history and heritage of the site, nor out of deference to the sacred burial ground. It was retained only because the site was waterlogged from numerous underground springs. What the developers had intended to be the sites of 37, 39, 41 and 43 Elmcastle Walk are still an open site. It is perhaps symbolic of the great void left in Tallaght by residential and commercial developers in the 1970s and since.

St Annes, Kilmesantan (variously Kylmesantan; Collmesantan; Kipcopsentan)

What is now well known as St Anne's Church in Bohernabreena is named after an earlier church – a much earlier church, some remains of which can still be seen in Glenasmole, on an elevated site overlooking the Waterworks. Also locally referred to as St Anne's for generations, the name was in fact an Anglicisation or corruption of 'Sanctán' or St Sanctán.

In the early sixth century, a church was founded here by Sanctán, Bishop and Abbot of *Cill-easpuig-Sanctán*, placing him around Tallaght some 200 years before St Mael Ruain and in the same period as St Eoghan and St Kevin in Kilnamanagh.

Sanctán was a Briton, born the son of two notable families, and indeed a brother and half-brother of other notable characters recorded in the history of these isles. According to the *Martyrology of Tallaght*, Bishop Sanctán was the son of Samuel Chendisel, 'the Low-headed', a King of Britain, and Drechura, a daughter of Muiredac Muinderg, 'the Red Necked', King of Ulster.

A brother of Sanctán, St Matoc Ailithir or 'Matoc the Pilgrim', came to Ireland first, and Sanctán may have followed his brother over. Sanctán, Matoc and Espoc Lethan, another brother, may have been closely connected with many of the Cambrian and Armorican (Breton) saints who came to Ireland in the late fifth and early sixth centuries. St Cybi of Holyhead may have been a half-brother.

Sanctán is included in the list of bishops in the *Book of Leinster*. His cult was later brought to the Isle of Man, where he is commemorated in the name of Santon Parish. Just as in Glenasmole, in the Parish of Santon on the Isle of Man, the name also erroneously morphed into 'St Ann'. Their Parish history acknowledges both the saint and the Church of St Sanctán in Glenasmole:

> Its Parish Church, which is dedicated to St Sanctain, who was an Irish saint and Bishop, and a disciple of St Patrick. Records show how the word 'Sanctain' has gone through different stages of spelling to arrive today at the more frequently used 'Santon'. 'Sanctain' appears as 'Sanctain', 'Santain', 'Santan', and 'Santon'. The latter two spellings are today recognised widely, but that of 'Santon', seems to have taken over and is the one that is more generally used … Sometime in the seventeenth century, in post-Reformation times, it would appear that St Sanctain's connection with Santon had been forgotten, for at that time there took place an even further corruption, which was quite erroneous, when the dedication was mistakenly attributed to St Ann. How this occurred is lost in antiquity, but it is not difficult to appreciate the easy way in which Santan could be mistaken for St Ann, and vice versa … It is interesting to note that in addition to Santon Church at least one Irish church had its name similarly altered in error, for Kell Easpuig Sanctain, near Dublin, was changed to St Ann's Chapel.

The church in Glenasmole endured, in one form or another, for close to 1000 years, from the early sixth century to the early 1600s. *The Annals of the Four Masters*, at 952, record the obit of 'Caenchomraic, abbot of Cill Easpuig Sanctán'. In 1179, this church and its lands were a sub-manor of Tallaght and from 1216, formed part of the extensive church lands of the See of Dublin.

The church of Mo Sanctán or *Cill Easpuig Sanctáin* was granted in 1192 to St Patrick's and in February 1207, John, Archbishop of Dublin, was granted permission by the King to build a deerpark and erect a deer leap here.

In 1547, in the taxation of the diocese of Dublin, it is called 'Temple Sauntan'. Repairs to the chancel and a curate's stipend were noted, suggesting the church was still, or again, in use. The church measured approximately 13.3m by 4.9m. It may have been in a nave-and-chancel form.

The church fell into disrepair by the early 1600s. It had been succeeded by the somewhat larger and later church at Templeogue (16m by 4.13m), likely reflecting the lawless character of the hills and mountains above Tallaght during that period, when the O'Tooles and O'Byrne's were at the height of their influence.

Remains of the medieval Church of St Sanctán, Glenasmole, 1988.

Máirín Ní Mharcaigh notes in 'The Medieval Parish Churches of South-West County Dublin':

> Earlier generations, from Neolithic to Early Christian, preferred upland habitations … possibly for defensive reasons but mainly because they were engaged in a predominantly pastoral economy. With the advent of the Anglo-Normans, the farming economy of the area was transformed into an arable one, based on the lowland plains. The churches were located on the lower ground to serve the greater number of people and also to distance them from possible aggression from the Irish chieftains of the Wicklow Mountains.

By 1875, what had once been the medieval church, built from coarse granite believed to have been quarried from Corrig Mountain, was in a ruinous state. The poorly preserved remnants of the church remain on the site. A pre-Norman font and St Sanctán's (or St Anne's) Holy Well also remain, bearing witness to this truly ancient ecclesiastical foundation.

The feast day of St Sanctán is 9 May. Local parishioners continue to celebrate mass in the graveyard in late July to mark the Feast of St Anne, rather than the Feast of St Sanctán. The local football team, St Anne's, further perpetuates the corruption of the ancient name. The old graveyard on this site was in use until the

St Anne's (St Sanctán's) Graveyard, 1988.

St Anne's Roman Catholic Church, Bohernabreena.

1950s, when concerns were expressed about water running off from the graveyard into the waterworks.

In August 1868, the foundation stone for the new Church of St Anne's on the Bohernabreena Road, Friarstown Upper, was laid. The Parish celebrated the 150th anniversary of the Church of St Anne in 2018. Rather curiously, according to the 'Inventory of Architectural Heritage', it was built in 1876. It was constructed on the site of an earlier chapel, dating from the penal times.

St Mael Ruain's Monastery

Saint Mael Ruain founded a monastery in Tallaght about the year 774 AD. The lands may have been granted by Cellach mac Dunchadh, King of Leinster, as an offering 'to God and St Michael and Mael Ruain in perpetual freedom'. Cellach is also understood to have been a major benefactor of Glendalough.

The old St Maelruain's Church, some time before it was rebuilt in 1829.

Little is known of the early life of St Mael Ruain (Mael means 'one who is tonsured', i.e. 'follower of', and *Ruan* (Ruadan) was the Abbot at Lorrha). It is believed he was likely born in Lorrha, north Tipperary, about 720 and studied in the monastery there under Ruadan. Relations between the monasteries at Lorrha and Tallaght would endure for several centuries.

The standards of monastic life had, it was felt, slipped in the period since the time of Eoghan in Kilnamanagh and Sanctán in Glenasmole. Mael Ruain became a central figure, perhaps even the founder, of the monastic reform movement known as the *Céilí Dé* or Culdees (the 'Servants of God'). He is credited as the author of the rule of the *Céilí Dé*, sometimes referred to as the Rule of Tallaght or the Rule of St Mael Ruain.

Austerity was a prevailing value in the monastery of Mael Ruain. Music was not allowed, save for the singing of office or vespers. The consumption of beer was strictly prohibited and a strict and modest diet, or pittance, was adhered too. The consumption of meat was a very rare privilege, and ordinarily only deer or wild swine was eaten on feast days or a portion may have been granted to a monk in poor health.

Mael Ruain was prevailed upon to allow his monks to consume beer, but only on long journeys or visits to other monasteries. (The monks of Tallaght maintained relationships with similar monasteries at Clonmacnoise, Terryglass, Lorrha and Iona.) He was reluctant to concede the principle, believing lust, sloth and other harmful inclinations were related to diet. Fasting and abstinence were encouraged to help regulate the body. In the years after Mael Ruain's death, his teachings continued to be transmitted, one of which noted:

> When at the end of a meal the body happens to be roused to lust, slightly or strongly, it was considered not amiss to cast that meal back upon the Lord in displeasure at him as if to say, 'there, keep thy meal for thyself', and believed that by this trial, will not often be made thereafter. Or else to subtract a part of a meal and to pray to God and repeat 'Lead us not into temptation' and *Deus in adiutorium* as far as *festina*.

Her pittance and her portion

The story of a monk's sister, as related in Tallaght during Mael Ruain's time (755–92) is instructive. The girl's name was Copar.

Desire lay heavy upon the girl, for it is a third part as strong again in woman as in men. Then he [the monk] regulated her portion and her pittance for a year: that is, a measured pittance. On that day year she came to him and confessed that her desire still persisted. Now he was busy sewing before her. Then he thrust the needle thrice into her palm and three streams of blood flowed from her hand. 'No wonder,' said he, 'If it is hard for the body, wherein are these strong currents, to contain itself.' Then he diminished her meals a second time. She was on that ration for a year, and her desire still persisted. So after that time he thrust the needle into her palm thrice, and three streams of blood flowed from it. So he reduced her meals again for a year, and at the end of the time, he thrust the needle again into her hand. This time however, not a drop of blood came out of her. 'In future,' said he, 'keep on this pittance until thy death.'

Individuality was a value not prized – everything was directed to the welfare of the community as a whole. A strict daily and weekly routine was maintained. Structure and routine were essential components of monastic life in Tallaght. Tonsuring, or head shaving, was ordinarily carried out on one Thursday a month. If, for whatever reason, it couldn't be carried out, it could be done on the Friday or Saturday of that week. If not, however, the monk would have to wait until a month later. No monk could have his head shaved on a Sunday.

Fifty years after its establishment, by the early ninth century, the monastery at Tallaght was an important and influential monastic centre. Tallaght, together with Finglas, became known as one of the 'two eyes of Ireland'.

St Mael Ruain died on 7 July 792. For almost 1100 years after, the annual Pattern of Tallaght was held on 7 July in his honour. (By the nineteenth century, the practice had descended into an annual occasion for drunkenness, revelry and debauchery, akin to the Donnybrook Fair. The Dominican Prior put an end to it in 1874.)

In 806, the Uí Néill – descendants of Niall, King of Ireland – plundered Tallaght, its sanctuary and termon lands. In response, the monks of Tallaght prevented the Taillteann Games from going ahead, pending compensation for the infringements of their rights and their material loss. The monks seized and retained their chariot horses on the eve of the Games, which were held annually at Taillteann, Co. Meath. Neither horse nor chariot were let run until the

King of Ireland had made full reparation for injuries inflicted on the monastery. Áed mac Néill afterwards gave full compensation to 'Tamhlacht', together with many gifts.

Only five years later, in 811, the monastery was again plundered, this time being devastated by Vikings. With resilience, faith, fortitude and some degree of optimism, the monks of Tallaght rebuilt their monastery. It not only endured but prospered for another 300 years, until about 1125.

After the Anglo-Norman invasion in 1170 and following the Third Lateran Council in 1179, Tallaght became part of the See of Dublin. It was listed among the lands confirmed to Archbishop Laurence O'Toole by Pope Alexander III and became, throughout the Middle Ages, one of the most important ecclesiastical manors in County Dublin.

By the sixteenth century, it was the Archbishop's principal residence outside the city (see Chapter 3). A medieval church was built on the ancient monastic site. The street pattern of this medieval borough was linear and appears to have consisted simply of a main street, which expanded at its west end to form the market place, where the road forked north past St Mael Ruain's Church and south towards Oldbawn. The Archbishop's Palace lay on the north side of the road and the long plots on the south side (now the Village Green and car park) are probably the remains of the medieval plot pattern.

A portion of John Rocque's map of County Dublin from 1760, showing Tallaght village and the surrounding area.

Martyrology, poetry and prose

Three important manuscripts, or at least manuscripts which have become important, were produced in early monastic Tallaght: the *Martyrology of Tallaght*, the *Martyrology of Óengus* (or *Félire Óengusso*) and the *Stowe Missal*. The three remain subjects of rigorous academic interest and scrutiny.

The Martyrology of Tallaght

A 'martyrology' is a list of the days of the year on which saints have died. The *Martyrology of Tallaght* was most likely written between the years 797 and 833 in the Monastery at Tallaght. Written in prose, it contains two sections for each day of the year – one general and one for Irish saints.

The earliest reference we have to this manuscript is in the twelfth-century *Martyrology of Gorman* (*Félire Uí Gormáin*), written between 1166 and 1174 by Mael Muire Ua Gormáin, Abbot of Knock, Co. Louth, which attributes the *Martyrology of Tallaght* to Mael Ruain. More recent scholarly work, however, casts doubt on this and it is perhaps more appropriate to attribute the *Martyrology* to Mael Ruain's Tallaght.

The *Martyrology of Tallaght* appears to have been a working document for what would come to be known as the *Martyrology of Óengus*, but itself became a holy relic, later venerated in Lorrha, Co. Tipperary. A prologue in the *Martyrology of Tallaght* describes the decline in pagan faith in Ireland and the rise of Christian monasticism in its place. It contains the following famous verse:

Senchatraig na ngente/iman roerud rudad/itfossa can adrad/amail Lathrach Lugdach.

Ind locáin rogabtha/dessib ocus trírib/it rúama co ndálib/co cétaib, co mílib.

which translates as:

The old cities of the pagans to which length of occupation has refused are deserts without worship like Lugaid's House-site. The little monastic sites that were settled by twos and threes are Romes with multitudes, with thousands.

If the early Christian foundations in Glenasmole and Kilnamanagh had been settled by twos and threes 200 years earlier, the Monastery at Tallaght was, poetically at least, likely home to multitudes and was becoming part of a network of such foundations around the country.

A leading authority on the subject is Irish Celticist and prominent hagiologist Dr Pádraig Ó Riain. He favours a later date for the texts, and has proposed that the composition of the *Martyrology of Tallaght* and the *Félire Óengusso* was a response to a decision at the church council of Aachen in 817 that every monastery should have a martyrology from which the monks should read a list of the saints at the hour of Prime (the first hour of daylight). An example of such a martyrology, according to Dr Ó Riain, arrived in Tallaght around 828, and work was immediately commenced in Tallaght, resulting in the addition of local, Leinster and Irish saints to the litany.

The facts in relation to both documents, however, remain uncertain and obscure and will no doubt provoke many more years of diligent study. Both compositions are believed to have been the work of St Óengus, a monk and Bishop at Tallaght. Most now agree that St Mael Ruain himself had gone to his eternal rest before the works were commenced.

The Martyrology of Óengus

The *Martyrology of Óengus* is a more sophisticated literary rendering of the *Martyrology of Tallaght*. It has been described by Hennig as 'the earliest, most original and most beautiful attempt ever made to raise the Christian calendar to the rank of real literature'. A literary masterpiece, it was the first text of its kind anywhere in the Christian world.

Where Ua Gormáin attributes the *Martyrology of Tallaght* to Mael Ruain, he notes that Óengus based his work on it: '… because it was thus in the *Martyrology of Tallaght of Mael Ruain*, out of which he [Óengus] composed his *félire*'. It is generally accepted that the *Martyrology of Óengus* was indeed the work of the man himself.

While the original manuscript has not survived, ten known early copies, dating from between circa 1400 and 1630, have survived. It is known that in the eleventh century, a copy of the *Martyrology of Óengus* arrived in a Benedictine monastery in Regensburg, Germany, and this document was to influence many continental texts. A preface, commentary and glosses were added, probably in a scriptorium in Armagh between 1170 and 1174.

St Óengus died on Friday, 11 March, and while the actual year of his death is uncertain, the day and date of his death suggests he died in 819, 824 or 830. In his *History and Antiquities of Tallaght*, Handcock states he died in 824, but without explanation of how he so confidently settled on that year. The contents of the *félire* – the last identifiable obit being at 828 – suggest it was completed sometime after that date and that, therefore, Óengus was alive and active.

What is certain, or at least understood, is that Óengus produced Tallaght's first great literary work and indeed perhaps its greatest yet. That should be reason enough for him to be remembered and celebrated in Tallaght. Óengus was buried in his birthplace of Clonenagh, Laois, having returned there from Tallaght.

The *Stowe Missal*

While the original manuscripts of both the *Martyrology of Tallaght* and the *Martyrology of Óengus* have been lost to history, one original manuscript that has survived from the period is the Stowe Missal, comparable in age to the *Book of Kells*.

The *Stowe Missal* is, strictly speaking, not a missal at all. Nor was it written in Stowe in England. One of the oldest surviving documents of the early Irish Church, it was most likely written in the Monastery of St Mael Ruain at Tallaght, not long after he had died there in 792.

The *Stowe Missal* has been the subject of enduring academic interest. It was discovered in 1819 in the library of Stowe House, the ancestral seat of the Marquess of Buckingham in England. The manuscript changed hands privately a number of times before finally being purchased by the British government and returned to Ireland in 1883. After 140 years of scholarly debate, there are some things we can say of the *Stowe Missal* with some degree of confidence.

A page from the Stowe Missal, written circa 800 AD.

Front and back of the silver shrine created in Lorrha to house the Stowe Missal.

Set down in the first half of the ninth century, it was written with a goose-feather quill on thick vellum – parchment made of calfskin. The manuscript was written in Latin and Irish and, notwithstanding later additions, it was probably written by a single scribe.

Unlike other surviving early Irish manuscripts, the *Stowe Missal* is a small and comparatively bland manuscript. It measures only 15cm x 12cm, and is almost devoid of decoration. The size and style of the manuscript suggests it was not for display, nor was it written to dazzle the reader. According to a leading expert on the subject, Dr Lars B Nooij of the Department of Early Irish at Maynooth University, it was a cheaply made, highly portable functional manuscript, enabling an itinerant monk to perform the basic rituals of the mass and to perform such sacraments as baptism, communion, the anointing of the sick and the last rites. It tells us much about the early Irish liturgy and how mass was said in Ireland in the early medieval period.

The theology of the *Stowe Missal* reflects the paramount importance of community over individuality. For the person who wrote it, being totally absorbed into a community was the goal – they freely gave up their individuality to belong to something greater than themselves.

Most likely written in the hand of its owner and intended user, the Latin text includes an incomplete Gospel of St John, the order of three special votive masses, a litany of saints and the sacraments of baptism and visitation of the sick. It is written in a large, formal and careful script, suggesting it was to be read perhaps from a distance, just as a priest might when saying mass.

A theological tract on the meaning of the symbols of the mass is written in Irish and is recorded in a smaller, ruder text. On the last page of the manuscript, also in Irish in a less formal script, are recorded three medicinal charms, cures or 'spells': one for an eye ailment; one for an injury from a thorn; and one for a urinary infection. It is unusual to find medicinal charms or cures in Irish liturgical documents of the period.

The smaller, less formal script of these later additions suggest they were rough notes by the monk, for private reflection only. They appear to have been written by the original scribe with different quills over an extended period of time. The Irish-language theological tract on the mass is of linguistic interest, as it is one of very few long passages of continuous text in Irish of that period to have survived.

The additions, over time but in the same hand, suggest the manuscript remained in the possession of the original scribe for a significant period, perhaps for his lifetime.

The monks of Tallaght, as elsewhere, routinely travelled and, even in St Mael Ruain's time, had interaction with other monasteries throughout the country. We know that a student of St Mael Ruain retired to Terryglass, and Óengus himself returned to his birthplace of Clonenagh, Co. Laois.

About 200 years after it was written, the manuscript was enclosed in a valuable and highly ornate silver and bronze reliquary or shrine, made in the monastery at Lorrha, Lower Ormond (Tipperary). It remained in Lorrha throughout the medieval period and the 200-year-old shrine was refurbished in the late 1300s at the behest of Philip O'Kennedy, Lord of Ormond, in whose possession it was at the time.

At some point thereafter, the missal and shrine were deposited in a wall in Lackeen Castle, near Lorrha, probably for safekeeping. And there they were discovered, in the eighteenth century. It is unclear how the missal and shrine came to be in Stowe House in Buckinghamshire in England, but it is of note that George Nugent Temple Grenville, the Marquess of Buckingham and owner of Stowe House, was twice Lord Lieutenant of Ireland.

A longstanding academic debate has raged as to whether the missal was written in Tallaght or, in fact, in Lorrha. On balance, the evidence suggests a Tallaght origin. This evidence includes the fact that the name of St Mael Ruain is the most recently added name to a litany of saints, all of whom had been dead for at least a century. His name was also given a capital letter, along with only a small number of elevated saints – notably St Peter and St Patrick – giving St Mael Ruain a privileged position in the litany. Nowhere else in Ireland would Mael Ruain have been held in such high esteem, other than in the monastery he had founded at Tallaght.

The litany also showed a Leinster bias, that is, it chiefly contained the names of saints with Leinster associations. For these reasons, it has long been thought, though not universally agreed, that the *Stowe Missal* was written in Tallaght. Is it a coincidence that the manuscript ended up in Lorrha, where Mael Ruain himself had been born and had studied before coming to Tallaght?

Having been bought by the State in 1883, the *Missal* and shrine were returned to Ireland. The *Missal* has been retained by the Royal Irish Academy. The shrine or reliquary in which it was held from the eleventh to the nineteenth century, made in Lorrha, Co. Tipperary sometime between 1027 and 1033, is now in the National Museum.

What is reasonably certain about Tallaght's three great early manuscripts – the *Martyrology of Tallaght*, the *Martyrology of Óengus* and the *Stowe Missal* – is that they were all written within a single lifetime – within a forty-year period between 793 and 833. They helped lay the foundations for Christian faith, tradition and worship in Tallaght and beyond for the next 1000 years.

Subsidiary churches

By the medieval period, the parish of Tallaght, with its principal church on the old monastic site of Mael Ruain's, had a number of subsidiary churches. In addition to those at Kilnamanagh and Kilmesantan (succeeded by Templeogue), they included Killinarden, Kiltalown and Killininny.

Killinarden (Cill an Ardáin and Ballymana – Townland of the Monks)
Little is recorded or known about the church in Killinarden. By 1837, little could be discerned of it, though an old adjoining graveyard was still distinguishable. The land on which it sat had by

then been cultivated for many years, suggesting the church had fallen out of use since the mid-1700s or earlier. The graveyard had not been used in living memory. At a height of 700 to 900 feet above sea level, it was even higher than that at Kilmesantan and may have been abandoned for similar reasons.

There was a burial ground in nearby Corballis that had been used by the people of the locality up to the 1780s, though that too had fallen into neglect. St Paul's holy well nearby was used by locals, who believed its water could cure stomach ailments.

Given the church of Killinarden's proximity to Ballymanagh (Ballymana), translated as 'Townland of the Monks', these may not be unrelated.

Kiltalown — the Church of the Elms

Now the site of Kiltalown House, built by John Robinson JP, a medieval subsidiary church stood close to this spot, the foundations of which were removed about 1821 for the construction of an earlier house by a Mr Carpenter.

Killininny — the Church of the Daughters

There was a pre-Norman subsidiary church at Killininny, believed to have been on the site of what later became Allenton House. The name Killininny was taken by O'Curry of the Ordnance Survey in 1837 to be a corruption of the name Killnaninghean – the 'Church of the Daughters' – an ancient name of a church 'south of Tallaght'. O'Curry was confident that the site of Allenton was one and the same and was certain that it had been the site of an old monastic establishment. This also aligned with local tradition. An archaeological assessment of the site in 1990, however, turned up little to support the assertion. O'Curry did note that another old church had existed in nearby Oldcourt, of which nothing at all remained.

Kiltalown House, once home to John Robinson, was constructed close to the site of the medieval Church of the Elms.

St. MAELRUANS CHURCH. TALLAGHT. Co. DUBLIN. 10535. W.L.

The rebuilt St Maelruain's Church and its seventeenth-century tower, on the site of the eighth-century monastery.

A Ramble About Tallaght

The rebuilding of St Mael Ruain's, 1829 — Semple's Tallaght temple

After the decline of the Monastery of St Mael Ruain, a medieval church was constructed on the site. In 1630, both the church and chancel were still in good repair. By the 1820s, the church was no longer fit for purpose. The protestant Archbishop Magee was keen to put structures in place to counteract the rise of Catholicism. As part of his ambitious programme of building between 1824 and 1834, St Mael Ruain's, along with seventeen other churches in Dublin, was redeveloped. The Catholic Emancipation Act of 1829 was passed in the same year as the redevelopment of St Mael Ruain's.

The architect of the new church was John Semple Jr. Both his father and grandfather had been notable and successful architects, engineers and builders. His grandfather's brother George was a renowned engineer, who designed St Patrick's Cathedral spire and Essex Bridge. George also designed St Patrick's Hospital for the mentally ill (or 'Swift's Hospital'), fulfilling Swift's bequest, one of Dean Jonathan Swift's many great legacies to the city of Dublin. Swift, of course, was the author of *Gulliver's Travels*, among other things.

Semple Jr trained at his father's knee, completing his papers about 1824. His father had been appointed architect to the Board of First Fruits for the ecclesiastical province of Dublin under the anti-Catholic Archbishop Magee.

Semple was only 28 when he designed St Mael Ruain's and had already completed the ambitious (some would say 'outrageous'!) design for Monkstown Church, the construction of which was hampered by an unfortunate series of setbacks. The design of St Mael Ruain's was likely tempered by the challenges faced by Semple in Monkstown.

The building of Monkstown Church did not run smoothly, and it took an incredible eight years before its eventual opening. The site and design changed at least seven times; four different Building Committees were appointed; the builders went on strike when money dried up; plans were lost; there were difficulties in raising money due to apathetic parishioners; personalities clashed; and, to cap it all, Archbishop Magee, who had masterminded the whole project, lost the wife he adored, was crippled by a series of strokes and died before seeing the church completed.

Semple's church in Monkstown opened on Christmas Day 1831. It was not received particularly well. A writer in *The Dublin Penny Journal* (12 July 1834) declared that he had never seen 'a greater perversion of judgment and taste' and that 'there [was] not a spot in the church where the eye [could] rest without pain'. The relative simplicity and more modest scale of St Mael Ruain's ensured a somewhat smoother completion.

In less than a decade, Semple designed a number of notable churches, many of which are still standing, though some have since been deconsecrated. Among the young architect's impressive portfolio in the period were the Church of Ireland churches in Abbeyleix (1825), Kilternan (1826), Whitechurch and Rathfarnham (1827) and St Mary's Chapel of Ease (the Black Church, 1830) in Broadstone, Dublin. Semple's Black Church is mentioned in Joyce's Ulysses in the chapter entitled 'Circe', as the location of one of Bloom's many sins: He went through a form of clandestine marriage with at least one woman in the shadow of the Black Church. The church was also a favourite of poet Austin Clarke, who named his memoir, *Twice Round the Black Church*, after it.

The early years of Semple's career were arguably his most productive and rewarding. He experienced his greatest success while still only in his twenties, and his greatest legacy is those buildings he designed before he was 30 years old. The death of Archbishop Magee in 1831, along with the disbandment of the Board of First Fruits and the reorganisation of the Church of Ireland's building activities in 1834, may have played an unwelcome role in Semple's career trajectory. After the death of his father, his career took something of a nosedive. With the decline in ecclesiastical commissions, he turned his attention to designing residential developments and prison extensions.

While overseeing the construction of St Mael Ruain's, a neighbour in Tallaght – the anti-Catholic Major James Palmer, who had recently constructed Tallaght House – held the position of Inspector General of Prisons in Ireland. Among the many responsibilities of that role was to rubber-stamp plans and designs for new prisons, or for their extension. From about 1835 until 1843, Semple was architect to the 'City Prisons, Roads and Pipe Water Works'.

One of the few residential streetscapes designed and completed by Semple was Seaview Terrace, Donnybrook, later home to novelist Anthony Trollope. It was one of the last major Georgian

Semple's Church of St Mael Ruain, under construction, circa 1829.

St Mael Ruain's Church, Tallaght, designed by John Semple Jr and built in 1829.

developments in what became a very Victorian and post-Victorian neighbourhood. Semple lived in a house called Lilliput (now Riversdale House), before later moving into one of the houses he had designed, named Eglinton.

Afterwards John Semple became involved in the development of Belgrave Square, Monkstown. He appears to have overstretched himself financially in relation to this development, and was declared bankrupt in 1849, twenty years after designing St Mael Ruain's. In later life, due to his financial embarrassment, he lived with one of his sons. He died in 1882.

When the old medieval church on the ancient monastic site of St Mael Ruain's in Tallaght was being removed and cleared, prior to the construction of Semple's church in 1829, workmen found a lead coffin, containing, it was believed, the remains of Archbishop Hoadly's wife. One of workmen cut the lead coffin into narrow strips. He rolled the strips around his arms, his legs and his trunk and walked into Dublin where he promptly sold the valuable metal. It was not revealed until sometime later where the lead had come from.

Some material from the earlier church was incorporated into the new building, as was the old tower. To the left of the present pathway from the entrance gate to the church was once the floor of the old church, and it is believed there were substantial vaults under the ground there. They may be there still.

Moll Rooney's Losset

Still in the grounds of St Mael Ruain's church, to the east of the tower, lies a rough and rude pre-Norman granite font. Similar fonts of the pre-Norman period have been found at the churches in Clondalkin, Cruagh, Kilmesantan (St Anne's) and Saggart. Handcock noted 150 years ago that 'neglected on the ground [is] a most curious ancient font of a horseshoe form'.

The fonts found in Clondalkin, Cruagh and Kilmesantan are of a rectangular form, while that in Saggart is circular, making Tallaght's font somewhat unusual. Its 'D' or horseshoe shape suggests it may once have been, or at least intended to be, placed against a wall, perhaps at the door of the church or monastery.

Locals in Tallaght took to calling the font 'Moll Rooney's Losset', a corruption of both 'Mael Ruain' and the Irish word losaid, meaning a wooden trough or kneading tray, used in the past for kneading bread. It is likely that this name was because of its shape.

The purpose of the font or trough has been debated for almost 200 years. It may have been a baptismal font – given its large size, it has been speculated that it was for the baptising of adult converts to Christianity. It is unnecessarily large for infants.

Its 'D' shape, however, presumably to be placed against a wall, suggests it may simply have been for monks to wash their feet before entering the monastery. Malachi Horan, in Dr Little's Malachi *Horan Remembers* (1943), suggests it was for the washing of pilgrims' feet – also entirely plausible.

Malachi Horan relayed events within his own lifetime relating to the font:

About fifty years ago [this would coincide approximately with the placing of the font on bricks in 1890] the congregation of the Church thought they would put it to similar use again [washing of pilgrims' feet]. Four men were ordered to bring it to the gate. There was Chris Barrett, John Boothman, Larry Dwyer, and Michael Lawlor. They were four big men and well used to labour. But they could not move that trough. No, not an inch could they get a stir in it. They brought sticks and crowbars, and strained till they near broke their backs, but as well try to shift Cruachan with a furze-root. But what could they expect? Was not the weight of the hand of God on it? At long last them that were there grew uneasy in themselves, and told the men to stop working and leave the Losset where it was.

St Mael Ruain's Losset, by William Frederick Wakeman, 1895.

A Ramble About Tallaght

There it rests to this very day. Chris Barrett, John Boothman, Larry Dwyer and Michael Lawlor (God help them) all were dead ere the year was out.

Malachi Horan's memory may have been failing. It was in fact likely to have been only thirty-five years earlier, rather than fifty. For Chris Barrett died on 12 October 1907, aged 54 years. John Boothman died on 19 December 1907, only nine weeks later. He was 57 years old. Laurence Dwyer, 48, died on Valentine's Day 1909. Within sixteen months of each other, three of the four named men were dead.

Tradition and lore in the village of Tallaght held that Cromwell's men once used the font for watering their horses. An account from St Mary's School, Tallaght, written in the 1930s for the Schools' Folklore Collection records:

> Some say it was St Mael Ruain's holy water font while older people maintain that it was on this stone St Mael Ruain divided the bread which the monks had baked to help the starving people of the district.

Another account from the 1930s' Schools' Collection, from Breeda Doyle of Mountain View, Main Street, Tallaght, recalls:

> There is an ancient Baptismal Font … which is believed to be that used by St Mael Ruain when baptising. But during the Reformation when the English seized the church the baptismal font was removed from the church to its present position … When Cromwell was marching from Drogheda

St Mael Ruain's Losset.

to Wexford he passed through Tallaght and having to stop the night and seeing the church, he and his soldiers decided to stable their horses in it. He also used the Holy Water Font as a trough for his horses to drink from but they could not take all the water out of it no matter how hard they tried, so they bored a hole in the bottom to drain it off. But a drain of water still remained which after all their efforts they did not succeed in moving it. Thousands of men and horses tried to pull it away but many were killed and a few were badly injured.

While the above story is most certainly an impressive embellishment, there is probably at least an element of truth in it. A Captain Allend is recorded as having desecrated the church when stationed there in 1651, and had most likely put the font to some practical use.

A hole was later drilled into the base of the font, and local lore tells us that the man who drilled the hole suffered a 'withered hand' within a year of having drilled it.

Cholera and comets — plague and faith

Conditions in Tallaght and indeed in Ireland in the summer of 1832 were grim. Poor potato crops in 1829 and again in 1830 were followed by an economic depression and a collapse in agricultural prices. The Catholic Emancipation Act had been passed in 1829 and the Tithe War was well under way. To add to the woes of both economic and political uncertainty, the arrival of cholera in Ireland that spring added to a general feeling of vulnerability and foreboding. For the poorly educated but newly emancipated Catholic population, in such circumstances, faith was more accessible, and perhaps more comforting, than facts.

On 18 March 1832, in Belfast, the first reported case of cholera in Ireland appeared. By 8 May, only seven weeks later, cholera had been reported in fourteen of the 32 counties, including the urban centres of Dublin and Cork. The fear of cholera spread even faster than the bacterial disease. A general panic quickly took root among the peasant classes.

Rumours of apparitions, apocalypse and cosmic catastrophe abounded. On Saturday, 9 June, an apparition of the Virgin Mary on an altar in the chapel in Charleville, north Cork, was reported. It was a timely appearance. She left on the altar 'sacred ashes', which, she had informed those who saw her, was the only protection against cholera. She ordered that small parcels of the ashes should be brought to the neighbours' houses and placed under the rafters. They were told the neighbours should then take ashes from their chimneys, and proceed to do the same to four neighbouring houses.

Within hours of the apparition, the news had spread across north Cork and within 48 hours had reached Queen's County and Westmeath. Within six days, most of the country, from Wexford to Donegal, had witnessed extraordinary scenes of dozens, sometimes hundreds of animated locals running from house to house carrying pieces of lighting-straw, burnt sticks or smouldering turf. The degree of hope of protection that accompanied the ashes was exceeded only by the panic of imminent and mortal danger.

On 11 June 1832, Humphrey O'Sullivan, a schoolteacher living in Callan, County Kilkenny, made the following entry in his diary:

> The lower classes of the Irish are a credulous people. Some practical joker sent a fool out with a small piece of charred stick, or some other bit of kindling, which had been extinguished in Easter-water, or holy water, and told him to divide it into four parts, and give it to four persons in four houses, telling them that the cholera would kill them unless each one of them did the same thing. By this means 16 persons, and 64, and 256, and 1,024, and 4,096 etc., etc., got this fire, until the entire country was a laughing stock for Protestants.

A finely built new Anglican church – St Mael Ruain's – had opened in Tallaght village only three years earlier, built upon the ancient monastic site and funded by the Board of First Fruits.

As the message spread throughout the country, so too did it evolve. In some localities people were asked to visit four houses, and in some, it was seven. In some localities, it was turf that was to be burnt, and in some a stick or a straw. In some localities the ashes were to be placed under the rafters of the home and in others, the sign of the cross was to be marked on the threshold or the door.

The message travelled across the national grapevine, accompanied by increasingly alarming accounts of how hundreds of people had just died of cholera in a locality not so far away. Accounts began to emerge of entire villages being virtually wiped out. When the message crossed the Wicklow Mountains to Rathdrum, it was claimed that several hundred people had just died on the other side of the mountain. There was no truth to the story. When the ashes reached Newtownmountkennedy, it was reported that 200 people had died in Hollywood. There was no truth to that story either.

But more extraordinarily, as the message and the ashes spread, so too did the rationale. What started in Charleville in north Cork as a holy apparition granting protection against cholera had, by the time it arrived in Bagenalstown, Co. Carlow, mutated into news that the town of Roscrea, Co. Tipperary, had been devastated by 'fire from Heaven'. Carlow town itself received news that the colliery district around Castlecomer had been destroyed by fire. In Dunlavin, Co. Wicklow, the blessed turf was distributed with news that Queen's County (the entire county) had been destroyed by a ball of fire from Heaven.

It was in that context that Patrick McDonald of Bohernabreena, having been approached by the five men from Kilbride at lunchtime on 12 June 1832, put down his shovel and went about the urgent business of distributing his blessed turf to protect his neighbours and friends around Tallaght and district from comets or cholera.

CHAPTER 3

Tallaght Castle and the Archiepiscopal Palace

From 1192, the archbishops of Dublin kept a manor at Swords, North County Dublin. In about 1200, the then-Archbishop built a substantial castle there, Swords Castle. For over 140 years, Swords served continually as the manorial residence for Dublin's archbishops. It had been founded close to the sixth-century monastic settlement of St Colmcille (St Columba).

Alexander de Bicknor was appointed Archbishop of Dublin in 1317, and would hold the post until his death in July 1349. He had already served as Lord Treasurer of Ireland (1307–09) and would hold several other important posts, such as Lord Chancellor of Ireland and Lord Deputy, sometimes while he was Archbishop. De Bicknor was, at times, effectively the chief representative of English rule in Ireland. At the time of his appointment to the see as Archbishop of Dublin, the Scottish invader Edward Bruce had just been crowned High King of Ireland, after a bloody campaign.

Many of the native Irish chieftains and lords supported Bruce against the English Crown and the Crown's representative in Ireland – the Archbishop of Dublin. On de Bicknor's return

Tallaght Castle and the Archiepiscopal Palace

A view of the ancient archiepiscopal palace at Tallaght by W Monck Mason, circa 1821.

from receiving his appointment to the Archbishopric, Bruce was marching on to the neighbourhood of Dublin. Bruce's campaign in Ireland in 1316 and 1317 devastated the country south of Dundalk to the gates of Dublin.

The Archbishop's residence in Swords was not a heavily fortified structure. While there is no direct evidence that Bruce attacked Swords Castle, it does appear to have been abandoned by the Archbishop at this time. The weakness of the structure highlighted its inadequacy during troubled times. Its proximity to the coast might also have been perceived as a weakness in times of strife. By 1326, Swords Castle is recorded as having fallen into disrepair.

In 1310, the year after de Bicknor relinquished his role as Lord Treasurer of Ireland, the inhabitants of Tallaght were provided with a grant to construct a wall enclosing the town, to protect it against the native Irish tribes, the O'Tooles and the O'Byrnes. Fourteen years later, de Bicknor, now Archbishop of Dublin, was provided with a grant to construct a castle there. It would serve both as a country residence and as a secure fortress, part of the Pale embattlements. As a fortress against the native Irish chieftains, it would prove to have limited utility.

Perhaps importantly, it was built close to the site of St Mael Ruain's ancient Monastery – one of the 'two bright suns of Ireland', the other being Howth – lending an ecclesiastical and sacred foundation and tradition to the Archbishop's authority. Described as 'half-monastic, half-baronial', it reflected de Bicknor's own ambitions as Archbishop. He had pretentions to challenge the Archbishop of Armagh, wishing to assert his own office for the Primacy of all Ireland.

The Archbishop's bawns in Tallaght were stocked with long and short horns, and his sheep grazed on the rich pastures along the banks of the Dodder, from Rathfarnham to Oldbawn.

In 1324, while the Archbishop of Dublin was having his castle built in Tallaght, some pressing ecclesiastical matters presented themselves – the Kilkenny witch trials.

Dame Alice Kyteler had married William Outlaw, a wealthy moneylender, in Kilkenny in 1280. They had a son of the same name before her husband died in 1301. She remarried shortly afterward, but was again widowed. A third time she married, and a third time she was widowed. She was living with her fourth husband, Sir John de Poer, a brother of the Seneschal of Kilkenny, when the Bishop of Ossory, the Very Reverend De Ledrede, paid a visit to that city. He accused Dame Alice Kyteler of being a witch. It was all the rage in Europe about that time, and the Very Reverend Bishop was a well-travelled man.

Kyteler was accused of poisoning her husbands, of demon worship, of having acquired the power of sorcery through sexual intercourse with a demon, and of sacrificing living animals to demons and devils, including one called 'Robert Artisson'. Alice Kyteler was connected with some of the most important families in the country. Her son William, her lady-in-waiting Petronilla de Midia, and eight other persons of the lower classes were also accused. The Chancellor of Ireland was Roger Outlaw, and he would come to her defence.

It was, as Bernadette Williams, a lecturer in medieval history at Trinity College, Dublin, notes,

> an occasion for a major confrontation between secular and ecclesiastical authority. In theory the state claimed control over the material life of its subjects and the church over the spiritual life. While this principle of separation was acknowledged by both parties, the dividing line was often disputed as each jealously and zealously guarded their own rights in their separate law courts.

There was a possibility that the Bishop of Ossory might find himself in a sticky wicket or, worse still, the Archbishop of Dublin. Something was brewing. A pungent stew of clerical authority, familial relations and Crown interests filled the toxic political cauldron in which the Archbishop now sat.

It would be resolved, to the satisfaction of almost all parties, with a witch's cunning, a bishop's grace and a chancellor's prudence. Alice Kyteler was spirited out of the country before formal charges could be brought against her. Her loyal and faithful servant, however, was not. Petronilla de Midia, her lady-in-waiting, was arraigned and found guilty of being a witch.

She was not related to anyone in high office. She was not secreted out of the country. She was whipped six times and burnt at the stake in Kilkenny. Her ashes were scattered to the four winds, much to the satisfaction of the Bishop of Ossory, the indifference of the Chancellor and the relief of the Archbishop. With the matter finally extinguished, de Bicknor could get back to building his castle in Tallaght.

It has been noted that the Kilkenny witch trials were very soon followed by a famine in Ireland. The newly built castle in Tallaght was better stocked than it was fortified, making it an attractive target for the hill men of Ballinascorney and the wild men of Imaal.

In 1331, the O'Tooles of Imaal came down from the hills with sparthe, skein and bow and forced their way into the castle at Tallaght, killing a number of the Archbishop's servants and driving off 300 beasts. A large body of Dublin citizens marched out to Tallaght, under Sir Philip Brett, to challenge the native tribe. After a pitched battle, few got to march back.

After this event, 'watch and ward' was consistently kept at the castle of Tallaght. In fact, this incident is sometimes credited with the foundation of the first public 'police force' in Ireland. The raid likely caused considerable damage to the episcopal mansion, and in 1340, de Bicknor rebuilt it.

Over their 500-year history, the Archbishop's castle, palace and manor house at Tallaght housed some of the most colourful, interesting and influential men in Irish history. They were for the most part highly educated, well-travelled and politically connected. From the time Tallaght Castle was built in 1324 until the Palace was levelled and the land sold in 1822, a total of 34 prelates were translated to the Archbishopric of Dublin. Tallaght was, for much of the time, an inhospitable quarter. Some, we might suppose, never used their country residence at all, while some visited it regularly. Few spent a great deal of time there, but those who did left their mark.

A Ramble About Tallaght

Archbishops Tregury, Browne, Bulkeley, Hoadly and Fowler were perhaps those who left the most lasting impressions – Tregury, through the restoration of the Palace; Browne, through his discontent at being domiciled in Tallaght; Bulkeley, through the building of Oldbawn House; Hoadly, through the redevelopment of the Palace and the gardens: and Fowler? Well, he was just remembered in Tallaght as a nice guy. All had a tough time of it in Tallaght, and had plenty to write home about.

The Most Reverend Michael Tregury (Archbishop of Dublin 1450–71)

Michael Tregury (Michael of Tregury, Cornwall) served the see of Dublin as Archbishop for 21 years and had previously been Chaplain to Henry VI of England.

His time in Tallaght was not without drama, and indeed even his journey to Dublin was filled with adventure. On the way to Dublin in 1451, his ship sank and he lost most of his valuables. It was perhaps an omen, a prelude to his troubled tenure as Archbishop.

In that same year, the Archbishop gave 'recommendatory certificates' to 50 people of his diocese to travel to Rome for the celebration of the Jubilee being held under Pope Nicholas V. It was to be one of the great gatherings of people from all over the Christian world, and Dublin would not be underrepresented. Such were the celebrations in Rome, seven of the 50 Irish pilgrims were pressed to death in the crowd and a number more died of fatigue on the return journey. The seven died at 'Adrian's Mole' (Mole Adriana), along with about 190 others caught up in the festivities. Many more drowned in the River Tiber.

In addition to their own bad news, the bedraggled band of survivors returning to Dublin in 1453 carried other tidings: Constantinople had fallen to the Turks, and Emperor Constantine Palaeologus was slain (After 1100 years, he would be the last Christian ruler of Constantinople, at least to date). Archbishop Tregury was deeply moved. He promptly declared a three-day fast throughout the Dublin diocese, promising indulgences for those who observed the fast. He led a procession of his clergy to Christ Church Cathedral dressed in no more than sackcloth and ashes.

Later that year, Archbishop Tregury travelled to England to bring a message from the Deputy Lieutenant, Edward Fitz Eustace. On his journey back to Ireland, he was kidnapped by Breton pirates. They took him aboard a ship in Dublin Bay and sailed toward Ardglass in County Down, holding the Prelate for ransom. The party was pursued and, amid the slaughter of 520 of the sea-rovers, the Archbishop was finally rescued.

Archbishop Tregury tended to avoid the political realm, focusing on his ecclesiastical role, but where land, power, taxes and rents were concerned, it was difficult to remain outside of that realm. As a member of the Privy Council, he received an annual salary of £20.

According to the *Dictionary of Irish Biography*, Archbishop Tregury

> … served as a commissioner to supervise the defences of Dublin and also received a grant in 1460 to re-enter all diocesan lands in south Dublin, any previous grants or alienations notwithstanding; the only exceptions were that the castles of Tallaght and Ballymore were to be garrisoned by English troops. In connection with this reassertion of diocesan rights, Tregury was kidnapped in 1461–2 by the Harolds and the O'Byrnes, who were subsequently excommunicated for their abuse and ill-treatment of him.

The exact circumstance of this 'kidnapping' are uncertain. In his *The Memoirs of the Archbishops of Dublin* (1838), D'Alton notes:

> There is extant in the Liber Niger of Christ Church, a copy of a bull of Pope Pius the Second, dated the 23rd of November 1462, and directed to the Bishop and Archdeacon of Ossory, commanding them to pronounce as excommunicated, Geoffrey Harold and two of his sons, Patrick Byrne, Thady Sherriff, Robert Burnell and others, laymen of the city and diocese of Dublin, for assaulting this prelate and committing him to prison, and to keep the offenders under this ban, until they personally sought absolution at Rome with the sanction and approval of the said bishop and archdeacon. These were, probably, some accessories in the transaction mentioned ante at 1453.

This suggests that the excommunication was related to the Breton pirates episode nine years earlier, which seems unlikely.

Shortly before his death, the elderly Prelate was pardoned by the Pope for failing to carry out an oath to visit the shrines of the apostles.

Archbishop Tregury was known to have a temper. In 1465, he was accused of assaulting Stephen fitz William and stealing a halberd (a weapon consisting of an axe blade topped with a spike mounted on a long shaft). Although he did not appear in court to clear his name, he was allowed to clear himself before the Earl of Desmond, the Deputy Lieutenant.

He is recorded as having been a lover of music and owned two organs, which he kindly bequeathed to St Patrick's Cathedral.

During his time in Tallaght, Tregury made substantial repairs to the Archbishop's 'manor house'. At a remove of 550 years, it is difficult to ascertain what life in Tallaght Palace may have been like in the 1460s. But only ten days before he died, Archbishop Tregury made a last will and testament. An inventory of his personal possessions was made and also a statement of his debts. It gives us some insight into the sorts of things we might have found in the palace at Tallaght:

In plate, one basin with a ewer [jug] of silver; two salt cellars of silver and overgilt, with one cover; two standing cups of silver and overgilt, with two covers; one standing cup of silver with a cover; three flat cups called flat pieces, with one cover; a chalice with a paten overgilt; a large scarlet robe used for parliament with suitable furred hood (in the keeping of Stephen Buttiler); five habits with their suitable hoods (four of which remain in the keeping of the said Stephen, and the other one with the Constable of Tallaght); a missal, a grayle, two brass candlesticks for the altar; one blue cloth of silk for the same; three bed coverings; five towels for the altar; a pair of organs; two chasubles with three albs and one trunk; two feather beds; a basin with a ewer of electrum; a white bed with three curtains; two red beds; four mantles; a black furred gown with a scarlet hood; a gown of russet furred with lamb skins; a red gown; a banner called a guidon; one trunk and one carshet coffer of spruce; two habits cut for riding; four bankers; a candlestick with flowers; a candlestick without flowers; a mattress. In the haggard in Tallaght 7 stacks or heaps of grain; in the barn at Finglas two heaps. In the barn at Swords three stacks; in the fields 40 acres sown in wheat; 14 horses for the plough; 6 horses for wains or carts; one cart horse with David Foulore; two horses; four mares with their foals; thirty cows; fourteen calves.

Tregury died in Tallaght Palace on 21 December 1471. He was 72 years old, a great age for that time. In accordance with his last wishes, his remains were brought to Dublin and he was buried in St Patrick's Cathedral. His epitaph reads:

> Preasul Metropolis
> Michael hic Dublinenus
> Marmore tumbatus,
> pro me Christum flagitetis

which translates as

> Here's Michael the Prelate
> of Dublin See,
> In marble intomb'd,
> Invoke Christ for me

Archbishop Tregury's tomb fell into neglect and obscurity for several hundred years. It was discovered under the rubbish in St Stephen's Chapel in St Patrick's Cathedral. In 1730, Dean Swift preserved the cover of his tomb and had it erected 'in the wall on the left hand after entering the west gate'.

Archbishop George Browne (Archbishop of Dublin 1535–54)

Archbishop George Browne spent a nervous and challenging time in Tallaght. He was nominated to the See of Dublin when a vacancy arose following the murder of his immediate predecessor, Archbishop Allen, in the Rising of Kildare in 1534.

Browne was nominated by Henry VIII. D'Alton's *Memoirs of the Archbishops of Dublin* and Alfred Webb's *A Compendium of Irish Biography* (1878) both suggest 19 March 1535 as the date of his consecration, although James Murray's *Dictionary of Irish Biography* suggests it was 19 March 1536.

Of even less certainty is when precisely he died, an unusual obscurity for someone who held such a prominent office for almost 20 years. But Archbishop George Browne, the first Archbishop of Dublin during the turbulent times of the Reformation, was ultimately 'expelled and driven from the see' in 1554 and is believed to have died sometime in 1556. What is somewhat more certain is how unhappy he was while in Tallaght.

Browne complained bitterly of the treatment of his tenants in Tallaght by the neighbouring O'Tooles. On 16 February 1538, Archbishop Browne took up his quill in Tallaght Palace to express to Lord Thomas Cromwell his sense of vulnerability, isolation and discontent:

> Other place had I none to repair unto but only Tallaght, which adjoineth upon the O'Tooles, being now my mortal enemies, daily oppressing my poor tenants, above all others, much doubting that they be somewhat encouraged so to do, for they now be at my Lord Deputy's peace, doth no manner robbery but upon my only tenants. His Lordship hath sundry times, said he would be even with me, but, indeed, if he constrain me to lie at Tallaght, it will be odd on my behalf, for in short time, I shall be in the same case with the O'Tooles, that my predecessors was with the Geraldines. For servants have I none, passing four and a chaplain, which is very slender company to resist so many malefactors as be of the O'Tooles and their adherents, at the least two hundred persons. How I am wrapped, God judge. If I endeavour not to preach the word of God, then am I assured to incur my prince's and your lordship's displeasure. If I repair and manure in my said house of Tallaght, then am I assured nigh to be my confusion. Thus am I on every side involved with sorrows and all I think too little if it were for my prince's honour.

The Lord Deputy, Lord Leonard Grey, arranged a meeting with Turlough O'Toole, under the guise of wishing to come to a settlement with the clan. They were to meet at the border of Dublin. The Lord Deputy proceeded with an armed force and after a brief diplomatic exchange with Turlough O'Toole, attempted to take him prisoner. The O'Tooles took flight and were unsuccessfully pursued by Grey's forces until nightfall. In response to this treachery, in 1540 the O'Tooles laid waste to Tallaght and the manors of Crumlin, Saggart and Newcastle. These were uncertain times for the Archbishop. Tallaght would remain a troubled district for bishop or beggar.

The Most Reverend Lancelot Bulkeley (Archbishop of Dublin 1619–50)

Lancelot Bulkeley was the son of Sir Richard Bulkeley, Knight of Beaumaris and Cheadle, Anglesey in Wales, and his second wife Agnes. On his father death's, Lancelot's mother was charged with adultery and the murder of her husband – Lancelot's eldest half-brother, also Sir Richard, accused her of poisoning him. She was found guilty of adultery, but acquitted by a local jury of murder. Lancelot Bulkeley was educated at Brasenose College in Oxford.

For most of his years as Archbishop of Dublin, he resided in Tallaght and in 1635, built Oldbawn House (see Chapter 4) for his son, Archdeacon William Bulkeley, on some of the 10,000 acres he then held. Not long after Oldbawn House was completed, it was burnt to the ground in the Catholic Rebellion of 1641.

D'Alton's *Memoirs of the Archbishops of Dublin* states that Archbishop Bulkeley's 'only known literary production was a pamphlet, entitled "Proposal for sending back the Nobility and Gentry of Ireland"'. This is incorrect, however. The pamphlet was in fact written by the Archbishop's grandson, Sir Richard Bulkeley, and published in 1690, some forty years after the Archbishop's death.

As Archbishop, Bulkeley had concerns that sedition was being cultivated among the Roman Catholic population by Jesuits and friars in the city. Bulkeley applied to the Lord Justices for a warrant and a file of musketeers to seize the offenders. On the feast of St Stephen, 1629, Bulkeley and his party set out to make a stand and let it be known that Catholic sedition would not be tolerated.

Mass-goers in the Carmelite Church on Cook Street would get a rude awakening. The celebration of High Mass was interrupted by a violent visitation by Archbishop Lancelot Bulkeley, Lord Mayor Foster, Alderman Kely and Sheriff Forster, together with a file of soldiers under the command of Captain Carey. The fastened doors of the Carmelite Church were broken open. Watched by a startled congregation, the intruders wrecked the altar, pulled down and defaced pictures and toppled statues, including one of St Francis. Archbishop Bulkeley was particularly energetic in tearing down the pulpit of the Catholic Church.

Two friars were arrested and, with prisoners and sacred treasures, the attacking party left the Church, but were immediately halted. The local population, a crowd estimated at 3000, had gathered in the street outside. Mainly through the intervention of local women, the two friars were freed.

The growing and angry crowd surrounded the Archbishop and his party as they attempted to flee to safety. They got as far as Skinner's Row, where they were forced to seek refuge in a building until they could be brought to safety by a military escort. The incident was followed by rioting in the city and a curfew was declared the following day. Many citizens were arrested, including the constables of Cook Street, Cornmarket and High Street – for failing to keep order in the district and for neglect of their duty.

On 8 September 1650, Archbishop Bulkeley died in Tallaght, in his 82nd year. Of all the prelates that resided in the Palace of Tallaght, he has left one of the more intangible but memorable legacies – his ghost. The ghost of Archbishop Bulkeley is believed to haunt the road from Oldbawn House (now Tymon Bawn Community Centre) to Tallaght Palace (now the Dominican Priory). For centuries, local people feared seeing the phantom carriage of the Archbishop as he travelled to Oldbawn from his Palace. Local superstition had it that anyone who laid eyes on the Archbishop's ghost would die within a year. It was no doubt an effective legend to deter the superstitious Catholic peasants from trespassing on two of the finest residences' and gardens in all of Uppercross.

The Most Reverend John Hoadly (Archbishop of Dublin 1729–42)

When Benjamin Hoadly and his younger brother John were little boys, their doting father Samuel predicted that one day his eldest son would be an archbishop and his younger boy a bishop. Samuel Hoadly was a schoolmaster and a writer of textbooks. His *The Natural Method of Teaching. Being the Accident in Questions and Answers, Explained, Amended, Abridged, and Fitted to the Capacity and use of the Lowest Form* (1683) was the most popular school manual of the age, and before 1773 reached its eleventh edition.

Like many parents, Sam Hoadly had the capacity to both overestimate and underestimate his children. He was wrong in his prediction, but there is a lot to be said for parental expectations and a liberal sprinkling of sibling rivalry. There is also a lot to be said for having a doting and affectionate schoolteacher for a father.

Benjamin Hoadly grew up to become Bishop of Winchester, and his younger brother John became Archbishop of Dublin and later of Armagh – Primate of All Ireland.

When Archbishop Hoadly succeeded to the Dublin See in 1729, he found Tallaght Castle in ruins. Perhaps wanting a bigger house than his Very Reverend brother, the Most Reverend John Hoadly promptly set about levelling the old manor house and rebuilding a plush new abode. Between 1730 and 1742, he expended £2500 in overturning the 400-year-old remains of the Castle and manor house and constructing from their material a 'convenient and elegant' episcopal palace.

By English standards, its design was poor. Even by Irish standards, it was nothing to write home about. Topographer and novelist James Norris Brewer (1826) described the palace as 'a spacious, but long and narrow building, composed of the grey stone of the country, and is destitute of pretensions to architectural beauty. The interior contains many apartments of ample proportions but none that are highly embellished'. Accommodation included a hall measuring twenty-one feet square, lit by two tiers of windows, and a drawing room thirty-three feet long and twenty-one feet wide.

The artistic images we have inherited of Tallaght Palace are of questionable accuracy. Berenger's watercolour is likely to better represent the design of the Palace than Monck-Masons later engraving, of which Weston St John Joyce commented:

> It is impossible not to conclude that the well-known engraving in the possession of the Dominican Fathers at Tallaght … representing this structure as a Lordly pile of imposing proportions, was largely due to the imagination of the artist who depicted it.

The artist Gabriel Berenger, visiting Tallaght in the 1760s, made notes on his subjects. The palace at Tallaght he described as

An old castle modernised … The right wing is modern, the steps still more so, being new and being made of cut mountain stone. I was told that it was intended to rebuild the left wing just in the same taste as the right.

Austin Cooper, antiquarian and associate of Berenger, surveying the pile in 1779, noted: 'For a thing of the kind it is the poorest I ever saw. It is a large piece of patchwork, so devoid of either order or regularity, that it is past describing.' (Austin Cooper liked nice buildings. He would acquire for himself an estate in Kinsealy and the great house Abbeville, later the home of An Taoiseach Charles J Haughey. Like Haughey, Cooper was fabulously wealthy and was said to have won £20,000 on a lottery ticket in the 1820s! He was, incidentally I am sure, married to a daughter of Timothy Turner, a lottery ticket agent of Clare Street, Dublin. Also like Haughey, he earned considerable sums of money from the public purse, through the various public offices he held.)

In the second issue of the *Dublin Journal*, dated May 1761, an unnamed gentleman, educated in France, and giving an account of 'A Journey through Ireland', says of the Palace at Tallaght, 'There is not any thing worthy [of] remark in it. The last Archbishop that resided here when it was in its original splendour was Michael Tregury who died in August 1449.' The antiquarian William Wilde speculated that this unnamed gentleman was Gabriel Berenger. It may have been. But the statement was incorrect, at least in part, for Archbishop Michael Tregury died almost 22 years later, in 1471. The unnamed gentleman continued: 'The town is very inconsiderable; there are two cabarets; two tippling houses …' The former part of that statement was true then. And the latter part still is. There are still only 'two tippling houses' in the old village!

In 1742, Archbishop Hoadly was further elevated, being made Archbishop of Armagh. The following year, he had his name annexed to a proclamation signed by the Privy Council, strictly enforcing the Penal Laws, enforcing the capture and imprisonment of papal (Catholic) bishops, Jesuits, friars and other ecclesiastics. Ninety years later, the site of his newly kitted-out palace in Tallaght would be owned by a Catholic. And thirty years after that, it would house a Dominican novitiate! Perhaps all ecclesiastical careers end in failure.

The Most Reverend John Hoadly was an inquisitive agriculturist and delighted in practical farming. He was described by a contemporary as 'pious without superstition; charitable without ostentation; learned without pride; facetious and entertaining without levity and capable of adapting his conversation to persons of all ages, manners and professions'.

Archbishop Hoadly had a strained relationship with Dean Swift of St Patrick's Cathedral, but this was eased by Hoadly's daughter having a warmth for the aged Dean, who had always enjoyed the company of younger ladies. Swift, on hearing that Sarah Bellingham (Hoadly's daughter) had contracted smallpox, was greatly distressed, as she had always been most kind to him. In one of his letters to her, he thanks her for the pig and the bowl of butter which she had sent him, and in jest criticises her handwriting and spelling, stating that they are 'more like a parson's than a lady's'.

After four years as Archbishop of Armagh, Hoadly bought Rathfarnham Castle, Co. Dublin, where he retired, dying of a fever in 1746. Defeated by life, he was buried privately at Tallaght in the same vault as his lady and her mother – his mother-in-law – for all eternity. Archbishop Hoadly didn't do purgatory. No monument has been found marking Hoadly's final resting place, nor was his interment recorded in the Burial Register there. When the old St Mael Ruain's Church was being removed in the late 1820s, workmen found a leaden coffin. It was believed to containing the remains of the Archbishop's wife.

His only daughter, Sarah, married Bellingham Boyle, MP for Bandon Bridge. Sarah inherited Rathfarnham Castle on her father's death, and there they resided extravagantly and impressively beyond their means.

John Hoadly's loyal and faithful older brother Benjamin, himself an influential and controversial figure, had, perhaps unbeknownst to his little brother, played an important role in his elevation to the posts of Bishop of Leighlin and Ferns and Archbishop of Dublin. Benjamin had written to Robert Walpole, the Prime Minister, recommending his brother's elevation.

The Most Reverend Robert Fowler (Archbishop of Dublin 1779–1801)

Archbishop Robert Fowler was the last prelate to occupy the palace of Tallaght with any regularity. During Fowler's period in Tallaght, the gardens of Tallaght Palace were brought to a high state of perfection. Fowler enclosed the gardens, perhaps as much for defensive reasons as

A Ramble About Tallaght

The Gate of Tallaght Castle, drawing by Gabriel Berenger, circa 1779

aesthetic ones. In 1783, the then-Archbishop of Dublin received a certificate from the Lord Lieutenant and Council stating he had expended the sum of £3582 in 'making several repairs and improvements at the palaces, offices, and gardens of St Sepulchre and Tallaght'. Four years later, in July 1787, a further sum of £1397 was spent for similar purposes. He and his wife took Tallaght Palace as their principal residence.

Fowler was described by an opponent as a 'paltry, pragmatic man of straw', but was remembered in Tallaght as a kind, courteous and affable gentleman, declining a throne that had been placed in Tallaght Church for him. On Monday, 16 June 1783, The Most Reverend Archbishop of Dublin entertained his Excellency the (recently appointed) Lord Lieutenant (the Earl of Northington), along with many of the nobility and gentry, at a dinner in Tallaght Palace. Such an event indicates that the Palace was still in a reasonable state of repair at this time.

In November 1787, a fire was discovered in four different compartments of the Archbishop's City Palace on Kevin Street in Dublin. A neighbouring cleric rushed to the Palace. He discovered that the locked palace doors had been opened and found an ancient, faithful porter lying slumped on the stairs near the great entrance. His throat had been cut. In fact, his head was almost severed from his body. In a small room upstairs, the only female servant of the house was found with her brains dashed out and otherwise mangled in the most shocking manner. 'Providentially', the Archbishop and his family were in Tallaght, as was all of his plate.

On a Friday morning in August 1788, the Archbishop was returning from his morning ride when his horse unexpectedly took flight, throwing His Grace to the ground. He was taken up 'senseless', but was well enough recovered in a few minutes to be able to ride home to Tallaght on his servant's horse, and felt 'no greater inconvenience, than a few slight contusions from the accident'.

Archbishop Fowler's wife died in the Palace in January 1793 and was buried at Tallaght Church. By 1797, the seventy-two-year-old Prelate was in a very poor state and so was the district. It was no country for an old man, or indeed for anyone who had the means to reside elsewhere.

In October 1797, three shocking armed raids were carried out in the neighbourhood, targeting the larger houses and the respectable gentlemen of the district. On 17 October, the country residence of the Right Hon. the Attorney General at Newlands was raided by 'banditti of ruffians', plundering it of arms and property. The same week, Heathfield Lodge, the country house in Tallaght of His Majesty's printer, Mr Grierson, was broken into by a 'gang of freebooters' and robbed of firearms, plate, a quantity of house linen and clothes.

And on 21 October, persons believed to be those responsible for other raids in the district attacked the house of a Mr Geary. The owner, however, determined to protect his property, fired on the bandits, obliging them to retreat without accomplishing their purpose. In the morning, a blunderbuss that appeared to have belonged to the Attorney General was found near the house, and a quantity of blood lay on the ground near it. At least one of the villains had been severely wounded. A search through the neighbourhood led to one of the party being discovered at the Green Hills, at the foot of a haycock, dreadfully wounded 'at diverse parts of his body'. The wretched man confessed to having attempted to rob Mr Geary, before promptly expiring.

That same week, at about 11pm on Saturday, two hackney coaches drove to the gate of the Archbishop's Palace at Tallaght. A number of men alighted from the coaches, knocked on the Palace door and demanded admittance. They were refused by the porter, who declared that as his Lord was not in the Kingdom, he could not permit them to enter. They threatened to force their way in, demanding five new muskets that had lately been brought there and whatever other arms were in the Palace.

A great number of men arrived on foot and joined those who had arrived by coach. The porter, taking the advice of one of the female servants who had come to him, and seeing opposition vain, let the banditti in. After taking possession of the muskets in question, together with some blunderbusses and what other arms they could find, they quietly left the palace.

The same gang were assumed to have been responsible for all the raids in the district that week.

A newspaper reported: 'For the last three nights the neighbourhood of Tallaght has been disturbed by a numerous banditti. The palace of the Archbishop of Dublin, the houses of Mr

Grierson, Mr Metcalf and Mr Myers, were on these nights attacked and plundered of arms, by these depredators.'

On 22 October, Mr Sherriff Paisley and a party of the Stephen's Green Cavalry raided a public house in a laneway off Thomas Street in Dublin and discovered six men. On their person was found broken plate, counterfeit coins and forged banknotes. They were thus assumed to be the notorious party of ruffians who had lately committed the outrages in the neighbourhood of Tallaght. One wonders from whom they had taken the forged banknotes and counterfeit coins! Their leader was George Mighton, who had only recently been sentenced to be transported. Justice was both swift and seen to be done. On 24 November 1797, a Mr McMahon, who had been found guilty of involvement in the raids, was escorted by the Earl of Ely's corps of cavalry to be executed in Tallaght.

Archbishop Fowler, reflecting back on the good old days, as old men tend to do, and bemoaning the fact that the neighbourhood of Tallaght had clearly gone to the dogs, as old men tend to do, resolved to up sticks and move away for a quieter life. The reality was that Tallaght had never been a particularly salubrious neighbourhood. As palace dwellers go, Fowler had enjoyed a relatively easy time of it.

Some years earlier, when the artist Gabriel Berenger passed through Tallaght, he recorded in his journal notes on the journey from Baltinglass to Dublin. In Baltinglass, he remained the night, but did not sleep, 'as the pigs and dogs of the town were at war the best part of the night, and made a horrid noise'. He returned with a relative to Ballymore Eustace and stated his intention to travel on to Dublin, through Tallaght. He was advised by the landlord of the Eagle Inn there to beware of robbers, who then infested the neighbourhood of Tallaght. (He arrived, however, safe in Dublin that night.)

Archbishop Robert Fowler leased an estate in Essex, England, whence he removed to, just in time to miss the excitement of the 1798 Rebellion in Ireland. He lived for his last years as Archbishop of Dublin as an absentee prelate. He resided in Bassingbourne Hall in England, where he died on 10 October 1801. On the occasion of his death, the *Freeman's Journal* reported that he had died 'amazingly rich'. He left one son, the Archdeacon of Dublin, and two daughters, the Countess of Kilkenny and the Countess of Mayo.

In 1789, the *Freeman's Journal* reported that on Monday, 22 May of that year, the Archbishop ordained his son a deacon in Tallaght Church. On Wednesday, 24 May, he was ordained a priest, and on Saturday, 24 June, he was installed as Chantor of St Patrick's! He was Dean of St Patrick's Cathedral, Dublin, in 1793, and Archdeacon of Dublin from 1794 until 1813. He served as Bishop of Ferns and Ossory from 1813 to 1841.

Stansted Airport outside London now occupies much of the site on which stood the last home of the Most Reverend Archbishop Robert Fowler of Tallaght Palace.

By 1800, following the 1798 rebellion, the Durham Fencibles (from 'Defensibles') were stationed for a time in the Palace at Tallaght of the now-absentee Archbishop of Dublin.

For many years, there was something of a mystery as to where the Most Reverend Robert Fowler had been laid to rest. It was recorded that he had been interred in the Holy Trinity Church in Takeley, Essex, but there was no memorial, tomb or tablet to mark his final resting place. It has recently come to light that he was buried under the chancel (or altar) of the Holy Trinity Church. During restoration works during the Victorian period, the vault had been filled in. His end is reminiscent of his predecessor Archbishop Michael Tregury, whose vault in St Patrick's shared a similar fate until it was rescued from obscurity by Dean Swift.

Archbishop Robert Fowler was the last Archbishop of Dublin to reside in the Palace at Tallaght. Between 1801 and 1821, the rambling old pile fell into ever greater disrepair. The Archbishop's city palace, St Sepulchre's on Kevin Street in Dublin, was, in 1804, vested in the Crown under the Archbishop's Palace Dublin Act, 1804. During Fowler's 20-year residency in Tallaght, the city palace had been somewhat abandoned.

According to the Act,

The said Mansion House hath of late years been suffered to go into very great decay, and cannot be rendered fit for the Habitation of an Archbishop of Dublin, without considerable expense … the said House and offices have been left in a very ruinous and neglected condition, and which Sum of nine hundred and twenty-three pounds twelve shillings and sevenpence is entirely inadequate to the expense necessary to put the said house and offices in complete repair, and render the same fit for the Residence of an Archbishop of Dublin.

It later became the first headquarters of the Dublin Metropolitan Police and, later still, Kevin Street Garda Station.

The Diocese had neither the need nor the means to maintain the Palace at Tallaght. In 1821, it met its end when an Act of Parliament was passed for the levelling and demise of the Palace and demesne. The Archbishop of Dublin at the time was the Most Reverend Lord John Beresford DD. No sooner was the Act passed than Beresford was translated to Archbishop of Armagh, Primate of All Ireland. He promptly set about restoring St Patrick's Cathedral in Armagh, appointing one of the most skilled architects of the time, Lewis Nockalls Cottingham.

We know, in some detail, what became of Tallaght Palace since it was disposed of in 1822. But what of its last residents? What became of the Fowlers, the last family to occupy the Palace? Robert Fowler's eldest son, Robert, Bishop of Ferns and Ossory from 1813 to 1841, married Louisa Gardiner, daughter of Luke Gardiner, Viscount Mountjoy, in 1796. Gardiner was an MP and property developer, perhaps best remembered for laying out Mountjoy Square and Gardiner Street in Dublin.

Their eldest son, Robert Fowler, was born in 1797 and married twice. He settled at Rahinstown, Co. Meath. From the written history of Rahinstown House, by Noel French of Meath History Hub, we can follow the trials and tribulations of the Archbishop's descendants. According to French, when Robert Fowler died in 1863, he was succeeded by his eldest son, also Robert, who was Deputy Lieutenant, Justice of the Peace and High Sheriff of Meath in 1871. He married Laetitia Mable Coddington of Oldbridge in 1856, and died in 1897.

Their second son, John Sharman Fowler, joined the Royal Engineers in 1886, serving on the frontiers of India, South Africa and Ireland. At the outbreak of the First World War, he became Director of Army Signals of the British Expeditionary Force, a position he held throughout the War. By the end of the War, Fowler was commanding 70,000 men. Fowler remained in the British Army after the war, serving in China until 1925.

Robert Henry Fowler, born in 1857, was sent to Sandhurst, before joining the British Army in 1878. In addition to attaining the position of Captain in the Army, he enjoyed a reputation as an international cricket player. He lived just one month short of his hundredth birthday, making him the longest-lived international cricket player at the time. By 1901, he had already retired from the Army, and in the 1901 census, Robert H Fowler, retired Army Captain and Justice of the Peace, his wife, their two sons, two visitors and thirteen servants were in residence at Rahinstown. Robert Henry served as High Sheriff of Co. Meath in 1899. In 1908, a number of cattle drives took place on the estate of Captain Fowler of Rahinstown.

He had two sons. Robert St Leger Fowler was also a highly regarded cricketer, being captain of the Eton team while at school there. Robert St Leger served as a captain in the First World War, winning a Military Cross during the defence of Amiens against the last German offensive of 1918. He died from leukaemia at Rahinstown in 1925.

George Glyn Fowler, Robert's second son, was killed at the battle of Loos on 26 September 1915, aged nineteen. There are a number of memorials to him in Rathmolyon Church, including the wooden cross originally erected at Lapugnoy Military Cemetery.

Bryan John Fowler of Rahinstown also served during the First World War. He was awarded the Military Cross and also won a Distinguished Service Order for his efforts in the Second World War. Brigadier Fowler was at Fairyhouse Races on Easter Monday 1916 when he was

Belgard, home to the Maude family.

summoned away to maintain control in Drogheda. He competed for Britain in polo in the 1936 Olympics in Berlin, winning a silver medal. On returning from England, the family lived for a while at Culmullen House, before moving to the family estate at Rahinstown. His son, John Fowler, became a well-known horse trainer. He represented Ireland in the Mexico Olympics of 1968. In December 2008 he was killed in a tree-felling accident on his farm.

Many of the families who occupied some of the finest houses in Tallaght – the Fowlers of Tallaght Palace, the Palmers of Tallaght House, the Lentaignes, later of Tallaght House, and the Maudes of Belgard, all served, and lost loved ones, in Britain's military and colonial adventures. Their privilege and position came with something akin to a Faustian pact. The beneficiaries of imperial patronage had dues to pay, often the lives of their sons or grandsons. High office often came at a higher price.

CHAPTER 4

Tallaght House

Major James Palmer of Tallaght House

James Palmer (b.1780) was the son of the Reverend Henry Palmer, Archdeacon of Ossory. His grandfather, father and brother all made their careers in the Church. In 1794, fifteen-year-old James broke with family tradition and joined the military. He joined the 105th Regiment of Foot and, on 30 April 1795, was made a Captain of the 107th Regiment of Foot. Later that year, he began service in the West Indies, as part of a 15,000-man force under the command of Sir Ralph Abercromby. Their mission was to 'reduce' the Caribbean Islands – that is, to make them British. The force landed in Jamaica in early 1796, after initially being driven back by a storm.

A profligate son

Palmer, as a young man and much to the disappointment of his father, enjoyed a liberal disposition. At the age of seventeen years, little more than a boy, he sired an illegitimate son with a Barbados woman, while out in the Caribbean. His son, James Jr, was born at sea. On returning to London, he enjoyed a lifestyle much beyond his means and was frequently found at the gaming table. At twenty years of age, he returned to Dublin and, in July 1800, married Ellen de Rinzi, the widow of an officer. His son, James Jr, would reside with Ellen in Baltinglass.

Palmer's father, the Archdeacon, on his deathbed that same year, offered his twenty-year-old son a little over £500 to sign a covenant essentially relinquishing his inheritance or any claim to his father's estate. The young Palmer, almost certainly already in debt, took the modest sum and signed the covenant, something he would later regret and in fact appeal in the courts eighteen years later.

In June 1803, he was promoted to 2nd Captain of the Imaal Infantry. Palmer achieved the full rank of Major in the Army on 25 April 1808 and continued to serve until about 1816, when, after twenty years' service, he retired on half-pay.

He appealed in writing to Sir Robert Peel for various appointments to public office, including as Commissioner for Cobh Harbour.

In 1820, forty-year-old James Palmer was appointed Governor of the House of Industry – the workhouse – a position he held for fourteen months. He resided on the premises and received an annual salary of £500.

In December 1821, he was appointed to the post of Inspector General of Prisons in Ireland, one of two recently created posts of that title and grade. Palmer would work closely for twenty years with his colleague Benjamin Blake Woodward. From their office in Dublin Castle, the two

Lentaigne's Tallaght House, now replaced by the Retreat Centre at St Mary's Priory.

men were responsible for inspecting all prisons on the island of Ireland. It was a post he was, arguably, poorly qualified for, and it appears to have been secured as much through patronage as aptitude. His salary started at £552 but only four years later, in 1826, it was increased to £900. By 1831, the base salary with costs including travel and expenses was topping out at almost £1200, a substantial annual income for the time. Major James Palmer lived on Dame Street in Dublin, before securing a lease for the demesne of Tallaght Palace.

Tallaght House

On 16 November 1824, Palmer signed a 21-year lease from the Archbishop of Dublin for 204 acres and nineteen perches – the demesne of Tallaght Palace. The lease came with a clause for renewal. He immediately set about erecting Tallaght House from the remains of the old Archbishop's Palace. In clearing the site of the derelict Palace, he salvaged Archbishop John Hoadly's firepiece and gifted it to his brother, Reverend Henry Palmer.

It contained the Hoadly coat of arms and was inscribed: '*Johannes Hoadly, hanc domum refecit,*' or, 'John Hoadly rebuilt this house.'

Reverend Palmer saved the stone-carved coat of arms from over the Palace's fireplace. His son, also named Reverend Henry Palmer, wrote the following in a letter, dated 21 October 1885, to Reverend CT McCready DD:

> I perfectly remember, when quite a boy, some sixty years ago, being taken up to Tallaght by my father to the handsome modern mansion, which my uncle, Major Palmer, Inspector-General of Prisons, built, having pulled down the fine old palace … My dear father saved, as spolia opima out of the ruins, the noble chimney-piece in question, and went to the expense of having it brought by sea to Waterford, and thence here [Tubrid Church, Diocese of Lismore], and erecting it in his church. I remember a mitre came with it; but it was not thought becoming to have it replaced on the summit of the apex after having fallen from its high estate!

Hancock, writing in 1876, suggested it was still there. Tubrid Church has long since fallen into disrepair. Recent (2021–22) efforts to trace the whereabouts of this important piece have not been successful. While not quite the Elgin Marbles, it would seem appropriate that such a piece should, if at all possible, be repatriated to its place of origin.

By the time Palmer finished building Tallaght House, he was already in considerable financial difficulty. The annual rent alone was more than £400, twice the value that had been placed on the land only three years earlier.

The lucrative appointment as Inspector General, with its escalating salary, perhaps underpinned Palmer's confidence in taking a lease on the Archbishop's land and constructing his country house at Tallaght, despite his already burgeoning debts.

To fund the construction of his country mansion and the development of his estate, Palmer borrowed substantial sums of money. In May 1825, he signed a deed with Thomas Popham Luscombe, a retired Deputy Commissary General of the British Army, for an annuity. James promised to pay Luscombe £210 per year for twenty years or his natural life – giving only some indication of the capital Palmer may have borrowed from Luscombe. Only months later, in January 1826, Palmer signed a deed of assignment, which transferred this debt from Luscombe to John Lentaigne of Dominick Steet, Dublin. He also transferred two acres of the land to Lentaigne.

Already wading through a sea of debt, Palmer signed another annuity in February 1829 to Francis Preston of Co. Meath, for a sum of £1,500. Palmer agreed to pay £132 per year for a life annuity, post a bond for £2,400, and acquire an insurance policy for £1,200, with a clause that he could redeem the annuity after five years.

Major Palmer had not long moved into Tallaght House when his wife of 27 years, Ellen, died in 1827. Ellen had been unable to bear children. Palmer had already sired two – James Jr while out in the Caribbean before he had met Ellen, and another out of wedlock in 1822.

Only six months after the death of his wife, Palmer remarried. Eliza Nash was already 'with child' – Palmer's – when they married in St Peter's Church in Cork in late November 1827. James and Eliza would, together, have two children – Henry 'Hal' Wellington and Priscilla, both born in Tallaght House.

Palmer now held a respectable position in society, resided in an impressive trophy home on a country estate, and had what appeared to be a gentleman's family. But Palmer was heavily indebted. In a futile attempt to extract himself from his financial quagmire, he agreed to transfer the lot to John Lentaigne. On 23 July 1831, after only five years in Tallaght House, he signed a deed of conveyance and deed poll that turned the entire property over to Lentaigne, a Catholic. This didn't save him from humiliation.

On 21 May 1832, James Palmer, the Inspector General of Prisons in Ireland, was incarcerated in the 'Warden's Apartment' of Kilmainham Gaol. He owed over £591 to Rev James Magee. It must have been awkward for the Warden, to be hosting the Inspector General as a prisoner. It must also have been deeply humiliating for Palmer to be imprisoned in an institution that he himself was appointed to inspect! On 21 June 1832, his insolvency petition was heard and one month later, he agreed to pay £250 a year from his annual salary to meet his debts.

It was around the time of his incarceration, and perhaps with an eye to promotion to a higher office in Great Britain, that Palmer wrote and published *A Treatise on the Modern System of Governing Gaols, Penitentiaries and Houses of Correction* (1832), in which he argued the liberal point that the purpose of a prison is to prevent crime and reform the criminal, rather than for revenge.

The Palmers spent no more than six years in Tallaght House, from 1825 until 1831. They moved to 4 Vergemount, at Clonskeagh near Milltown in Dublin, residing there for some years before moving to Baggot Street, closer to the city, in 1841.

For the next decade, Palmer would remain on the brink of bankruptcy, despite his lucrative position. By 1843, Palmer had paid £5000 to his creditors, but still owed up to £7000. He would spend the remainder of his life heavily in debt.

Inspector General of Prisons

Palmer's career as Inspector General of Prisons in Ireland was not without controversy and after twenty years, was irreparably tainted by allegations of fraud and nepotism. It became apparent that many 'turnkeys' in Kilmainham Gaol were former servants in Palmer's household. One fellow gave testimony that he was told he could secure a job of turnkey if he gave Palmer's wife £30. Palmer had most certainly given his wife's brother, Andrew Nash, a job – 'an ill-defined but sensitive position' – that had never been formally approved. This was not refuted.

Furthermore, Palmer employed a man named John Lamb, to 'carry messages' between his office in Dublin Castle and Kilmainham Gaol. Lamb received an annual salary of between £65 and £70 for the job. Lamb carried messages by hiring a cab for the journey, at regular and considerable expense. The post had never been approved, and the job was essentially a part of Palmer's own duties. It was widely believed among prison staff that Lamb was Major Palmer's illegitimate son. When challenged by the Commissioners, Palmer responded, 'This is a gross and utter falsehood.' The Commissioners were not convinced.

Palmer started his career as a political moderate, but with age and maturity became a Tory. In 1842, he wrote to his son, 'I am turned a complete Tory, more than yourself if possible.'

Palmer held the post of Inspector General of Prisons and Lunatic Asylums throughout Ireland for almost 25 years, from 1821 until his retirement in 1846. As retirement approached, Palmer was a disappointed man, disillusioned with the country at large. In a letter to a friend, James Buchanon, dated 14 August 1845, he states: 'In this land we have nothing but strife, Popery & folly – well for us there is another beyond the Flood.'

At the time of his retirement in 1846, Palmer had been in receipt of approximately £1000 per year in salary plus expenses. He retired on a pension of £150 per annum. After his retirement, Major Palmer lived in a fine Georgian House at 92 Lower Baggot Street in Dublin.

Contribution to the Irish prison system

Palmer proved to be a liberal reformer, at least by the standards of the day. Architectural plans for new prisons to be built in Ireland had to be approved by him and his office, and as a consequence, Palmer had some influence on the architecture and skyline of many Irish towns.

According to one Dr JP De Long, 'James was instrumental in overseeing reforms that made imprisonment less harsh, safer, better organised and regulated, and more humane.'

On 31 March 1846, a gathering of esteemed gentleman was held in Radley's Hotel on College Green. They were resolved to mark the recent retirement and great contribution Major James Palmer had made to the country at large, and to note the great loss he would be to the prisons of Ireland. He was honoured by his colleagues for the 'zeal, intelligence, courtesy and kindness' that marked his official life, and was presented with silver plate.

In the years after his retirement, Palmer travelled a little, visiting Liverpool, the Isle of Man and London. He had £150 a year to live on, considerably less than the four-figure salary he had always struggled to survive on.

Palmer's retirement coincided with the deepening of Ireland's Great Famine. To his son Thomas he wrote on 26 February 1848: 'Poor Ireland is as bad as ever in starvation & wicked ways. Popery & potatoes are the ruin of Ireland. If both were abolished, she would recover herself – In a very few years say from 4 to 8.'

Major James Palmer died in London while visiting a friend, on 1 May 1850, at the age of 70. On his demise, he left little but debt. He left 'not a penny' to his son Thomas and owed money to Mr Robert Taaffe, a solicitor and his daughter Priscilla's soon-to-be husband (they would marry the following January).

His wife, Eliza Palmer, died on 27 February 1852 at her daughter's residence in Hardwicke Street, Dublin.

On the occasion of his father's death, Henry 'Hal' Palmer wrote to his half-brother Tom, to impart the sad and unexpected news.

London

fourteenth of May 1850

My Dear Tom,

    I regret to have to write you word that the poor Governor departed this life on the 1st of this month. His death was rather sudden as although I came here the instant I heard of his danger yet the poor man had died the day before I got there. Uncle and Aunt Margaret & Mr Taaffe came over in time for his interment ... I regret also to tell you that he not only did not leave a penny after him but had anticipated his next quarter which poor Taaffe is at the loss of – the post goes out for America this day. So I must conclude although indeed if I had even plenty of time I could scarcely say more. I wish you would write to me directed to the care of Mr Taaffe & as soon as I get back to Clonmel where I am now stationed I will write to you more fully. In the meantime believe me ever.

Your affectionate brother

Henry

Losing his trophy home, Tallaght House, to John Lentaigne, a very successful Catholic who would later be knighted, must have been a humiliation for Palmer, who had a clear dislike of Catholics. It was perhaps fortunate that Palmer would not live long enough to see Sir John Lentaigne occupy the post of Inspector General of Prisons in Ireland.

The Lentaignes of Tallaght House

From 1832 until 1855, Tallaght House was the country seat of John Lentaigne. Lentaigne, an antiquarian and collector, not only succeeded Major Palmer in his country estate, but later succeeded him in his post as Inspector General of Prisons in Ireland. Lentaigne assumed the position in 1853, three years after the Major's death and seven years after his retirement. John Lentaigne's brother Joe, a successful barrister, was a regular visitor to Tallaght House and took a keen interest in the affairs of the district.

The name Lentaigne was not native to the parish, nor was it common in Ireland. When Eugene Curry visited Tallaght House in 1837 with the Ordnance Survey, it was a name he struggled to write, spelling it variously 'Laingtaing' and 'Laningtaing', perhaps reflecting how it may have been pronounced by those working Lentaigne's estate at the time.

John and Joe Lentaigne's father, Benjamin Lentaigne, had come to Dublin from France – fleeing one homeland caught up in republican fervour only to settle in another. Arriving in Ireland in 1797, he had a walk-on part in one of the most dramatic moments in Irish republican history. Indeed, he may have played a greater role!

The Lentaignes were a noble French family of Catholic royalist extraction, with deep roots in Normandy. Two of Benjamin's older brothers, Jean François and Joseph, were executed by guillotine in 1793, during the French revolution.

The fourteen-year-old Benjamin was spared Robespierre's terror only on account of his age. He was instead imprisoned. He reportedly used his boyish good looks and not inconsiderable charm on his gaoler's wife, who, taking a liking to the lad, allowed him to escape. And escape he did – travelling to Jersey first, and then to Flanders, where he joined the army. He later travelled on to England, where he trained to be a surgeon, serving with the 5th Dragoon Guards. In that role, he was stationed in Dublin in 1797.

Benjamin Lentaigne was the surgeon who attended to Theobald Wolfe Tone in the final week of his life, after Tone's throat was cut. History records that Wolfe Tone cut his own throat. William Sandys, who was in charge of the Provost Prison, and the sentinel who guarded Tone, told an inquest on 20 November 1798 that Tone acknowledged 'he had given himself the wound in his throat'.

On the morning of his death, 19 November 1798, Lentaigne reportedly warned Tone that any sudden movement would be fatal. Tone famously described this warning as 'welcome news' and then, moving his head suddenly, caused a further haemorrhage that resulted in his death.

It might have occurred to any independent observer that Lentaigne had motive – his two older brothers had both been executed by republican revolutionaries. He also had a weapon, the skills, the opportunity and perhaps even an alibi, should he have had the inclination to murder Theobald Wolfe Tone! Tone allegedly told Lentaigne, 'I am but a poor physician.' Lentaigne was a very fine one.

After Tone's death, Lentaigne resigned his commission in 1799 and set up a private medical practice in Dublin. For the following decade, in addition to seeing private patients, he provided free medical care to the poor of the neighbourhood. For two hours every weekday, his doors were opened to Dublin's poor in need of medical attention.

Benjamin Lentaigne kept a country house in Corlatt, Co. Monaghan, and his son John would later become High Sheriff of that county. Benjamin Lentaigne died from typhoid fever on 30 October 1813, contracted while tending to the poor of Dublin. He is buried in Drumcondra graveyard. Two of his three sons survived infancy.

Joseph Lentaigne

Joseph Lentaigne was born in Dublin on 27 July 1805. After studying in the recently opened Clongowes Wood College, despite being a Roman Catholic, he took an MA in Trinity College, Dublin, winning the Vice-Chancellor's prize for Greek and Latin verse and a number of other honours.

In 1827, the 22-year-old Joe Lentaigne was called to the bar, and he threw himself earnestly into his profession. In 1839, Joe Lentaigne was nominated for election for the Board of Guardians in the South Dublin Union. Lentaigne's address at the time was his brother's country seat, Tallaght House. In 1843, after a number of years struggling with a vocational calling, he gave up his worldly possessions and entered the noviciate of the Society of Jesus – the Jesuits.

He was 40 years old by the time he had completed his noviciate and went to Vala in the south of France to complete his theological studies and formation. He studied under Père Gury, a notable scholar and author of a well-known treatise on moral theology. On return to Ireland, Father Joseph Lentaigne served as Professor of Rhetoric and President of Clongowes Wood. He was appointed first Provincial of the Order in Ireland on 8 December 1860.

In 1865, at 60 years of age, Father Joseph Lentaigne was sent to Australia, along with Father William Kelly (brother to the then-Rector of Clongowes), and was the founder of the first Jesuit missions in Australia. That July, Father Lentaigne and Father Kelly sailed in the giant ship the SS Great Britain, designed by famed engineer Isambard Kingdom Brunel. The Great Britain was considered a great feat of engineering, one of the most advanced and largest ocean-going vessels of the day. It was a truly modern ship, being built of metal rather than wood; powered by an engine rather than wind or oars; and driven by propeller rather than paddle wheel. The two men arrived in Melbourne after 58 days at sea.

Arriving on 21 September 1865, the ship anchored in Hobson's Bay, where her passengers disembarked by boat. As the launch-tender carrying the two Jesuits rather unsteadily beached at Sandridge (Port Melbourne), Father Kelly stood back to allow Joe Lentaigne to climb out of the boat first. Father Lentaigne signalled to Kelly to go first. Father Kelly objected, 'No, Father! You are the Superior, so you should go first!', to which Lentaigne replied, 'Yes, I am the Superior and I order you to land first!' And this is how Father William Kelly became the first, and Father Joseph Lentaigne the second, Irish Jesuit missionaries to arrive in Melbourne. They were followed over by 30 young Irish Jesuits, who established churches and colleges in Sydney and Melbourne.

Among their modest possessions transported to Melbourne from Dublin was what has since become known as the 'Lentaigne Triptych: The Easter Story'. The work depicts three scenes from Christ's Passion: the larger, central panel depicts the Crucifixion; that on the left, one of Christ's falls when carrying the Cross; and that on the right, his Entombment. In 1866, the Society of Jesus took over the Richmond parish, Melbourne, and it is believed that Father Lentaigne's triptych has been there, in several locations, ever since. It was placed in St Stanislaus's Chapel in South Richmond, built in the 1920s, and it remained there until the closure of the chapel in the 1980s. It was then moved to St Ignatius's Presbytery, Richmond.

Father Joe Lentaigne became the first Jesuit Rector of St Patrick's College in East Melbourne. He was remembered as a mild disciplinarian, respected and loved by his students and their families. Lentaigne described his young students, many the sons of tavern keepers and public servants, as 'lively, precocious little colonials who preferred play to study'. He described some of the older boys as 'wild as kangaroos'. Lentaigne resisted the temptation to correct the boys' accents.

Among Lentaigne's teaching colleagues was a lay teacher, Thomas W Rogers, a Jesuit scholar from Stoneyhurst College in England. Rogers left St Patrick's after only one term, attracted by higher wages. He was not mourned by Lentaigne, as he reportedly 'flogged too hard and too often' for Lentaigne's liking.

The workload took a strain on Father Lentaigne and on 18 March 1867, Lentaigne again boarded the SS Great Britain and returned to Ireland. In the week before Lentaigne departed Melbourne for home, one of his young students wrote:

> I have got a holiday today and Father Lentaigne was presented with a silver inkstand, a pencil case, and nice gold cross. It was presented to him by one of the boys preparing for University. We were all collected into one of the classrooms and Father Lentaigne came in, and I spoke a few words and then one of the boys presented the things to him. The boys were all very sorry because he is going away and one of the students who was brought up under him was crying bitterly. It was quite a scene down there this morning, the servants were crying as well. The boys gave him three cheers and three for all the Jesuits.
>
> The other day Father Lentaigne ordered one out of each class to be presented to him. There were five candidates in each class and I got the most votes in my class and then went in to see him. Father Lentaigne gave us a short lecture and seemed to feel having to part with us very much.

Father Lentaigne was only in Melbourne for eighteen months, from September 1865 to March 1867. It is striking how much of an impact he had – on individuals, as indicated by the passage above, and on the wider community of Melbourne. His contribution to the School in Melbourne was recorded and celebrated over 130 years later in *More than a School: A History of St Patrick's College, East Melbourne 1854–1968*.

Father Joseph Lentaigne, a cultivated and educated man, was expected to be of considerable further service to the Church. However, he spent many later years in inaction, rarely leaving the house, due to ill health. Indeed, he rarely left his own room. He amused himself in his room with the largely forgotten art of Latin verse-making. One example, described in the Irish Jesuit Journal as an 'ungallant couplet', survives:

Men have many faults, woman only two;
Right they never say; right they never do.

It was, perhaps, of its time.

A few minutes before midnight on Christmas Eve 1884, Father Joseph Lentaigne died in the Presbytery at Gardiner Street, Dublin. At the moment of his passing, his religious brothers were singing the words of the *Invitatorium of Matins*: 'Today you shall know that the Lord will come. And in the Morning you shall see him.' Father Lentaigne was buried in the Jesuit's Plot in Glasnevin Cemetery.

Sir John Lentaigne of Tallaght

John Lentaigne was born in Dublin in 1803 and was educated at Clongowes Wood, Co. Kildare. He studied medicine at the University of Dublin, where he graduated MA in 1825 and MB in 1828, becoming a licentiate of the Royal College of Surgeons of Ireland in 1830 and a fellow of the Royal College of Physicians of Ireland in 1844. In 1841, John Lentaigne married Mary Magan, a daughter of Francis Magan of Emoe, Co. Westmeath. The Magans were a long-established family of means and influence in Westmeath (one of whom was Francis Magan, also called The Traitor Magan, who betrayed Lord Edward Fitzgerald to the British authorities in 1798).

John Lentaigne was a favourite of the Irish administration at Dublin Castle. He served in a variety of senior roles, including Commissioner of Loan Funds (1841), Inspector of Reform and Industrial Schools (1870–86) and Commissioner of National Education (1861–86), as well as Justice of the Peace.

Somewhat coincidentally, Lentaigne also held the role as Inspector General of Prisons for over twenty years, from 1853 to 1877, just as Major Palmer of Tallaght House had done some years earlier. In the 1840s, he served as High Sheriff for the County of Monaghan, a role his son would later also hold.

Lentaigne unsuccessfully contested the Dublin County seat in the liberal interest in the general election of July 1852. Proper treatment and care of the insane was one of his great interests and he served on the Board of Governors of the Richmond Asylum in Dublin from 1875 to 1886. He was president of the Royal Zoological Society of Ireland and the Statistical and Social Inquiry Society of Ireland and a member of the Royal Irish Academy.

He was knighted for his services, becoming Sir John Lentaigne in 1880, before later being appointed to the Irish Privy Council in 1886, thereby becoming the Right Honourable Sir John Lentaigne of Tallaght.

On securing Tallaght House from Major James Palmer in 1832, Lentaigne took a great interest in the estate and neighbourhood of Tallaght. He allowed £42 a year and three tons of coal for the support of the school for the poor of the village. The National Board made an annual contribution of £8 per year.

He set about improving the gardens and grounds around Tallaght House and assembled an impressive collection of curios, antiquities and artefacts. Some of these he housed in the ancient surviving tower house of Tallaght Castle, some he kept in Tallaght House itself and some he set about the gardens.

Perhaps the most extraordinary installation was the skeletal carcass of a whale that had been washed up on the shores of north Mayo about 1840. The whale bones were brought to Tallaght House by Lentaigne, at some considerable expense, and erected into a great arch over the Friars' Walk – an elevated path, passing St Maelruain's Tree, leading to the 'Bishop's Seat', dating from the time of the Archbishop's Palace. The arch was erected on poles embedded in two large millstones that had been brought by Lentaigne to Tallaght House from Corkagh gunpowder mills in Clondalkin. The mills had been destroyed in a great explosion in 1787. Two large millwheels still sit in the grounds of the Dominican Priory, close to the retreat centre.

The Friars' Walk at St Mary's Priory.

Among Lentaigne's impressive collection of antiquities was an important manuscript, which has since come to be known as the 'Lentaigne Manuscript', now housed in the Royal College of Surgeons in Ireland (RCSI).

This early fifteenth-century manuscript was presented to the library of the RCSI by John Lentaigne in March 1851. The manuscript is a copy of the works of English surgeon John of Arderne (1307–92). A contemporary of Chaucer, John of Arderne served Edward III as an army surgeon at the battle of Crécy in 1346. He is considered one of the fathers of surgery and is sometimes referred to as 'the first surgeon'. He was a favourite of King Edward's eldest son, the Black Prince, who granted him land in Connacht. John of Arderne developed several treatments for knights, most notably for an affliction called 'fistula In ano', a condition where a large, painful lump appears between the base of the spine and the anus – caused by long periods of time spent sitting on a horse!

John of Arderne's writings are among the earliest documents in Britain and Ireland on surgery whose source is known. A census by the late Professor JD Widdess of Arderne's

Pages from the Lentaigne Manuscript.

surviving manuscripts showed a total of 43, of which 40 are in England. As most of them are imperfect, the Lentaigne manuscript, a rare source of information on medieval surgical practice, is very important as it is in an excellent state of preservation. It is not known how the manuscript came into John Lentaigne's possession. It may well have come from his father, who, like Arderne, had been a military surgeon in England.

In May 1846, during the height of the Great Famine, a robbery took place at Lentaigne's house at Tallaght. Eight months later, in January 1847, a Mr Bernard McGouran appeared before the bench and admitted involvement in the robbery. He, reportedly, confessed his involvement so that he could get transported out of the county.

Tallaght Industrial School

At any one time, the Lentaignes would have two women from the refuge attached to Golden-Bridge Convent in service in their household. They would stay with the Lentaignes, serving the family for a year or two, until Lentaigne could find respectable positions for them elsewhere. They would then employ two new servants from Golden-Bridge, on the recommendation of the Reverend Mother. Lentaigne kept neither plate nor silver under lock and key. Most of these women had served time in Mountjoy Prison before being admitted to the refuge in Golden-Bridge to see out their sentence. They must have received a 'ticket-of-leave' before being admitted to Golden-Bridge.

It was, by today's standards, an obvious blurring of professional boundaries, and indeed in the contemporary context, could be seen as exploitative. However, at the time it was recognised as an extraordinarily charitable and Christian act. Even too Christian perhaps. A joke circulated in polite society that John Lentaigne would often rise in the morning to find the only spoon left in his house was himself! The bon-mot was attributed to none other than Archbishop Whately.

Over a seven-year period, from 1858 to 1865, having accepted fourteen women into service in his household, Lentaigne found only two of these women 'unsatisfactory'.

One of these was an elderly lady who had, her whole life, been so notorious a thief that even friends of Lentaigne were surprised that he would consider taking her into his home. She was in his service for two years, when she stole some tea and sugar. The theft was trifling, but it was felt that even the slightest deviation from honesty could not be overlooked. She was told she must depart, but no charges were pressed. She was encouraged to emigrate. Lentaigne continued to befriend the lady, and while awaiting the arrangements for her emigration, she was permitted to remain in their service for several more months.

Another of the women had 'never settled' into the Lentaigne household, and after only a few months, left the Lentaignes' home of her own accord. She had never seemed contented there. Lentaigne felt she had an irrepressible desire to return to her old haunts and habits. He believed she left his service to prevent herself from robbing him.

As early as 1853, Mary Lentaigne had taken girls into service in Tallaght House. When muslin and lacework were displayed at the Great Exhibition by Mary Lentaigne that year, they were presented as 'worked by the children of Tallaght Industrial School'. In that same year, John Lentaigne was appointed to the position of Inspector General of Prisons in Ireland. He and his wife both held a deep personal interest in the reform of the young.

John Lentaigne became involved with Bishop Charles McNally in late 1858 to develop the concept of establishing a reformatory school for girls in Monaghan Town. Bishop McNally wrote to the St Louis Order Superior in Juilly to invite the Order to Monaghan, and it was on this basis that Sister Genevieve Beale arrived as the first Mother Superior of the St Louis Order in Monaghan in January 1859.

Given their strict Catholic faith, their inclination to activism, their institutional connections and Joseph Lentaigne's senior position in the Jesuit Order, it is not beyond the realm of possibility that if John Lentaigne hadn't come to an arrangement with the Dominican Order in 1855, the demesne at Tallaght could quite possibly have become the site of a reformatory or boarding school rather than a Dominican novitiate.

The Children of Tallaght House

In March 1855, the Lentaigne household in Tallaght was struck with tragedy when their thirteen-year-old son Benjamin Joseph was struck down with fever and died in Tallaght House. Shortly after, the Lentaignes decided to leave Tallaght House and, later that year, leased it to the Dominican Order, who arrived in Tallaght the following September.

Some years later, the family would experience a relentless spate of tragedy and loss.

In February 1867, their sixteen-year-old son Gerald Fitzgerald Lentaigne died while in school in France. Gerald was a student at the Saint Francis Xavier School in Vannes in Morbihan, France, when he died. The declaration of death was made on 26 February 1867 by Father Pacaud, Attorney at the school, and M. Aug. Maurey, Professor. Father Pacaud, on behalf of the family, bought the perpetual concession and erected an Irish cross to mark the final resting place of Gerald Fitzgerald Lentaigne, born in Tallaght House.

The Irish cross in the cemetery of Boismoreau, Vannes, is a striking monument in the local context. The limestone cross was likely made in Paris, from a drawing sent from Ireland. In 1937, it was classified as a historical monument.

The following year, 1868, their twenty-two-year-old son Francis died. Further tragedy was to visit the family only one year later, when their nine-year-old daughter Josephine Ida died of fever. John's brother, Father Joe, would around this time be inspired to translate into Latin Coleridge's quatrain on a child's death, 'Epitaph on an Infant':

'Ere sin could blight, or sorrow fade,
Death comes with friendly care;
The opening bud to heaven conveyed
And bade it blossom there.

It was a harrowing time for the Lentaigne family. Even by the expectations of the day, to bury three of their children in three successive years must have sorely tested their faith in a loving God. That faith would be further tested in the years ahead. In 1874, Victoria Lentaigne, their fifteen-year-old daughter, was struck down with typhoid. John sat downstairs in their city residence on Great Denmark Street as his daughter succumbed to the fever that had taken his father when John was only a boy.

In just seven years, the couple buried five of their children. A son who survived them died tragically only a year after the death of Sir John. Sir John Lentaigne died in November 1886. On his headstone in Glasnevin Cemetery, he is recorded as Sir John Lentaigne 'of Tallaght', despite having vacated Tallaght House 31 years earlier. His wife Mary neither grieved nor lingered too long after him. She died only six months later, in May 1887. One of their four surviving sons, Henry, then resident in Hunter's Hill in Sydney, Australia, was beside himself with grief when the news came through from Ireland.

Henry Westenra Lentaigne, a medical doctor from Tallaght House, was a kind and generous man. He was partially paralysed on the right side. Henry had a good medical practice, was financially sound and was on the happiest and most affectionate of terms with his wife. He was, however, 'nervous and fanciful' since the death of his father. This was compounded after receiving the news of his mother's passing.

On a Saturday evening in late September 1887, Margaret Lynch, a servant girl, put the Lentaignes' baby to bed and served Henry his tea, before leaving him to read his newspaper. She returned to the scullery to clean up.

Henry's wife was out visiting some friends that evening. He had told her earlier in the day he was expecting friends to call for dinner the following afternoon. Margaret Lynch, labouring away in the scullery, heard a loud bang, like a lamp exploding. She rushed into the room in which she had just left Henry and found the doctor lying with his shoulder to the door and his head on the floor. There was a stream of blood coming from his head and running across the floor. A single bullet was found on the floor and a revolver at his knee. There was nobody else in the house. He appeared to be dead, and Margaret raised the alarm with neighbours.

An empty cartridge was found in the chamber of the revolver that had evidently been recently discharged. Death had been caused by haemorrhage and damage to the brain caused by a single gunshot. A jury found that 'Henry Westenra Lentaigne died from the effects of a pistol shot wound in the head inflicted by himself, but whether intentionally or accidentally the evidence does not enable us to decide.'

What became of the Lentaignes of Tallaght?

John Vincent Lentaigne was born in Dublin in July 1855 – the summer his parents vacated Tallaght House for the last time. Like most of the Lentaigne boys, he was educated at Clongowes Wood College and at Vannes in Brittany. He later entered the Catholic University of Ireland, and the Dublin University in 1880, and the Royal College of Surgeons of Ireland (RCSI).

He was appointed Resident Surgeon at the Richmond Hospital in 1882, later moving to the Mater Misericordiae Hospital in 1886. He was elected fellow of the RCSI in 1886, the year his father died, and served as Vice President in 1906, before serving as President from 1908 to 1909. In 1911, he was appointed Surgeon General to the household of the Lord Lieutenant of Ireland.

Like his father before him, John Vincent was knighted in 1910. He married Phyllis Mary Coffey in February 1882, and they had two daughters and three sons. Lentaigne died at his home in Dublin on 30 March 1915, only one month after his brother Joseph. Like his paternal grandfather, Benjamin, he is buried in Drumcondra.

On 25 February 1915, Joseph Hussey Nugent Lentaigne JP, Barrister at Law – the 69-year-old, eldest surviving son of the Right Honourable Sir John Lentaigne of Tallaght House – died after a short illness. He had been Clerk of the Crown and Hanaper for 30 years and Permanent Secretary to the Lord Chancellor. He was very interested in zoology – birds in particular – and attended the Saturday breakfast parties in the Royal Zoological Gardens, where he was considered an institution. He had inherited the family property in Monaghan. He never married and died on a salary of €900 a year. According to an obituary, 'His social charm and the "distractions of society" may have prevented him from obtaining a very large practice at the bar though he had some remarkable qualities such as industry and tenacity of purpose which had generally led to success.'

Benjamin Plunkett Lentaigne was called after his deceased brother and grandfather. Educated in the family tradition in Clongowes Wood College, he chaired the Debating Society in 1882. Winning first class medals in Natural Philosophy, Chemistry, Euclid, Algebra and French, he was a gifted scholar in Greek, Latin and English. He went on to become a High Court Judge in Rangoon, Burma, before returning to Ireland and retiring to Stackallen Glebe, outside Navan, Co. Meath. He died in March 1941, leaving two sons, both of whom were serving in the British armed forces.

Colonel Edward Charles Lentaigne of Tallaght, Co. Dublin, of the 4th Gurkha Rifles, grandson and heir to Sir John Lentaigne, married Cecilia Mary Bunbury, second daughter of Thomas and Lady Harriot Bunbury, on 30 April 1919. Their wedding appeared in *The Gentlewoman* of Saturday, 31 May 1919:

CAPTAIN EC LENTAIGNE, DSO (of the 4th Gurkha Rifles), the eldest son of the late Sir John Lentaigne, and Miss Cecilia M Bunbury the youngest daughter of Lady Harriot Bunbury (of 'Cotswold House,' Winchester), were married just recently at the Oratory, Brompton. Major CH Bunbury gave away his sister, who was attended by Master Ian Selby-Nevill and Master Philip Morris, and Mr Joseph Lentaigne was best man to his brother. The ceremony was performed by Father Crewse, the Superior of the Oratory, and a very large congregation witnessed the wedding, including:—Lady Harriot Bunbury, Mr and Mrs Bertram Bunbury, Miss Lentaigne, Mr HJ Bunbury, Lady Alice Dundas, Colonel and Mrs Hew Thompson, Captain Dundas and Miss Dundas, the Hon. Mrs William Dundas, Mr Robert Dundas, Marie Lady de Freyne and the Hon. Lily and the Hon. Muriel French, Lady Hamilton Dalrymple, Captain the Hon. Hubert and Mrs Preston, and Sir Henry and Lady Adamson.

Their only son, John Lentaigne, was killed at El Alamein on 25 July 1942, while serving with the Rifle Brigade.

Their daughter Mollie Lentaigne (b.1920) became a noted medical artist and a Red Cross Voluntary Aid Detachment nurse during the Second World War. Mollie Lentaigne is remembered for her medical drawings, of which some 300 are preserved in the East Grinstead Museum in the United Kingdom. She later became Mollie Lock and settled in Zimbabwe. In May 2021, to celebrate her 101st birthday, she zip-wired across the Batoka Gorge.

The Hidden Gem

Josephine O'Reilly Lyons (nee Lentaigne), a granddaughter of Sir John and Lady Lentaigne of Tallaght House, became a writer, an artist and a model for Pond's Creams. She was, by the age of 24 in 1945, already widowed twice. She took art classes from Jack B Yeats and was the author of *The Hidden Gem*, reminiscences of her first husband, published in 1944.

Jo-Jo Lyons took her place in society circles in Dublin in the 1950s. Her son (one of her twelve children) Victor O'Reilly became a successful writer, and was the author of *Games of the Hangman* (1991); *Games of Vengeance* (1994); *Rules of the Hunt* (1995); and *The Devil's Footprint* (1996). Victor O'Reilly, great-grandson of Sir John Lentaigne of Tallaght House, died in 2022.

By 1992, Jo-Jo Lyons was styled Countess Sliwinska and lived in Spain, where she spent her later years painting.

The last Lentaigne lands in Tallaght

The Lentaigne family retained an interest in lands at Tallaght until 1919. Four months before EC Lentaigne married Cecilia Mary Bunbury, in January 1919, he liquidated the last of his family's holdings in Tallaght. Tallaght Courthouse and the old Royal Irish Constabulary barracks in the village were both built on lands once owned by the Lentaigne family. The auction was held in Tallaght Courthouse in the first week of January 1919. The auctioneer was quite literally auctioning the land beneath his feet. Among the lots put up for auction were the following (lands measured in acres (a), roods (r) and perches (p) – there are four roods in an acre, and 40 perches a rood):

Lot 6: 2r, 3p, held by Dublin County Council for 99 years from April 1905 at a rent of £2. The new Tallaght Courthouse is built on this lot.

Lot 7: 3a, 3r, 1p, upon which is situated the dwelling house known as Rose Villa, let to a yearly tenant at the rent of £9.3s.6d.

Lot 10: House and yard with out-offices and presently let at £1 monthly, free of rates.

Lot 12: House and yard adjoining Barrett's, at present let at £7 yearly. Tenants paying rates.

Lots 9–14: Cottages and gardens containing about one rood each, let at weekly rents of 3s to 8s.

Lot 16: House standing on 1r 30p, containing two sitting rooms, three bedrooms, kitchen, scullery, yard, out-offices, stable and gat, also a small cottage, clear possession will be given.

Lots 17: RIC Barracks situated on main-street, let to Chief Commissioner at yearly rent of £20.

A total of seventeen lots were auctioned off on Lentaigne's behalf, comprising over 100 acres of land in and around the village of Tallaght.

It proved an opportune time, after almost 90 years, for Colonel Edward Charles Lentaigne, a serving British Army officer, to dispose of his family's holdings in Tallaght. Ireland's War of Independence broke out only two weeks later.

CHAPTER 5

The Battle of Tallaght, 1867 – What the Dickens?

For 100 years and more, up to March 1867, there was an expression in Dublin and indeed Ireland: 'Tallaght hill talk', meaning to give vent to one's feelings as soon as danger has passed. The expression is believed to have originated in reference to those who had been confined by the Archbishop's Court at St Sepulchre's (Kevin Street, Dublin). On returning to their native mountains, as soon as they had reached Tallaght Hill (outside the jurisdiction of the Archbishop), they would raise a fist to Dublin and curse him.

Rebels gathered on Tallaght Hill during the uprising of 1798, and they would gather there again on 5 March 1867, seeking to overthrow the British yoke. A certain mythology has grown up around the 'Battle of Tallaght' of 1867. A plaque celebrating 'The Bold Fenian Men' was erected on the walls of the Dominican Priory in Tallaght in 1967 by the National Graves Association, 100 years after the event, and a year after the fiftieth anniversary of the 1916 Easter Rising. The plaque went missing for many years, having been taken down during remedial works on the wall. It has since been reinstated.

In the months leading up to March 1867, military authorities in Ireland were frequently informed of the plans of the Irish Republican Brotherhood or the IRB – the Fenians – by a network of senior, reliable and well-paid informants. At times, Dublin Castle was better informed of IRB plans than many members of that august body. To ensure secrecy, junior members were not informed of plans until 24 hours before those plans were to be executed, and plans were thus executed by those with little understanding, if any, of a strategy. A remote and disorganised leadership often failed to coalesce or agree on cohesive plans of action.

A plan of sorts was cobbled together to mount an insurrection in Ireland on 5 March 1867. The date was not without symbolism. It was Shrove Tuesday, a day in the Christian calendar preceding a long period of sacrifice – reflecting the 40 days Jesus spent fasting in the desert, resisting the temptations of the devil. The leaders of the insurrection clearly expected the Rising to lead to a significant period of sacrifice – and, perhaps, temptation.

The day before the Rising, after written confirmation of the plans had been received in Dublin Castle from a reliable informant, police barracks in and around Dublin and further afield were put on high alert and instructed to prepare for the event.

Excitement was not confined to Tallaght. This was to be a national uprising and Fenian cells in Clonmel, Limerick, Kilmallock, Bray and Cork were all put on notice, ready to rise.

But Tallaght Hill was to be the *pièce de résistance* of the Fenian rising nationally. Several thousand Fenians were called on to assemble on Tallaght Hill, to draw the military authorities out of the city and from the surrounding counties. They were then expected to disperse throughout the surrounding countryside and to engage troops in a fragmented and prolonged guerrilla war. Expected, rather than instructed.

The Fenians, quite literally taking the high ground, would entice the military away from key strategic targets in Dublin – the Castle, railway stations and barracks – allowing Fenians in the city to wage an assault on the poorly defended capital. Meanwhile Fenians throughout the country were called on to rise up in their own respective localities, to preoccupy troops and prevent them from being redeployed to defend key strategic targets elsewhere. As a strategy, it was not without merit, and as an enterprise, not without manpower. Nor was it without risk.

The Battle of Tallaght, 1867 – What the Dickens?

A number of elements went according to plan. Several thousand Fenians did indeed gather on Tallaght Hill that night, largely unimpeded on their journeys there by the forewarned military authorities and local constabularies. Estimates ranged from 2000, a realistic approximation, to 8000 Fenians, a less credible figure. They were allowed to assemble, at a safe distance from almost any meaningful target. Key strategic centres in the city remained guarded and appropriately fortified. Around 30,000 British troops were stationed in Ireland at the time. Many remained in Dublin city that night.

Fenians on the ground were only given 24 hours' notice from the 'centres', some of whom had learned of the plans on 26 February.

In preparation for what was to transpire, the usual complement of five constables in Tallaght barracks was supplemented with ten reinforcements, drawn from Rathfarnham and other stations, bringing the local force in Tallaght that night to fifteen men. They did not underestimate the capacity of the Fenians to wreak havoc. A number of the constables in Tallaght crossed the road to visit the Dominicans in Tallaght House (the Dominican Novitiate was still under construction) to confess their sins, mindful that it might be their last opportunity before meeting their maker. Father Dominic Scanlan OP gave them their penance and his blessing.

As evening fell, a frosty air descended on the town. Temperatures were low in Dublin that night, at 4.6°C, and somewhat colder in the hills around Tallaght. Sleet and rain began to fall. The weather would deteriorate further later in the week, giving rise to a mythology that the Fenians were greatly hampered in their enterprise on the night by heavy snow drifts and blizzard-like conditions.

Throngs of Fenians arrived at the foot of Tallaght Hill, and from late evening, Clarke's public house in Jobstown did a roaring trade. The house was crowded with persons in arms. As the night wore on, some said they would go home as the thing was sold. Others said they would not go home without a fight. *Plus ça change!*

Over 700 acres of land at Mount Seskin was held by Henry O'Connell FitzSimon, a grandson of The Liberator, Daniel O'Connell, and a son of the poet Ellen FitzSimon. He was one of the largest Catholic landholders in Tallaght around that time.

Following orders, at about 11.30pm, Sub-Inspector Dominick Francis Burke and Sub-Constable James Kenny were travelling from Rathfarnham to Tallaght Barracks, in preparation for the arrival of the Fenians. Between the bridge at Templeogue and the church at Templeogue, they came upon a horse and cart with five or six men around it. Kenny put his hand into the cart and found it to be full of ammunition. The men ran away.

A few minutes later, a number of men returned, one approaching Kenny with a cutlass. Kenny fixed his sword to the muzzle of his rifle. The man made a cut at Kenny. Kenny lunged at him with his bayonet, and, according to his own later testimony, hit him 'on the hand or arm'. Another man tried to take the reins of the horse. Kenny made a stab at him with a bayonet and he ran away. The first man was injured and was carried off by his comrades.

Burke and Kenny took possession of the horse and laden cart and made their way in the direction of Tallaght Barracks. Looking behind them, at some distance was a body of some 100 Fenians following briskly in their direction. The horse was not spared as Burke and Kenny hastened toward Tallaght.

The man wounded by Sub-Constable James Kenny was Thomas Farrell, a 30-year-old confectioner and Fenian from Williamstown (Blackrock). He had received a bayonet wound to the abdomen. He died in the Meath Hospital the following day, 6 March, after being found on the roadside near Roundtown. No member of his family attended his inquest.

Burke and Kenny arrived into Tallaght shortly after midnight with the confiscated cartload of ammunition. The cart had been stolen from J Reilly of Upper Abbey Street earlier that day. It had since been loaded with 1000lb of Fenian ammunition, destined for Tallaght Hill. It was now safely in custody at Tallaght Barracks.

Shortly after Sub-Inspector Burke's arrival, the tramp of a great body of men, coming up the Greenhills Road toward Tallaght Village could be heard. They were only minutes away from the barracks.

Sub-Inspector Burke took an offensive position rather than wait and be forced to adopt a defensive one. He ordered his men out of the barracks. They formed a line, facing north, directly down the Greenhills Road outside the barracks. This initiative prevented them from being blockaded into their own barracks. Burke's fourteen men were armed, experienced and disciplined.

When the gathering of Fenians approached to within 30 paces of the village, Burke shouted out 'Halt' to the men. He called on them, in the name of the Queen, to surrender, warning that if

How The Irishman *newspaper reported on the Battle of Tallaght.*

they did not, he would fire on them. The group fell back in a disorderly array. A few stones were thrown in the direction of the officers, and a few moments later, shots could be heard in the distance as the Fenians retreated. The shots may have been fired by Fenian centres at their own men, in an attempt to compel them to advance.

Burke's officers remained in formation for some time after, until a sentinel arrived to inform them that another troop of Fenians was approaching from Roundtown (Terenure) and proceeding to approach the village from Boldbrook. These were likely the men Burke and Kenny had seen advancing less than an hour earlier.

Still outside the barracks, Burke faced his men east. In the still night air, they could hear the growing sound of up to 200 men marching toward the village – that and the sound of their own hearts beating in their chests. It was close to 1am.

As before, when the group came within 30 paces, Burke called out to the men to disperse. As he proceeded to roar out parts of the Riot Act into the frosty blackness, the Fenians discharged a volley of shots at Burke's men. Burke immediately commanded his men to return fire. Kneeling in formation, the fourteen officers discharged a low volley into the darkness. The sound of arms being dropped or thrown to the ground could be heard, accompanied by the great shuffle of men retreating into the distance.

Shortly after the shots and shuffle, moans and wails could be heard a little way down the road. After several minutes, Burke declared his intention to go and investigate the source of the wails. His men expressed concern, noting that some Fenians may be lying in wait to mount an attack. Burke asked for two volunteers to accompany him. They collected a table from the barracks to use as a stretcher.

The three men – Burke, Denis Kelly and Martin McCormack – set off into the inky black night. Only 40 paces from the barracks they found Stephen O'Donoghue, a Fenian centre, seriously wounded. He was lying on a footpath, his head toward Tallaght, wailing, 'Oh! Men, oh! Men.' He appeared to have been shot in the back. The bullet had passed close to the spine, fracturing the fifth rib, and had passed through his right lung. He was lying face down on the pavement, 'breathing through his wound', clawing at the gravel.

Burke ripped open the man's clothes to examine the wound. Several rounds of ammunition fell from O'Donoghue's pockets. A revolver case was found on his person. O'Donoghue was moaning, calling out for water. Seven discarded rifles lay on the ground, five close to the man. O'Donoghue was placed on the table and removed to the barracks, where Burke gave him some 'stimulants', some wine and brandy.

Later that morning, before dawn, Burke returned to Rathfarnham. He summoned Dr Seward to go to Tallaght to tend to the wounded man. When Dr Seward arrived at 7am, he found Dr Doherty, a military surgeon from the 52nd Regiment, who had been en route to Tallaght Hill, already present.

The prognosis for O'Donoghue was poor. Father Dominic Scanlan OP from the Dominican Novitiate, the priest who had heard the confessions of some of the constabulary men, was called over to the barracks. He gave the Last Rites to the wounded Fenian. O'Donoghue died sometime after 10am, some nine hours after the shooting. Stephen O'Donoghue, from Werburgh Street in Dublin, was a 35-year-old solicitor's clerk and father of four young children. His wife was left a pregnant widow.

At the inquest, Burke said that he would regret to the last day of his life that any of his countrymen had been shot, but that if it were to be done again, he would do it. Burke and his men were commended for their decisiveness and their humanity in executing their duty that night.

The officers of the Irish Constabulary who served in the Tallaght district that night were: Sub-Inspector: Dominick Francis Burke; Head Constable: John Kennedy; Constables: John Shannon, George Hall and Jason Pickerton; Sub-Constables: James Kenny, Martin McCormack, Samuel Nickel, Michael H Kelly, George Hare, Charles Graham, Michael McGlinchy, Jeremiah Murrey, Denis Kelly, Patrick Kavanagh, James O'Neill, Richard Shortall, John Coffey, John Ferrer.

Fenian centre Stephen O'Donoghue had, it was suggested, not properly drilled his men. A Fenian prisoner under his command later testified that rifles were given to 'some who knew, and some who boasted they knew how to use them'. The Fenians, opening fire on Burke and his men, were acting contrary to orders. They had been ordered not to attack the barracks. Their job was simply to assemble on Tallaght Hill, to draw the military out of the city.

Some of the Fenians were as young as sixteen and seventeen, and they appeared to have been among those who rallied the group to attack the barracks. After the attack, these young fellows were reportedly the first to run. O'Donoghue had failed to keep his own men in line. There was a possibility that O'Donoghue had in fact been shot in the back by his own poorly trained and undisciplined men.

Whatever the facts, what is certain is that he paid the ultimate price for the failure – his own and that of the senior Fenian leadership. The name of the deceased, Stephen O'Donoghue, is incorrectly recorded in the Civil Records as Stephen Donougher. Many mistakes were made.

Further casualties of 'the Affair at Tallaght' were reported in the following days. John Roche, a plasterer by trade, was wounded by a gunshot in the leg. He was carried a distance by comrades, until they could carry him no more. Michael Nolan, of Ross Lane off Bride Street, was found lying at the side of a ditch in the vicinity of Tallaght. He had received two bullet wounds in one leg, and was rendered wholly unable to make any attempt at flight. He remained there until a group of Scots Greys, with cabs and cars, reached him the next day.

Roche and Nolan, along with another casualty, Kerwin, were brought to the Meath Hospital. Nolan and Kerwin later managed to escape, both fleeing to the United States. Roche, however, was so seriously injured that he required his right leg to be amputated. He remained in hospital for a considerable period. Perhaps as a consequence, he was never charged with involvement in the affair. John Roche lived until June 1894. When he died, he was buried as a celebrated Fenian in Glasnevin Cemetery. Among the mourners at his funeral was Arthur Griffith.

Thomas Moran, a labourer, also received a gunshot wound to the leg. Another young man, named only as Byrne, was also reportedly wounded and remained in Tallaght Barracks.

In the hours after the attack, the police at Tallaght arrested over 50 Fenians and detained them in Tallaght Barracks. Troops, proceeding from Dublin to Tallaght Hill, deposited more detainees in the barracks at Tallaght before advancing on. The detainees were held in the yard of the Barracks. Lancers arrived at 6.30am at Tallaght Hill and arrested 83 insurgents.

Fenians dispersed in various directions, some to Ballinascorney and some to Killakee. Some made out cross-country in the direction of Celbridge. One Fenian took refuge in the old tower house of the Dominican Novitiate in the village. There he stayed for several days, until it was safe to leave.

One of the men arrested was Patrick Keogh, a 25-year-old tailor from Plunkett Street in Dublin, then a place of decaying buildings and old clothes shops and a neighbourhood frequented by sailors of the lowest class. In 1863, Keogh had joined the Fenians and taken the Oath. Each man who paid half-a-crown was given a pike-head. Keogh testified that on the night of 5 March 1867, he didn't actually know what a 'republic' was, but that it had since been explained to him: 'that every man would be like every other man, and all respected alike'.

Between three and four o'clock on the afternoon of 6 March, prisoners were removed from Tallaght under an escort of a detachment of the 52nd light infantry, cavalry and mounted police. Between lines of infantry, the insurgents marched, with mounted police to the front and cavalry to the rear. Sub-Inspector Burke and his men accompanied the procession. In total, 140 Fenian prisoners were marched from Tallaght into the city, some to the Lower Castle Yard in Dublin Castle and some to the city's jails at Kilmainham and Richmond Barracks.

One young Tallaght man caught up in the affair was seventeen-year-old Robert Boardman, of Boardman's Mill at Boldbrook. He later testified that on the night of 5 March, he met several parties on the road to Tallaght who were armed with pikes and rifles. They compelled him to go with them to Tallaght Hill. On the way, he saw rockets fired on the hill. The men said that 'that was the place they should go to'. The Fenians fired rockets from Tallaght Hill to indicate the rendezvous point to those approaching the area.

Boardman informed the court that 'they treated me very kindly along the road and wanted to treat me at every public house we met', much to the amusement of those gathered in the courthouse. Boardman was not, thereafter, cross-examined. Robert Boardman, from a well-heeled family in the district – the owners of Boardman's Papermills at Boldbrook – would later go on to become a magistrate (JP) at Tallaght Petty Sessions.

Several Fenian flags were confiscated in Tallaght and around Dublin that night. Thirty-one Fenians, many of them armed, were arrested the next morning in the neighbourhood of Kilmainham, as they returned from Tallaght. A green flag carried by the men was confiscated. A flag confiscated by Sub-Inspector Burke in Tallaght was retained by him as a souvenir of that extraordinary night. It would, many years later, be presented to the National Museum of Ireland by his family.

General Halpin, an Irish-American, was the Fenian military leader for the Dublin District. On 6 March 1867, the day after the Rising, Halpin was seen playing billiards in a public house in Rathfarnham, waiting for the dust to settle before returning to the city. The Rising was described by General Massey, another senior Fenian, as 'a futile, leaderless and aimless adventure'.

The daily papers were giddy with excitement at events around the country. *The Irish Examiner* of 8 March stated that a troop of 4000 men and boys had been faced down by Sub-Inspector Burke and his fourteen men in Tallaght. From such headlines, a mythology was born. In fact, it was probably about 200 men, based on Burke's own account in the days immediately following the event.

In the weeks after, Sub-Inspector Burke gave a number of accounts of the night. These accounts were not entirely consistent with each other, nor were they entirely consistent with the testimony of other serving officers.

A 'Special Commission' into the charge of High Treason against a number of Fenian prisoners commenced on 24 April 1867. Of 109 witnesses presented by the Crown, only three residents of Tallaght were listed: James McDermott, a labourer from Newtown; Robert Boardman from Boldbrook Mills; and James McHugh, another labourer from Tallaght.

The following September, Dominick Francis Burke was one of eight officers who had their service during the Rising recognised by the Crown. Burke was awarded the Constabulary Medal for his bravery in defending the barracks, presented to him by the Marchioness of Abercorn at the Constabulary Depot in the Phoenix Park. After the presentation of medals, the Lord Lieutenant informed those present that, as proof of Her Majesty's satisfaction at the conduct of the Irish Constabulary, she was pleased to command that the force should thereafter be called the 'Royal' Irish Constabulary. They would have the harp and crown as badges of that force.

Burke received one of only three medals awarded. They were among the first medals awarded by the force. Sub-Inspector Burke was also awarded £104. Head Constable John Kennedy was awarded £50. Constables John Shannon, George Hall and Jason Pickerton each received £20. Another fourteen sub-constables were each awarded £15. It had been a good night's work.

That same month, Stephen O'Donoghue's widow, Annie O'Donoghue of Werburgh Street in Dublin, gave birth to a fifth child, a son. She named him Stephen.

Dominick Francis Burke retired from the Force in November 1870. He had been promoted to First Inspector.

In the 1940s, over 70 years after the event, many Dublin men claimed to have been among those on Tallaght Hill on 5 March 1867. Stories of fallen Fenian comrades, dying of exposure and hunger as they held out in the mountains after the event, appear to have been somewhat exaggerated. James North, one of the last remaining 'survivors' of the Rising, related his tale in 1940:

> I was only a lad of seventeen the day my company marched up through Rathmines. I joined them at Dartry, then a green countryside. I escaped in a bread van. We were unarmed and had scarcely assembled when we saw the soldiers – a regiment called the Holy Ninth Boys – coming in all directions across the fields, along the roads, until they completely surrounded us. But I got away and a bread van driver carried me in one of his baskets and let me off near Massy's Estate. I was three weeks in the mountains. The poor people who had scarcely enough themselves were always good to us and gave us a bit to eat. We were only a handful. But if James Stephens hadn't have been arrested it would have been a far different story.

The Battle of Tallaght, 1867 – What the Dickens?

'Only a handful' they were most certainly not.

Malachi Horan of Killinarden hill, who was about nineteen at the time, also recalled the event, 76 years later, and perhaps gives us an insight into what the people of Tallaght thought of the affair:

> Battle indeed! It was not even a fight. The Fenians took their stand before the Tallaght Barracks and they without a plan or a leader or any hope of either. An' well, the police in Dublin knew it, too. Head-Constable [Sub-Inspector] Burke ordered his men to fire on them. One was killed and some more wounded. That was the battle, glory be!

In his *History and Antiquities of Tallaght* (1876), William Domville Handcock included a version of events that night. His account, only nine years after the event, already indicated a degree of mythologising. He states, 'Sub-Inspector Burke challenged the advance party, estimated to

Kiltalown House, where some assistance was given to the Fenian rebels.

have numbered about a thousand.' In fact, Burke had, the day after the event, at the inquest into the death of Stephen O'Donoghue, stated that the party numbered about 200 men. It may have been more, but in the darkness it was impossible to estimate beyond that.

Handcock noted that an uncle of his, Robinson, who had Kiltalown House at the time, observed men, Fenians, wandering around his front lawn in the morning after the Rising. Handcock failed to note, however, what Malachi Horan would reveal many years later – that Robinson, a magistrate, assisted many Fenians to escape from troops – Scots Greys – arriving to round them up. According to Horan, Robinson fed and watered a number of men before providing safe passage through his lands. When the Fenians were out of sight, Robinson, according to Horan, stood at his garden gate for three hours to head off any soldiers following their trail.

On the occasion of the retirement of Dominick Francis Burke (a nephew of Sir Joseph Burke, Glenisk, Co. Galway, and Sir Dominick Daly, Governor of South Australia), a letter of appreciation and thanks was addressed to him and published in the Freeman's Journal. It was signed by over 100 gentlemen, including the Lord Mayer of Dublin. Among the signatories was one John Robinson of Kiltalown House.

What the Dickens?

One month after the Battle of Tallaght, on 6 April 1867, world-renowned English novelist Charles Dickens, then at the height of his international fame and celebrity, published an extraordinary account of the Rising in Tallaght on that fateful night. An unnamed correspondent claims to have left his lodgings and walked behind the Fenians as far as Rathmines and then jumped into a Dublin friend's jaunting car, in which they travelled out to Tallaght village before the Fenians arrived there en masse.

The writer details an exchange he had early that morning with a maid, while breakfasting in his lodging house. The writer had just received a telegram urgently summoning him back to Dublin, where Dickens was scheduled to give a number of readings ten days later in the Rotunda Hall. As he read his telegram, it was clear to the maid that he had received important, perhaps even sensational, news from Dublin. 'Have they kept their word?' the maid enquired. He looked at her quizzically. 'Are the boys up in Dublin?' she asked. 'They said they would rise today!'

The Battle of Tallaght, 1867 – What the Dickens?

The writer details how he left his country lodgings in haste and travelled by the Great Southern and Western rail line, stopping in Straffan, Celbridge, Lucan and Clondalkin before arriving in Dublin. He travelled in a third-class carriage, so as to be able to hear the talk of the countrymen. Returning to his city lodgings on Harcourt street in Dublin, he was greeted by a servant girl, who announced, 'The Fenians have riz.' From there, the writer claims to have progressed to Tallaght, to bear witness to a once-in-a-lifetime event.

Some people, reading Dickens's journal, believed the author himself was in Tallaght, Co. Dublin, on the occasion of the Battle of Tallaght. And indeed, some people still do.

According to Dickens's own diary for that week, however, he was in the north of England. On the night of 5 March 1867, he was in Newcastle. However, he travelled to Dublin nine days later and spent four days there. He gave four readings in the Rotunda Hall before travelling on to Belfast for three days, where he gave further readings. It is unlikely that he had time to visit Tallaght during his stay. But having been so impressed by the sensational international news coverage of events in Tallaght the previous weeks, perhaps the great master of fiction couldn't resist the temptation to associate himself with the story of the battle, and therefore with the history of Tallaght. He was one of the first, but certainly not the last, to help construct the mythology of the Rising at Tallaght.

On 5 March 2017, the 150th anniversary of the Battle of Tallaght was marked by an appropriately modest parade through Tallaght village, organised by the local branch of Sinn Féin. The fine

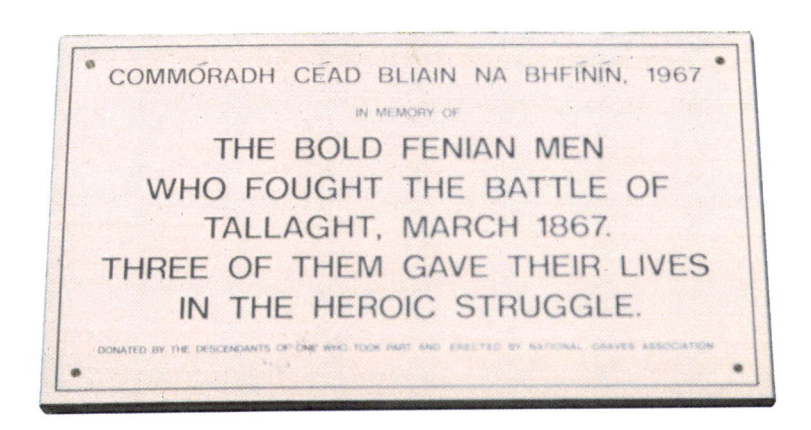

Plaque commemorating the 'bold Fenian men' of 1867.

A Ramble About Tallaght

Fenian historian, author and respected Tallaght man, Dr Shane Kenna, was scheduled to be the keynote speaker at the event. Tragically, Shane died only the week before, after a long battle with cancer. He was 33 years old. He was buried in Newlands Cemetery, beside the notable Clondalkin singer-songwriter Mic Christopher. Shane was one of the foremost authorities on 'The Invincibles' and the IRB, and was one of generations of Tallaght school boys inspired by the lore, the mythology and the history of the Bold Fenian Men and the Battle of Tallaght.

The Hill of Killenarden

Though time effaces memory, and griefs the bosom harden,

I'll ne'er forget where'er I be, that day at Killenarden;

For there, while fancy revelled wide, the summer's day flew o'er me,

The friends I loved were at my side, and Irish fields before me.

The road was steep; the pelting showers had covered the sod beneath us,

And there were lots of mountain flowers, a garland to enreath us,

Far, far below the landscape shone with wheat and new-mown meadows,

And as o'erhead the clouds flew on, beneath swept on their shadows

O' friends, beyond the Atlantic foam there may be noble mountains,

And in our new far western home green fields and brighter fountains;

But as for me, let time destroy all dreams, but this one pardon,

And barren memory long enjoy that day on Killenarden.

Charles Graham Halpine (circa 1860), Young Irelander, Editor of the *New York Leader* and Assistant Adjutant General with the rank of Major during the American Civil War

CHAPTER 6

The Big Houses

Oldbawn and Oldbawn House since 1635

As a village, 'Oldbawn' dates to March 1627, to the granting of lands by English King Charles I to Archbishop Launcelot Bulkeley, then resident at the Archbishop's Palace at Tallaght. Archbishop Bulkeley was the son of Sir Richard Bulkeley of Beaumaris, Wales, and could trace his lineage back to Eaton in Cheshire in 1341, where an ancestor (also Richard) was the Sheriff of the Shire. The family can be traced even further back to the reign of King John (1199–1216). William Bulkeley supported the Lancastrian side in the Wars of the Roses during the reign of King Henry VI (1422–61).

Launcelot married Alice Bulkeley, daughter of Rowland Bulkeley of Conway in Wales. They had at least one son, William, and two daughters, Grissel and Mary.

Among those lands granted by Charles I was a significant holding at Oldbawn, which the Archbishop presented to his son William Bulkeley, along with lands he had purchased in Dunlavin, Co. Wicklow.

About 1635, upon this land in Oldbawn, a wild and desolate place, was built a Jacobean or Caroline manor house, which would stand for 340 years and would be occupied as a residence for almost 290 years. The house was likely designed and built by a Welsh architect and builders, brought over to Tallaght for the task. The Tudor 'H' plan to which it was built was falling out of favour in England by 1635, but was still popular among Welsh builders. In 1636, around the time of its construction, William Bulkeley became Archdeacon.

The Bulkeley family, like many new English settlers, introduced new, English-style houses and English farming methods. Archdeacon William Bulkeley, a man of middle height and slender build with brown hair and a grey beard, spent much of his time and talents over the next four decades in the development and improvement of the estate, setting out formal gardens and turning Oldbawn into 'a most delightful patrimony'. His wife, a tall and slender lady with long tresses of brown hair, spent much time with her mother – Bulkeley's mother-in-law – who resided with the family.

Among the household in Oldbawn was William's seven-year-old son Richard (later Sir Richard), a daughter and his 'cousin-german', Roland Bulkeley. Richard Bulkeley would go on to become High Sheriff of Wicklow in 1660 and sit in the Irish House of Commons for Baltinglass in 1665–66.

We know from the 1664 'Hearth Money Roll' that Archdeacon Bulkeley declared twelve hearths at Oldbawn, giving some indication of the extent and wealth of the household. Later visitors to the house would note that in fact Oldbawn House had fifteen hearths, perhaps reflecting later additions to the house. By comparison, the Archbishop's Palace at Tallaght had only eight hearths.

It was the only house in the district occupied by a family of position, and as the estate grew, so a little village developed around the great house. By the mid-1600s, Oldbawn had about 100 inhabitants, many of whom were dependent on the estate for employment. Among the Archdeacon's immediate staff were a cook, a dairyman, a porter, brewers, a cook-boy, a scullion-boy, a ploughman, a stable or 'garron-keeper', a horse boy and a footman, along with boys for tending cattle, sheep and swine. And in the village of Oldbawn could be found a tailor, a brogue-maker, a smith, a carpenter and a fowler. It has been suggested that some of these people may have come to Oldbawn from Conway and/or Beaumaris in Wales to serve the household.

Oldbawn House was one of the earliest substantial houses in Ireland built not purely for defensive purposes. The rebellion of 1641 would challenge the thinking behind constructing such a house. The recently built house was attacked and burnt, causing extensive damage, estimated at £3000. According to depositions of the Bulkeleys' servants and tenants, the house's offices, garden and orchard were completely ravaged.

The Big Houses

Views of Oldbawn House in 1890, showing the front (top and bottom left) as well as the clock tower and the yard (bottom right).

A Ramble About Tallaght

By mid-November 1641, the O'Byrnes were in revolt, creating terror within a few miles of Dublin. The district was engulfed in violence. Robbery and the destruction of property were commonplace, bringing the process of Anglicisation to a sudden halt. Unrest in the region would last for almost a decade.

William Bulkeley, Archdeacon of Dublin, died in 1671. The following year, his son Richard was created Sir Richard Bulkeley, 1st Baronet of Oldbawn in the County of Dublin and Dunlavin in the County of Wicklow. The Archdeacon's father, Lancelot Bulkeley, would be best remembered in the district and immortalised in the lore of Oldbawn and Tallaght, by later reports of his ghost appearing. He would be seen dressed in the robes of state, travelling in his carriage from his Palace in Tallaght village to his son's stately home in Oldbawn. The local peasantry, which was, well, pretty much everyone but the Bulkeley heirs, believed that if they looked upon the face of the phantom Archbishop, they would die before the year was out. The tradition lived on into the early twentieth century and almost outlived Oldbawn House itself. (Some accounts state that the Bulkeley ghost was in fact the Archdeacon. The earliest written account I can find is from 1867, from James M'Donnell of Oldbawn Papermills. He relates that

Detail from the Down Survey of Ireland (1656–58).

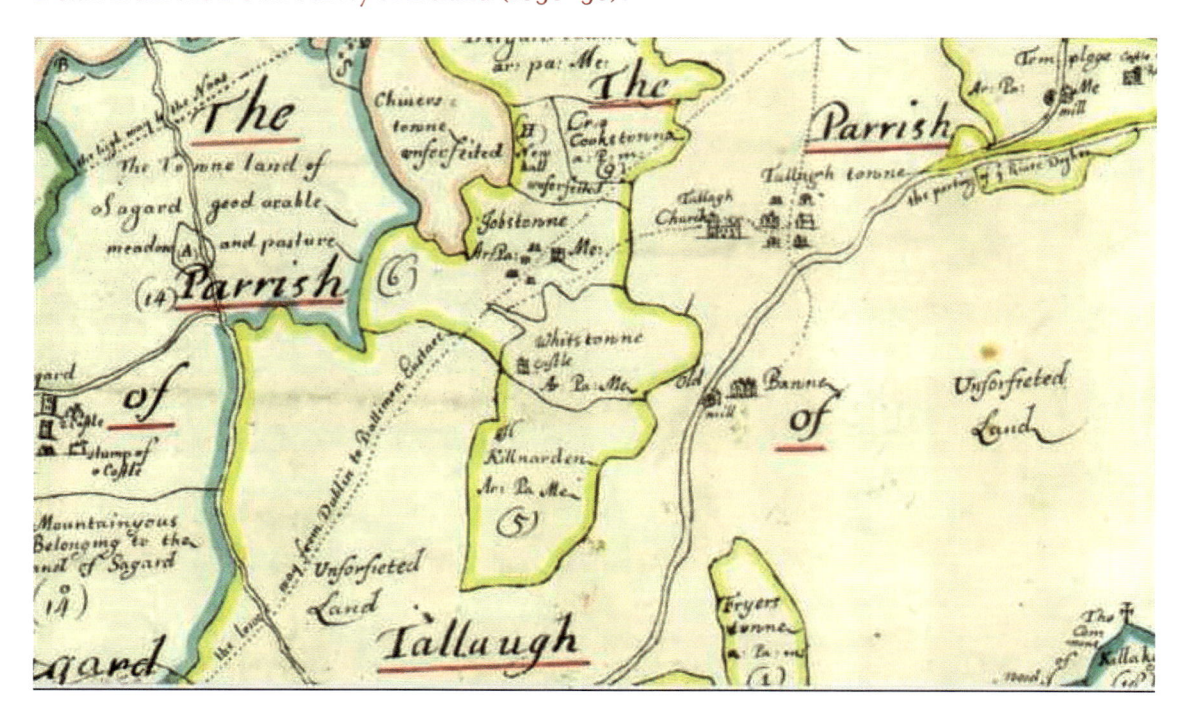

his childhood nurse believed the ghost of the Archbishop visited the house every year on the anniversary of his death.)

Sir Richard, 1st Baronet, having spent some years travelling and horse breeding, married in 1659. His wife died after only five years of marriage, leaving him with two young sons. He would marry again in later life, in 1684. He died the following year and was succeeded by his son, also Richard, 2nd Baronet of Oldbawn and Dunlavin.

Richard Bulkeley, 2nd Baronet, was an extraordinary and curious fellow. He was as learned as he was inventive, and as industrious as he was devout. He was educated and privileged, but suffered from a condition of the spine, perhaps scoliosis. Edmund Calamy, in *An Historical Account of My Own Life*, describes him as 'a gentleman of learning who was very short and crooked, but fully expected, under this dispensation, to be made straight in a miraculous way, though he happened to die before the miracle was ever wrought upon him, to his no small mortification and disappointment'. To be disappointed in life is perhaps to be expected. But to be disappointed in death must be mortifying indeed.

Dr Hillel Schwartz mentions that Sir Richard was 'afflicted with sciatica, "hectic fevers" and gonorrhoea … [an] hypochondriac struggling with headaches or fevers one day in three, often bedridden'. Brought up in an extremely devout household, Bulkeley was convinced that he could be made whole by divine intervention and claimed to have been cured of continuous headache, a stone and of a rupture (so that he ceased to need a truss).

A leisured crank, with much learning and more time on his hands than most, Richard, 2nd Baronet, spent at least some of his time in invention and prophecy. A Fellow of the Royal Society in 1686, be presented a paper on a 'self-propelled chariot that could not be toppled'. The chariot or 'calesh' would, according to Bulkeley, be very comfortable for invalids and would be almost impossible to overturn. But it could 'only hold one person, was ready to take fire every ten miles and it created an almost insufferable noise'. The paper was received with some amusement. The chariot never went into production. Sir Richard was also one of the first people to draw greater public attention to the Giant's Causeway in Antrim.

Richard, 2nd Baronet, was instrumental in establishing, developing and settling the village of Dunlavin in west Wicklow, and laid the foundations for a linen industry on land originally purchased by his great-grandfather from the Sarsfield family before the troubles in 1641. His father had been responsible for erecting some of the first houses in that village. Among Richard's many ambitions was a desire to develop a University of Dunlavin. In that regard, he was very much a man ahead of his time. Very, very much ahead. He failed to secure the support of the Church of Ireland for the proposal, and it may have been this that caused him to distance himself from that body.

His religious thinking at times set him at odds with his family. He fell in with a group called the 'French Prophets' and wrote and published several pamphlets in their defence. He was preparing to sell Oldbawn House and donate his assets to the group when fate overtook him and he expired. Owing to his financial support of the French Prophets, and later of Abraham Whitrow's breakaway movement, which preached the doctrine of 'levelling' (that the rich must part with all their estates and become poor, if ever they deigned to enter the Kingdom of Heaven), Bulkeley went heavily into debt.

Bishop George Berkeley stated that 'Sir Richard 2nd Baronet was resolved to sell his estate and give all to the poor. But I am told the Chancery opposed him as non-compos mentis'. There was then, as there is now, a fine line, though perhaps not very fine, between charity and *non-compos mentis*!

Between invention and faith, and despite his physical affliction, Sir Richard, as was perhaps expected for a man of his position, took to soldiering. He fought on the Protestant side, at the battle of the Boyne. On his return from the battlefield, he passed St Doulagh's Church in north County Dublin. The interior walls had been decorated in 1609 with frescoes depicting the Descent of the Holy Ghost; St Patrick; St Bridget; St Colmcille; and St Doulagh dressed as an anchorite. Bulkeley, in the name of William, his new sovereign, couldn't resist the temptation to deface the sacred frescoes and destroy the site. His great-grandfather, the Archbishop, who had done similar sixty-one years earlier in Cook Street Carmelite Church, would have been proud of him!

Richard's preoccupations did not hold him back professionally or socially. Nor did it prevent him from marrying well. He served briefly in the Irish House of Commons for Fetherd, Co. Wexford. The year after his father's death, he married Lucy Downing, the daughter of Sir George Downing, the Anglo-Irish statesman, soldier, preacher, spymaster and diplomat (after whom Downing Street in London is named). Lucy and Richard had one child, a son who died in infancy.

> Here lieth the body of Sir RICHARD BULKELEY, Bart. Who departed this life, April the 7th, 1710, in the 47th year of his age.
> And also of Lucy his wife Who departed this life October the ninth, 1710, in the 47th year of her age.

Remains of Sir Richard Bulkeley's gravestone, relaid close to the foot of the old church tower in St Mary's churchyard in Ewell, Surrey, UK.

Richard, 2nd Baronet, died in 1710. His wife survived him, according to some sources, only six months, and others eighteen months. Some of his letters survive among the papers of William King in Trinity College, Dublin, and in those of Martin Lister in the Bodleian Library. He is buried in Ewell, Surrey, where he spent his last years. His estate passed to a niece, Hester (Esther) but … well, it's complicated!

After the death of Richard Bulkeley, 1st Baronet, his second wife and widow remarried and became the third wife of the Hon. William Worth. Worth promptly moved into Oldbawn House. When she died, and after the death of Richard, 2nd Baronet, Worth took as a fourth wife his stepson's widow, the daughter of Sir George Downing. So, having married the widow of Sir Richard, 1st Baronet of Oldbawn, Worth went on to marry the widow of Sir Richard, 2nd Baronet of Oldbawn. The marriage was short-lived, as Lucy died shortly after, in 1710 or 1711. She is interred with Sir Richard, 2nd Baronet of Oldbawn, in Ewell, Surrey.

The Tyntes of Oldbawn and Dunlavin – keeping it in the family

James, son of William Worth by his second wife, a daughter of Sir Henry Tynte, succeeded him on his death in 1721 and took his maternal uncle's name, Tynte. Like father, like son, he went and married Hester, a granddaughter of the first Sir Richard, who was heir to Sir Richard, 2nd Baronet. Do keep up! By this somewhat convoluted turn of events, Oldbawn House came into the possession of the Tynte Family. The Right Hon. James Worth Tynte played a prominent role in politics.

James was succeeded by his son Robert Tynte in 1758. He married Elisabeth Stratford that same year. Robert died only two years later, on his way to Bath in England 'for the recovery of his health which was much impaired'. His wife Elisabeth was with child when he died. Lady Elisabeth Tynte remained a widow for the rest of her days, and died about 1816. Their son, the future Sir James Stratford Tynte, was made a Baronet in 1778, while still a minor. He married a first cousin, Hannah Saunders. The Tyntes of Tynte Park in Dunlavin, Co. Wicklow, are descended from Robert Tynte of Oldbawn House.

The neighbourhood of Oldbawn remained a challenging quarter, as it had been a century earlier. In 1788, there were reports of 'wanton barbarity on the neighbourhood of Oldbawn' – four calves were killed and their skins stripped. The carcases of the calves were otherwise left untouched. A suspect by the name of Madden was picked up on Winetavern Street in Dublin city the following morning, in possession of the, err, four skins. He was detained in the new prison.

Weston St John Joyce tells us that an 'eccentric resident' of Oldbawn House in the eighteenth century imported a herd of reindeer from Lapland and kept them in a deer park. After only a few seasons, however, they died, due to the moderate and disagreeable climate. If true, we might deduce that this 'eccentric' resident was Sir Richard Bulkeley, 2nd Baronet.

The house, having passed to Lady Elizabeth Tynte, was leased for a number of years before finally being purchased in the 1800s by the McDonnell family, who established a paper mill behind the house (see Chapter 7). The daughters of the house were educated in a Catholic Convent in Arras, France.

As late as 1912, when Weston St John Joyce visited and wrote about Oldbawn in his *The Neighbourhood of Dublin*, a large cypress tree known locally as 'the Informers Tree' still stood in the grounds, close to three neighbouring stumps of trees long felled. The Informer's Tree appeared in Oldbawn lore as relating to the 1798 rebellion – as the tree from which a rebel was about to be hanged. He was reputedly pardoned for giving information on three of his fellows, who were subsequently hanged on the trees that once grew beside it. The Informer's Tree was allowed to flourish.

This story, however, may in fact relate to a much older incident in the locality. In 1691, a party of rapparees, coming near Tallaght, stole away several horses and four men belonging to Colonel Donep's regiment of Danish horse. Believing that this could not have been done without the knowledge of inhabitants of the village, the Colonel ordered that several locals be taken up and threatened to be hanged, unless the horses and men were brought back by a certain day. This was accordingly done and some of the men that stole them were delivered up. It is possible that this incident is the origin of the Informer's Tree at Oldbawn.

With the demise and eventual closure of Oldbawn Paper Mills in 1874, Oldbawn House was effectively abandoned. It steadily declined. It hadn't been used as a principal residence for some time. By 1867, James M'Donnell of the Oldbawn Paper Mills resided in the neighbouring Park House. Oldbawn House was still in reasonable condition in November of that year, when it was visited by JR Flanagan and members of the Royal Irish Academy, who were given a tour of the old Tudor pile by M'Donnell himself. The main hall in the house accommodated a billiard table.

The ruins of Oldbawn House.

The old fireplace, rescued from Oldbawn House.

In 1890, the house was still roofed, though in a poor state of repair. By 1899, much of the lands at Oldbawn House were in the possession of Thomas Case of Rathgar, a large dairy contractor and prominent member the Dublin Cowkeepers' Association. In the early years of the twentieth century, he let 60 acres annually.

In 1907, the staircase and chimneypiece were removed from Oldbawn House to the National Museum and by 1910, the old house was in a ruinous condition. In May 1909, a fine row of beech trees were removed and two years later in 1911, on the retirement of Thomas Case, 100 acres of land known as Oldbawn Farm, containing the remains of the old house and paper mills, was put up for auction. It failed to sell. Case died in 1914. Much of the land was farmed by the Jordan family until the late 1960s.

Avant-garde painter and member of the White Stagg group, Thurloe Conolly, came out to Tallaght in 1944, to paint what remained of Oldbawn House. The area had long been of interest to Irish artists. Maurice MacGonigal had visited the area ten years earlier to paint 'The Dodder near Oldbawn'. By 1944, the decrepit ruin was beyond repair, and it would continue to fall into decay. Its last known use was as a storehouse for plant when the lands were being cleared for residential development in the late 1960s.

The ruins of what had been one of Tallaght's finest and earliest private residences were finally cleared in the early 1970s. All that remain are a celebrated stucco chimney piece from the dining room, depicting the building of the walls of Jerusalem and dated 1635; a carved oak staircase (both now in the National Museum); and a few old photographs of a clock tower with the year inscribed 1721 – likely the date of its construction – and 1747 – likely the date of its repair.

The Big Houses

The ghost of Archbishop Bulkeley now roams the grounds of Tymon Bawn Community Centre in Oldbawn and the Catholic Church of St Martin de Porres.

The Browns of Fettercairn and Brookfield

In the late 1870s, Brookfield House and Fettercairn House were two of the finest houses in Tallaght, situated just half a mile apart from each other. They were occupied by two brothers, William D Brown and James Brown, and relationships between the two were poor. This made for uncomfortable moments, such as when the families would see each other at Sunday service in the small Anglican Church of St Maelruain's in Tallaght village.

William D Brown had married Elizabeth Stubbs, daughter of Robert Stubbs of Newtown, in 1854. William lived in Fettercairn House, or 'New Hall' as it was sometimes called, with his two sons, Robert Stubbs Brown and James Hawkins Brown, and his daughters Charlotte, Adelaide and Mary Anne. In February 1878, Robert Stubbs Brown married Betsy Boardman of Boardmans Mills, in Boldbrook. Caroline, an older sister of the girls, had recently married John Barr, a Scottish-born farmer.

Fettercairn House was a comfortable, six-roomed, two-storey residence with a walled fruit garden, filled with flowers, fruit and vegetables. The house had a 100-acre farm attached to it – present day Fettercairn Estate.

William D Brown didn't own the farm, but paid an annual rent of £300 for the house and land. In 1882, he was £200 in arrears. William's brother James and his nephew James Verschoyle Brown, both of Brookfield House, were the rent collectors.

William D Brown was, to put it delicately, mad – quite literally, insane. He had previously spent time in a lunatic asylum. Shortly after his discharge and return to Fettercairn in 1880, his wife and the mother of his children, 47-year-old Elizabeth Brown, died of typhoid fever. This did little to help his mental health. And he was about to get madder.

A cousin comes a-courtin'

In 1880, sixteen-year-old Charlotte Brown was a pretty, gregarious and giddy young lady. Due to her father's instability, emotional distance and occasional prolonged absences from home, Charlotte had been very close to her mother. After her father's return from the asylum and her mother's death, Charlotte increasingly spent time outside of Fettercairn House. Her older sister Caroline and her brothers Robert and James kept a watchful eye on her.

Shortly after her mother's passing, Charlotte Brown regularly met her first cousin, James Verschoyle Brown of Brookfield House. Though almost ten years her senior, they had much in common. James had been very close to his sister, also called Charlotte, who had died of a lingering consumption in Brookfield House two years earlier, at 27 years old. He knew the pain and suffering his cousin was going through, having recently lost a loved one.

Although their fathers didn't get on and rarely spoke, the cousins had always been polite and courteous and had no quarrel with each other. As was customary for the time, Charlotte would often be chaperoned by one of her brothers when she went out walking with James.

For the next two years, James Verschoyle Brown and Charlotte were regularly seen walking the meadows of Fettercairn, Jobstown and Brookfield. James often brought little gifts for Charlotte. He gave her a £3 wristwatch, so she wouldn't be late for their walks together. On another occasion, he brought her a necktie and fur. She returned the kindness, presenting him with a cigar case.

Sometimes they were seen walking hand in hand, and sometimes James would have his arm around Charlotte's waist. In 1882, this could only mean one thing! Well, perhaps. For two years, Charlotte Brown 'loved too truly' James Verschoyle Brown, and he 'could not leave Charlotte out of his sight'.

In the autumn of 1882, James Verschoyle Brown received a letter in the post, sent to Brookfield House. He didn't recognise the handwriting. Sitting at a writing desk, he took a letter opener and proceeded to cut open the envelope addressed to him. After reading that letter, James would never walk with Charlotte again. In fact, he would refuse to speak to her again. He 'could not care for the girl'. What had been assumed by some, or at least by Charlotte and her father – that the couple were pledged to marry – would, some years later, become a debate of national interest.

The letter was from Caroline Barr, Charlotte's older, married sister. In it, Caroline wrote to say that she had seen her sister out walking with a young Royal Irish Constabulary officer, a man much below her sister's station in life. She saw them more than once, and often watched them together through her opera glass. On one occasion, the RIC officer was wearing the wristwatch that James had given Charlotte as a gift.

With that same opera glass, Caroline had seen her other young sister, Mary Anne, frolicking 'with a ploughman'. As a consequence, Caroline Barr had ordered the girls out of the house. They were disgracing the family for all to see. Charlotte responded to Caroline, telling her that the RIC man was as good a person as she would ever be.

James Verschoyle Brown was heartbroken. After two years of courting, he felt cheated and humiliated. He could not even look at Charlotte Brown again, let alone care for her. He never raised the letter with Charlotte. He just withdrew completely from her. Charlotte, now almost nineteen, didn't know why and nor did her father. He had been very keen on the match. They were to be married after all, weren't they? Everyone thought so. Perhaps time would heal whatever it was that was ailing James Verschoyle Brown.

A year passed without any reunion, and then another. Charlotte wrote an extremely abusive letter to James, calling him all manner of names and telling him never to visit her home again. He didn't reply. And he never visited her home again.

William D Brown was growing increasingly erratic. He owed his brother, James's father, £200 in rent, and he didn't have it. And he was about to lose one of his best farm hands, on account of him having tried to take liberties with the farm hand's wife.

In William's mind, James Verschoyle Brown was sitting over in Brookfield House, having tried to have his way with his daughter, and then snubbing her. He didn't understand what had happened.

For two years, William D Brown bullied, berated and abused his daughter Charlotte, to convince her to take a Breach of Promise lawsuit against her cousin. She declined. William bought a revolver, with the intention of shooting his nephew. Eventually Charlotte relented. In 1885, two and half years after they had parted company, she sought £2000 in damages in the courts from James Verschoyle Brown for Breach of Promise, claiming they had agreed to be married. But there was one small problem.

Before a jury, the fragmented Brown family were, one by one, called as witnesses in the case. All of the family's private affairs were put before the court and the national newspapers – their father's time in an asylum and the £200 he owed his brother; his meddling with his farmhand's wife; the purchase of a revolver; Caroline's letter to James, setting out in writing what she had seen; Mary Anne's cavorting with a ploughman; William's relentless bullying of Charlotte to take the case; Caroline ordering her sisters out of the house for having disgraced the family; Charlotte's abusive letter to James.

Fettercairn House, even with its high ceilings and fanlight, its walled and bountiful gardens, was not a home anyone would wish to live in.

George Hewitt, Sub-Constable of the Royal Irish Constabulary, was called to give testimony. He had walked with Charlotte Brown on a number of occasions, sometimes from church on a Sunday morning. They had walked in the evenings too. He had had in his possession her wristwatch – the watch she had received from Verschoyle Brown – for about a month. She had been walking from church one Sunday morning and 'let it fall'. George Hewitt was walking immediately behind her. She knew it. She wrote to him after, telling him to keep it until he saw her again. Hewitt wore the watch on his own wrist for a month, waiting to see the girl again and return the property. Hewitt didn't see Charlotte for two Sundays. On the third Sunday, he refused to give her the watch, but promised to give it to her the following Sunday. In exchange for the watch, she gave him her handkerchief.

On the other side, set out before the world, was James Verschoyle Brown's consideration and kindness to his young cousin during her grief after her mother's death. His generosity and thoughtfulness – giving her a wristwatch, necktie and fur. He had put nothing in writing. He hadn't even replied to Charlotte's abusive letters.

After several days of hearings, the prosecution and the defence brought their cases to a close. The Jury was asked to make a ruling as to whether James Verschoyle Brown had breached a promise to marry Charlotte Brown. The judge advised the jury that if they were to award damages to Charlotte Brown, the less damages awarded, the more likely she was to receive them.

The jury promptly found in favour of James Verschoyle Brown. No promise had been made and no promise broken.

Six months after the case, on 20 August 1885, James Verschoyle Brown of Brookfield House died of cerebrospinal fever. He was 31 years old.

In April 1886, fourteen months after the case, William D Brown announced that he and his family were leaving Fettercairn House. Patrick 'Pa' Mooney, a farmer from Stanaway Cottages in Crumlin, Dublin, acquired an interest in the holding.

Charlotte Brown went on to marry Patrick Warner Barr, a widower and her sister Caroline's brother-in-law, in 1893. He was eleven years her senior. They lived in Airlie House in Lucan and had no children. Charlotte (Brown) Barr died in 1932 in 'Montrose', Temple Gardens in Rathmines, the home of her brother, Robert Stubbs Brown. She was 68. Her husband died in 1939, leaving an estate of £10,826. The manse, glebe and church lands in Lucan were a gift to the Church by Patrick, after Charlotte's death.

In 1893, eight years after Brown vs Brown, Charlotte's father William D Brown died in Bethnal House in London, a mixed-gender asylum for 'pauper lunatics'. He was 67 years old.

Brookfield House remained in the extended Brown Family until 1924. In October 1936, it was inspected by the joint boards of Grangegorman Mental Hospital as a possible site for a new mental Institution. Brookfield House was lived in until 1965, at that time by Sarah Hannah Lambert.

The Mooney family would farm the land at Fettercairn up to 1971, when they sold it in advance of it being CPO-ed for development. In 1974, both Fettercairn House and Brookfield House were subject to Compulsory Purchase Orders by Dublin County Council. In 1974, 51 acres of land attached to Brookfield House and 133 acres attached to Fettercairn House were let, by public tender, for grazing.

Brookfield House was levelled and the site completely cleared in the late 1970s, for the construction of public housing at Jobstown Estate. It stood on the site of what is now Kilclare Gardens.

Fettercairn House was used as a parks depot for a number of years. In 1983, the house was given to St Mark's Youth Club, established in 1973, after their original clubhouse blew down in a storm. It remains St Marks Youth and Community Centre.

CHAPTER 7

Oldbawn Paper Mills

Paper mill raided

On Wednesday, 12 January 1831, between the hours of one and two o'clock in the morning, up to 150 armed men scaled the gates of Oldbawn Paper Mills and posted armed sentries on the walls of the concern. The men sized the watchman and an engineer, tied them up and locked them in the ragstore. There they were found the next morning, almost suffocated. The body of men set about destroying the machinery of the Paper Mill. They took away a quantity of paper and the arms of the persons residing within the mill.

The following week, the case was brought to the attention of the Lord Lieutenant. His Excellency, in endeavouring to bring the perpetrators of this daring outrage to justice, was pleased to offer His Majesty's pardon to any of the persons concerned, who would, within six months of that date, 'declare his accomplices, so that all or any of them may be apprehended and brought to justice'. The perpetrators were never found.

Only seven weeks earlier, on the night of Monday, 23 November 1830, Michael M'Donnell's Oldbawn Paper Mills had been entered and a valuable and costly paper machine destroyed. The mill had been locked up at 8pm, and at 5am on the Tuesday morning, a labourer entering the mill discovered rag, the base material in the last state of preparation for the manufacture of paper, strewn about the place. Two long ash rollers had been cut with a tenon saw, brass cocks and leaden pipes were destroyed, and thirty-six copper rollers were battered and rendered completely useless.

Much of the land surrounding the Mill was held by Sir William McMahon. The night before the attack on the Mill, a labourer in the employment of Sir William was visited by three men and told to resign his position of employment by noon the next day, or he would be visited with vengeance. The three men informed the labourer they were followers of Captain Rock, or Rockites (a group similar to the White Boys).

Further to the events of the previous two months, Michael M'Donnell travelled to England, where he purchased a quantity of new plant to replace the machinery that had been destroyed. On returning to Oldbawn, he wrote to Frederick Darley and John Tuder, Chief Magistrates of Police, requesting that the Constabulary stationed in Tallaght be temporarily assigned to his mill for a few months, as protection against further attacks. He noted there was ample accommodation available to house the men. They in turn wrote to Lieutenant Colonel Sir William Gosset, Under Secretary, recommending that permission be granted to station the men in Oldbawn.

The paper mills at Oldbawn, originally established on the banks of the Dodder near Kiltipper, was an important employer in the district, employing up to 100 hands. On 6 December 1802, they suffered their first serious setback. On that night, 'tempestuous weather' – torrential and intermittent rains – damaged or destroyed a number of mills close to Dublin. The bank, weirs and extensive mill works in Oldbawn were entirely swept away. There was fear that

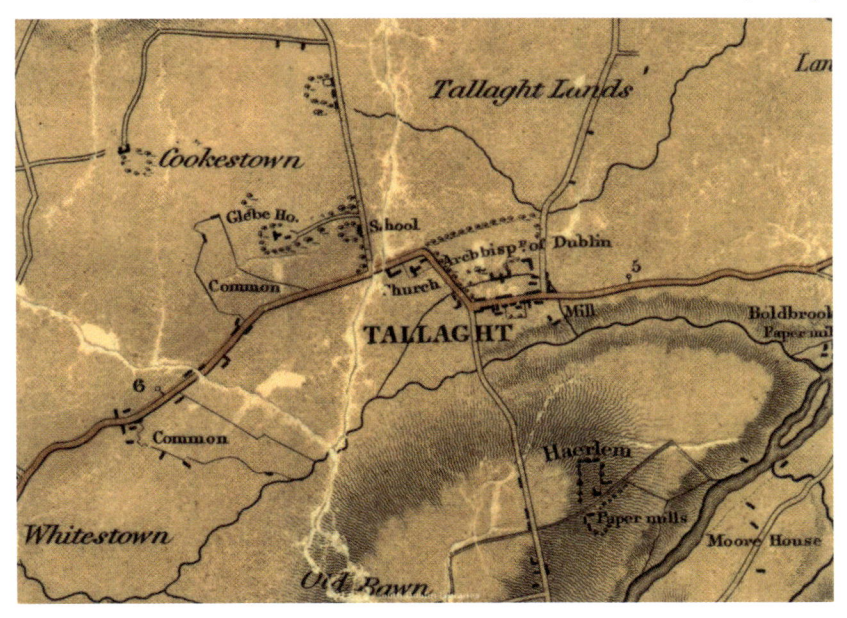

Tallaght as seen on William Duncan's 1821 map.

the local labourers would be ruined as a result. Nearly an acre and a half of Mr Wildridge's meadow, adjacent to the mill, was severed from the rest of his land by the violence of the flood and 'carried completely off'.

The Mill was later reconstructed at a safe distance from the river, on the site of Oldbawn House, giving it only some protection from the elements. Nature would intervene in its operations again many years later. On 7 January 1839 – the 'night of the big wind' – the great chimney stack of Oldbawn Paper Mills was 'blown across the road'.

In 1816, Andrew Auttersan, a Foreman of Taylor's Mill in Ballyboden since 1810, was recruited to take up the job as Foreman in Oldbawn Paper Mills. He would oversee operations there for the next ten years. It wasn't always possible to get or retain competent foremen, and competition was stiff with neighbouring mills on the Dodder. In 1842, Michael M'Donnell sacked his foreman, William McKay, due to what he considered gross incompetence. McKay, a native of Scotland, had signed a twelve-month contract, providing him with a salary, accommodation and coals for the year. However, after a series of blunders, only fourteen weeks into his employment, he was dismissed. McKay took a case against M'Donnell for loss of earnings and the cost of accommodation for the year, but M'Donnell won the case, with costs awarded. McKay, having been discharged from Oldbawn, went to America.

For 100 years, Oldbawn Paper Mills was in the ownership and management of the M'Donnell family and, from about 1818 until 1870, Michael M'Donnell and his two sons, James and Michael (Jr). The wider M'Donnell family had other milling interests in Saggart, Killeen and Bella Vista, and Michael M'Donnell and Sons had interests on William Street in Dublin city. Michael M'Donnell (Sr) resided in William Street in Dublin.

Oldbawn Paper Mills and the Young Irelanders

When leading nationalist and Young Irelander Charles Gavin Duffy, co-founder, owner and at the time editor of *The Nation* newspaper, was arrested on charges of felony in July 1848, James M'Donnell of Oldbawn Paper Mills accompanied him before the magistrate and offered to pay his bail. Gavin Duffy had transformed *The Nation* from a literary voice to a 'rebellious

The River Dodder at Tallaght.

A sluice gate on the Dodder, to control the flow.

organisation', and M'Donnell's Mills in Oldbawn supplied the paper (Oldbawn Paper Mills had supplied the paper to Grattan's Parliament 60 years earlier).

When the charges were read out against Charles Gavin Duffy, James M'Donnell enquired, 'May I ask your Worship if this case is not a bailable case? I came here prepared to tender bail in my own person if the case is held bailable.' The magistrate replied, 'It is a case in which I can take no bail.' Gavin Duffy interjected, 'I am obliged to you, Mr M'Donnell, but the magistrate has no power in this case. I suppose I am to be consigned to Newgate [Prison].' The magistrate, Mr Tyndall, inclined his head in the affirmative. While Charles Gavin Duffy made no protest as to his own arrest and the charges laid against him, he did protest the raiding of his offices and was supported in this by James M'Donnell.

On 7 August 1851, the Inland Revenue office in the Custom House issued notice for the auction of the contents of Oldbawn Paper Mills to satisfy a warrant in force for duty due to the Crown from Michael M'Donnell. Messrs Michael M'Donnell and Sons, Oldbawn Paper Mills and William Street, Dublin, were compelled to suspend payments to their staff. The liabilities were £8,000, principally in Dublin. A large number of operatives and labourers were in danger of being thrown out of employment, augmenting pauperism in Oldbawn. The company appears to have traded through its difficulties and satisfied the demands of the Crown.

In the summer of 1856, following the death of Michael M'Donnell (Sr), Oldbawn Paper Mills was put up for auction. It was acquired in full by James M'Donnell. The private residence was described as of a superior class, with very extensive stabling, cowsheds and out-offices, and fifteen neat, substantial cottages for workers. Included in the purchase was an interest in the lease of the house, offices and land – a sixty-year lease dated from 1845 – and two well-arranged gardens.

In October 1857, James's brother Michael M'Donnell (Jr) left Ireland, sailing out from Liverpool for Melbourne, Australia, on the ship *Red Jacket*. He was never seen in Oldbawn, or indeed in Ireland, again. James M'Donnell endeavoured to trace his brother, and received a letter from an officer suggesting that Michael had travelled on the same *Red Jacket* from Melbourne on to Auckland and that while boarding the ship, 'he appeared to be partially deranged'. Michael M'Donnell had made a will before leaving Ireland, appointing his brother James and a William Fox as executors. It was assumed that Michael M'Donnell was dead and that he had died unmarried and without issue. In 1871, Michael M'Donnell had still been neither seen nor heard of, prompting his brother James to seek probate of his brother's will.

The 1864 Great Exhibition

Paper from Oldbawn Paper Mills was exhibited at the Industrial exhibition in Dublin in 1864. The largest roll of paper was one and a quarter miles long, while a smaller roll was a mile long without a break or joint. The larger roll was an example of the paper on which the daily *Freeman's Journal* appeared, while the smaller roll was an example of the paper on which the *Penny Weekly Dispatch* was printed. M'Donnell had by this time the contract for both papers, in addition to *The Nation*, the *Weekly News*, the *Daily Express* and the *General Advertiser*, and was employing 120 people. The *Weekly News* alone accounted for 257,000 sheets of newspaper per month, or

1,040,500 sheets in a six-month period. Oldbawn Paper Mills was churning out well in excess of 2.5 million sheets of newsprint paper a year.

In 1871, around the time James M'Donnell sought the probate of his missing brother's will, Oldbawn Paper Mills was incorporated into a private company with nine shareholders. What had been a family concern now became the Oldbawn Papermills Company (Limited). James M'Donnell was its Managing Director and over £10,000 was invested in the latest technology and machinery.

Environmental concerns

For over twenty years, concern had been growing downstream about the defilement of the Dodder from the mills at Oldbawn, Haarlem (Milbrook) and Bolbrook. A case had been before the courts as early as 1854 in relation to chronic pollution of the watercourse. On 6 October 1875, Oldbawn Paper Mills Company (Limited) was summoned under Section 41 of the Dublin Waterworks Act for alleged fouling of the River Dodder at Oldbawn, through the discharge into the river of certain chemicals. The mill used up to one puncheon, or 318 litres, of human urine a week in the paper-making process. The urine was generously provided by the South Dublin Union workhouse.

The company was represented by a Mr Dunne, and when the case was called, Dunne applied for a postponement, as the company was not yet prepared to go into evidence. While cases were also scheduled against other mills on the river, Oldbawn Paper Mills, being the first, was seen as a test case. Under Section 61 of the Dublin Waterworks Act, any person or person throwing or allowing to issue into any stream within the jurisdiction of the Act, any impure or deleterious matter, was liable on conviction to a penalty of £5, and a further penalty of 20 shillings per day for each day the offence was repeated.

The paper mill couldn't operate without discharging its waste into the river. Twelve months after being summoned before the court, in October 1876, Oldbawn Papermills Company (Limited) was put into voluntary liquidation. Purchasers of goods at the mill were requested to settle their accounts at the offices and have their goods removed, as the liquidator could not be accountable for their safety. After approximately 104 years of paper-making by M'Donnells' Oldbawn

Paper Mills, the last ream of paper had been rolled. In its last weeks of operation, the mill had the capacity to turn out eighteen tons of paper a week.

On 3 April 1934, workmen arrived in Oldbawn, Tallaght, to fell the long-standing chimney stack of Oldbawn Paper Mills, as it had become unstable and was a hazard to public safety. At almost 300 feet, it was the tallest manmade structure in the district, towering over the townland for almost 100 years. Newspapers at the time described the stack as 'almost 200 years old'. While a great stack might have stood on this site for many years, this was not the original. That one had been blown 'across the road' on 7 January 1839, the night of the big wind.

The elusive Michael M'Donnell

The mystery of the fate of Michael M'Donnell Jr was never solved. His last known whereabouts was Melbourne in Australia in late 1857, after he disembarked from *Red Jacket*.

By the time Michael M'Donnell arrived in Melbourne, the M'Donnells' old friend Charles Gavin Duffy had become one of the region's most influential citizens. In 1856, despairing of the prospects for Irish independence, Charles Gavin Duffy had resigned from the House of Commons and emigrated with his family to Australia.

After being fêted in Sydney and Melbourne, Duffy settled in the newly formed colony of Victoria. A public appeal was held to enable him to buy the freehold property necessary to stand for the colonial Parliament. He was immediately elected to the Legislative Assembly for Villiers and Heytesbury in the Western District. A Melbourne Punch cartoon of the time depicts Duffy entering Parliament as a bog Irishman, carrying a shillelagh atop the parliamentary benches.

In 1857, the year of Michael M'Donnell's arrival in Melbourne, an Irish Catholic, John O'Shanassy, unexpectedly became Premier. He made Charles Gavin Duffy his second-in-command, as well as appointing him Commissioner for Public Works, President of the Board of Land and Works, and Commissioner for Crown Lands and Survey.

If M'Donnell departed Melbourne for Auckland, as was suggested in writing by an officer, given his now-very influential connections, he must surely have been at least partially deranged. For Charles Gavin Duffy owed the M'Donnell's of Oldbawn a favour.

CHAPTER 8

Those Damned Inquisitors – The Dominicans in Tallaght

On Saturday, 1 November 1755, the city of Lisbon in Portugal was hit by a great earthquake, reducing the city to rubble and killing an estimated 60,000 citizens. Among them were four Irish Dominican priests, who perished in the rubble of the Irish college there. Along with 12,000 dwellings in the city, all that remained of the Irish College of Corpo Santo at Cais do Sodré was a pile of debris. A tremor was felt in Cork, Ireland, and a massive sea swell swept into the bay of Kinsale that afternoon. But one effect of the earthquake would be felt in Tallaght, Co. Dublin, 100 years later.

A surviving priest in Lisbon, Father Charles O'Kelly OP, set out on a mission to rebuild the Irish Dominican College there. The institution had for many years contributed toward keeping the light of faith alive 'in the old country' during penal times, training Irish priests and sending them back to Ireland. Father O'Kelly put his wish before Pope Benedict XIV, who in turn recommended the project to the charity of all the bishops of Spain and the Indies. In the following decade, almost £40,000 was raised from across the region. The successor of Pope Benedict XIV, Pope Clement XIII, followed his predecessor's lead and addressed briefs to the Archbishop of Toledo, recommending the support of the Diocese for the Irish Dominican College of Corpo Santo.

Fifteen years after the earthquake, in 1770, a magnificent new Dominican college and church was built. It became colloquially known as the 'Martyrs' Seminary', as it trained Dominican priests who would often return to Ireland. Here, if discovered, they faced persecution in the days before Catholic Emancipation. The contribution from Spain to the Irish College of Corpo Santo could not be over-estimated.

By 1795, due to the French occupation of Lisbon, the college fell into decline. A suppression of religious houses in the early 1830s hastened its demise. After the introduction of Catholic Emancipation in Ireland in 1829, there was no longer an impediment to the Dominican Order establishing its own novitiate in Ireland. In the early 1850s, a portion of the buildings at Corpo Santo were sold, and from the sale of these buildings capital was raised for the establishment of a new Dominican novitiate in Ireland.

Two Dominican brothers, both in blood and in habit, played a central role in the establishment of the Dominican Novitiate at Tallaght – Patrick and Bartholomew Russell, two Cork men who had studied at Corpo Santo. Patrick Russell was responsible for the sale of Dominican holdings in Lisbon. After his brother Bartholomew took a lease out on Fingal House, outside Dublin, to provide for the establishment of a new novitiate in Ireland, Patrick discovered that John Lentaigne (later Sir John Lentaigne) was selling his modest mansion, Tallaght House on 33 acres.

Patrick persuaded Bartholomew to drop the lease on Fingal House. The purchase of Tallaght House was approved in 1855 by Father Vincent Jandel, head of the Dominican Order. A 1000-year lease from John Lentaigne was secured at an initial annual rent of £100. (It would later, by agreement, be increased to £130.)

And so it was that two Cork men, with Spanish money, contributed to Tallaght once again becoming an important centre of Christian teaching and learning – as it had been back in the eighth century.

When the Protestant Archbishop of Dublin heard that the site in Tallaght had been sold – a site that had, up to only 40 years earlier, been in the possession of his office for 500 years – he asked, 'And who has bought it?' When informed, 'The Dominicans,' he reputedly exclaimed, 'Ah! Those damned Inquisitors. What a calamity!' – referring to the role of the Dominican Order in the Spanish Inquisition.

House of the four Toms

In late summer 1855, three priests, all called Tom and all from Galway, moved into Tallaght House.

Father Tom Mullins, Father Tom Rush and Father Thomas Burke set about establishing the Dominican novitiate of Tallaght. They were joined the following year by a Mullingar man, Nicholas Duffy. A student, Duffy was promptly given the Dominican habit and his religious name – Tom – becoming Brother Tom Duffy. Having four Toms under the same roof must have made for occasional confusion. Coincidentally, Father Tom Burke had himself been called Nicholas before he joined the Order.

The porch of Tallaght House was converted into a temporary oratory for divine office and mass, until Mr Lentaigne's old timber barn adjoining the ancient tower house was converted into a chapel that would serve the community for 32 years. In 1859, a bell was placed on the tower, to compete with that ringing from the nearby Church of Ireland St Maelruain's.

Father Tom Burke OP – Ireland's Lacordaire

Nicholas Burke was born in the Claddagh in Galway on 8 September 1830. His father was a baker by trade, often humorously referred to by his son as the 'Master of the Rolls'. His mother was a serious and pious woman and a harsh disciplinarian. The family were of modest means and worked hard to give their son a good education. When he was seventeen years old, at the height of the Irish Famine in 1847, Nicholas was accepted as a postulant into the Dominican Order, and later that year he was sent to Perugia in Italy to begin his novitiate and to receive the Dominican habit. In later life, he recalled scenes of despair and destitution during the Famine in Ireland: 'If I were to live a thousand years, never could I banish from my memory or shut out from my eyes the terrible sights I then beheld.'

In the Dominican Order, Nicholas Burke was given the name Thomas after the eminent Dominican philosopher, theologian and jurist St Thomas Aquinas, becoming Father Thomas Burke, or Tom to his friends. He was ordained in March 1853. In 1855, he was recalled to Ireland to head up the novitiate of the Irish Province of the Dominican Order in Tallaght.

Burke's exceptional gifts as an orator were first noticed in 1859, when the 29-year-old priest delivered a sermon in the Star of the Sea Church in Sandymount, Dublin, titled 'Music in Catholic Worship'. This was on the occasion of the installation of a new organ in the church.

Throughout the 1860s, Father Burke's reputation as a preacher and orator steadily grew, not just in Ireland, but in England, throughout Europe and later in America. In May 1869, when the remains of Daniel O'Connell were being reinterred under the round tower in Glasnevin Cemetery, it fell to Father Tom Burke, as the most renowned preacher in Ireland, to deliver the oration. For two hours, Father Burke held captive an estimated audience of 50,000 Dubliners.

Burke's reputation was such that he was often compared to Jean-Baptiste Henri-Dominique Lacordaire, the French Dominican preacher, journalist, theologian and political activist. Lacordaire re-established the Dominican Order in post-revolutionary France and was considered the greatest pulpit orator of the nineteenth century.

Phase One

From 1855 until 1867, the Dominicans in Tallaght occupied Tallaght House or what came to be called the White House – previously the country residence of John Lentaigne. In 1863, the Order engaged architect Joseph James (JJ) McCarthy to draw up plans for a purpose-built novitiate. McCarthy drew up an ambitious and costly plan for a quadrangle of buildings to include a novitiate, college and church. To this day, JJ McCarthy's plan has never been fully realised.

When he was only twenty-three years old, McCarthy had designed St Columba's Catholic Church in Derry City. He was a member of the Young Ireland movement and a personal friend of Charles Gavin Duffy (as was the Dominicans' near neighbour in Oldbawn, Joseph M'Donnell, proprietor of Oldbawn Paper Mills). In the early 1860s, McCarthy was in a brief professional partnership with Daniel O'Connell, a grandson of the Liberator.

JJ McCarthy was known as an irascible and intemperate master. In the months in which McCarthy was finalising plans for the Dominican novitiate in Tallaght, an apprentice of McCarthy, O'Malley, filed a case against him for assault, heard before the Court of Common Pleas. In December 1863, McCarthy was charged with 'several acts of violence and assault'. McCarthy claimed that O'Malley's behaviour was unsatisfactory and admitted to having 'slapped the

Those Damned Inquisitors – The Dominicans in Tallaght

A portrait of Father Tom Burke.

plaintiff in the face for looking cross' and to 'striking him with a square'. O'Malley was awarded £70 damages.

When McCarthy died on 6 February 1882, he was buried in Glasnevin. His son Charles married the English artist Clara Christian, resident of Tymon Lodge, Firhouse, and when she died young in 1905, she was buried with JJ in the McCarthy family plot in Glasnevin. She had previously been a lover of the writer George Moore and was immortalised as the character Stella in Moore's *Hail and Farewell*.

On 29 May 1864, Father Bernard Goodman OP, Prior Provincial, laid the foundation stone for the new novitiate, a three-storey building orientated east to west, parallel with the main street of Tallaght. The first stone was suspended from a shears, ready to be lowered at the appointed time by JJ McCarthy and Mathew Gahan, the builder. A hermitically sealed bottle containing coins of the realm and a scroll written in Latin naming the dignitaries in attendance on the day was placed beneath the foundation stone. An exquisitely manufactured silver trowel was handed to Father Goodman, inscribed with the words, 'Presented to the Very Rev. Bernard J Goodman OP, Provincial of the Irish Dominicans on the occasion of this blessing and laying of the first stone of St Mary's Priory, County Dublin, by Mathew Gahan and his son Michael, builders, JJ McCarthy RHA, architect, 29 May 1864.'

Father Goodman mortared the foundation stone for the building. The day after the ceremony, the *Freemans Journal* concluded that 'A great and holy work has commenced on one of the ruins of the old temples of the national faith, which, like the fabled Phoenix, rises from the ashes in which it was thought to have been consumed, in the newness and vigour of a deathless life.'

A Ramble About Tallaght

It would take over three years for Mathew and Michael Gahan of Whitechurch, Rathfarnham, to complete the building, at a cost of almost £4000. The new novitiate was finally occupied on 14 September 1867. A telescope was installed in the Priory to allow the brethren to study the heavens and a library of 3000 volumes was brought to Tallaght from Lisbon. Father Tom Duffy had a keen interest in astronomy.

Studying the original architectural plans, it can be seen that the building originally had three great lateral chimney stacks. These were removed in 1933 to provide for the creation of fourteen attic rooms to match those constructed in a later wing. The attic area would become known as Mount Rascal.

By 1873, there was still a substantial debt owing on the building of the novitiate. This was cleared when Father Burke returned from a preaching tour of the United States with £2000 he had raised there.

The following year, the Prior, Father Francis Purcell OP, put an end to a 1000-year-old tradition – the Pattern of Tallaght. It was perhaps a sign of their growing confidence and influence in Tallaght, that after 1000 years of the custom, the Dominican Prior could effectively prevail upon the local people to discontinue the practice. It had for many years been little more than an excuse for public drunkenness and debauchery.

Shortly after the opening of the new Priory, Father Tom Burke was granted leave to bring a class of his novices from Tallaght to Rome, to introduce them to the Holy Father, Pio Nono (Pope Pius IX). After proudly introducing the group of young Irish men to the Pope, Burke was crestfallen when the Pope turned away, and was heard to mutter to an aide, 'Feniani.' The rising at Tallaght had happened not long before and the Fenians had made headlines throughout Christendom.

Phase Two

In 1878, Father Burke completed a second lecture tour of America, raising a substantial sum of money, some of which was used to buy the freehold of lands in Tallaght from the Trustees of the Church of Ireland. (The Trustees had little compunction about taking monies from the Damned Inquisitors!) This added considerably to the Dominicans' existing holding of 33 acres.

Those Damned Inquisitors – The Dominicans in Tallaght

Architect George Coppinger Ashlin was commissioned by the Dominicans in 1882 to draw up plans for a church – the Church of St Mary of the Rosary. JJ McCarthy had died earlier that year and his original plans were set aside. Ashlin was married to the daughter of Augustus Pugin, the architect who designed the clock tower (now Elizabeth Tower) that houses the bell known as Big Ben in London, and had been in a professional partnership with his son, Edward Welby Pugin. The design of the Dominican Church in Tallaght had some of the hallmarks of Pugin, under whom Ashlin had studied and completed his articles. Ashlin, a tall, commanding figure with an appearance of distinction, was of a quiet, retiring and somewhat shy disposition.

On 1 October 1882, the foundation stone was laid for the Church of St Mary of the Rosary. Father Tom Burke died in 1883, before the completion of the project. Burke had raised £3000 for the project by giving further lectures in America and the UK. Public subscribers in Ireland contributed over £4300, including £440 from members of the Royal Irish Constabulary.

A further £5000 was needed to complete the project. After Father Burke's passing, the public were called on to contribute to the building costs of the 'Father Thomas Burke Memorial

Church of St Mary of the Rosary or Tom Burke Memorial Church.

A Ramble About Tallaght

Church', as a monument to his legacy. A lottery at the Mansion House in Dublin was also held.

The building was constructed by Joseph Meade and Sons, from bricks made in Athy. The grey stone on the face of the building was quarried in Clondalkin and the dressing was cut limestone from Navan. The buttress and dressing were of white Ardbraccon stone. After thirty years of using the temporary Rustic Chapel, the Dominicans now had their own fine church.

Statues of St Maelruain and St Aengus took their place in the church, honouring the local Christian heritage of Tallaght. They stand side by side with statues of the Dominican Louis Bertrand OP, the Apostle to the Americas; Pope Pius V; the Dominican martyr John of Cologne; and Antoninus, Dominican Archbishop of Florence. St Aengus is, perhaps playfully, represented wearing a Dominican habit, despite having predeceased St Dominic, the founder of the Order, by 400 years.

A grinning gargoyle

Among those who knew him, Father Tom Burke was as celebrated as a raconteur, a wit and a mimic as he was as an orator and a preacher. Some observers believed that his wit was one of the only reasons he was never appointed a bishop. On hearing Pope Leo XIII express surprise one time that a very large aristocratic English lady had come all the way to Rome to receive a papal blessing, Father Burke remarked, 'Does not your holiness know that faith moves mountains?'

On his return from America, during a lecture tour in England, while in the home of a distinguished person in London, Burke was, in private company, going through some of his extraordinary mimicries. A notable ecclesiastical architect was present and was so struck by Father Burke's grotesque representations, that he offered him a great inducement, if he would give him a few sittings for these faces and figures, to ornament a grand new Gothic church he was about to undertake. Father Burke was exceedingly tickled at the idea and at the possibility of one day visiting that very church, to be confronted with a distorted stony self, gaping at him from the capital of a column. Burke replied, 'I wish to be a pillar of the Church. You want to make me only a grinning gargoyle.'

Father T Burke Memorial Church.

Interior of Father T Burke Memorial Church.

The old entrance to the church in Tallaght, completed shortly after Father Burke's death, is ornamented with two faces. One is believed to be a likeness of Father Tom Burke, the other of St Thomas Aquinas.

A number of stained-glass windows in the church were donated or sponsored by Victoire Martyn, Mary and Michael Mahon of Killinarden and a Mrs Welpy.

Victoire Martyn, a spinster of independent means from an old, established Galway family, had held Father Tom Burke in high regard. She also sponsored the Tom Burke Memorial Plaque, erected internally on the garden wall, now opposite High Street. (The Martyn family were one of the 'fourteen tribes' of Galway, the City of Tribes.)

Michael Mahon, a comfortable farmer in Killinarden, in whose name a memorial window illuminates the church, met a ghastly and gruesome end, becoming the victim in one of the most shocking murder cases in Tallaght's history in 1900.

Phase Three

From 1867 until 1886, the Dominicans occupied the Priory and Tallaght House, which they called the White House. When the new Church of St Mary of the Rosary, built parallel to the Priory and Main Street, was constructed, the friars now had to brave the elements – the outdoors – to get from the Priory to the Church. In 1901, a new, third wing, the east wing, was constructed, connecting the two. Electric lighting was also introduced into the building for the first time.

The new wing provided thirty-three extra cells for students, a larger kitchen and refectory and three classrooms. Due to a shortage of funds, only the west side of the new wing was faced with cut stone, reducing the total cost of the build by £900, to £10,500. So tight was the budget that postulants moving into the new wing were required, if they could afford it, to buy their own furniture for their cells.

On Christmas Eve 1901, at Vespers, electric lights were turned on for the first time in St Mary's.

A fire in the laundry

By 1906, after the construction of the new east wing, the old Tallaght House was underutilised and a decision was taken to use it as a laundry. At 5am on a Wednesday in March 1907, a serious fire occurred in the Dominican Laundry. When the fire was discovered, William Fox, a neighbouring publican and grocer on Main Street, sent a boy on a bicycle into Dublin to raise the alarm and summon the fire brigade. A fire engine was promptly dispatched from Chatham Row Fire Station. By the time it arrived in Tallaght, the fire had made significant headway.

Father Tom Burke OP, 'a pillar of the Church'.

Father Tom Burke Memorial Church some time before 1901. Note the old tower house of the Archbishop's Palace, to the left.

There was a good water supply from a pond in the grounds and heroic efforts were made by the Fire Brigade, the friars and some locals to quell the inferno. Despite four hours spent attempting to extinguish the fire, the building was completely gutted. Initial estimates of the cost of the damage were put at £500.

The building was, however, insured. After its refurbishment, it continued to be used as a laundry, an infirmary, a vestiary, a storage space and as occasional overflow accommodation.

As the one-hundredth anniversary of the Dominicans' arrival in Tallaght approached in 1955, a flurry of development activity got underway. Tallaght House – the White House – was now 130 years old and not much had been done with it since its refurbishment following the laundry fire in 1907. It was over 50 years since the last significant 'extension' of the Dominican buildings in 1901. After fifteen years of debate, a proposal from Father Ned Foley to extend the White House to create a dedicated Retreat Centre was accepted in 1954.

A Dominican brother constructed a summer house and seating around 1910 from whale bones brought to the site by John Lentaigne eighty years earlier. The summer house stood for a number of years and the metal poles on which the bones were placed still remain, close to the back wall in the grounds of the priory. The whale bones, however, are long gone.

The White House – Dominican Retreat Centre

A £45,000 redevelopment of Tallaght House got underway. Clearing of the site was commenced by Sisk & Co on 23 May 1955 and, five weeks later on 30 June, the foundations for the new Retreat Centre were blessed. The new development would completely enclose, at the western end, the old Tallaght House. A substantial four-storey extension to the east would expand the capacity of the building, providing 30 rooms for retreatants. The concrete blocks used in the construction of the building were manufactured onsite by a man from Blessington.

An impressive and elegant new red-brick entrance to the Dominican campus was opened on to the Greenhills Road, providing direct access to the Retreat Centre. On 4 August 1956, almost 101 years to the day since the three Toms had arrived in Tallaght House, the new Retreat Centre was officially opened by Dr John Charles McQuaid, Archbishop of Dublin. The development was largely funded through the charitable patronage of a consortium of Dublin businessmen.

During construction of the Retreat Centre, a long-forgotten underground tunnel was uncovered. It was believed to connect the Tallaght House site with St Maelruain's. It wasn't fully explored. Some years later, a subsidence or sinkhole appeared at the priory wall on Barrack Street and revealed what appeared to be an underground souterrain, consistent with a tunnel from the old Tallaght House to St Maelruain's. This sinkhole too was promptly backfilled without any great investigation.

The basement kitchen of the old Tallaght House, dating back to 1825, can still be seen in the basement of the Retreat Centre. The walls are approximately two feet thick.

The new wing

Parallel to the development of the Retreat Centre, plans were being advanced for another new wing, adjoining the tower house. While the first sod was cut on 17 August 1955, to mark the centenary of the Dominicans coming to Tallaght, the actual tender for the work was not put out until June 1956. The quantity surveyor was a Mr Cross and the builders selected were Maher and Murphy.

The architect for the new wing was Cyril Ashlin Harrington (1890–1973), a Cork man and principal in the firm Beckett and Harrington (Beckett was a relative of the writer Samuel Beckett). Harrington had recently completed the design for the Church of the Good Shepherd in Churchtown, which would open in 1957. Twenty years earlier, in 1936, Cyril Ashlin Harrington had completed a similar project for the Dominican Order, designing the new Dominican Novitiate, an extension to St Mary's Priory in Cork City. On that occasion, he gifted a tabernacle of chaste design to sit on the oratory altar. That extension had facilitated the transfer of the Dominican Novitiate from Tallaght to Cork, leaving Tallaght as a dedicated House of Studies.

Harrington was, for a time, President of the Royal Institute of Architects and a President and Captain of Rathfarnham Golf Club. A nephew of prominent Cork industrialist and banker Sir Stanley Harrington, Cyril lived in Butterfield Park, Rathfarnham. One of his last designs was for a church on Inishmore, completed pro bono in 1958. He died in 1973.

Students of architecture may note that the style and form of the building shares characteristics with the Player's Will's factory on the South Circular Road in Dublin, designed by Beckett and Harrington some twenty years earlier.

A new library — the lector's wing

With the centenary of their arrival in Tallaght behind them, the Dominicans continued apace with development. In March 1957, the first sod was cut on the site for a new library, also designed by Cyril D Ashlin Harrington. It was first used in October 1958, only eighteen months after the first sod was cut. The second floor contained eleven comfortable reading cells for teachers, earning it the name 'the lector's wing'. The original library, in the 1867 wing, was converted into another classroom.

The 1969 extension to St Mary's Church

The 1886 Church of St Mary of the Rosary could accommodate only 240 people. By 1965, the Dominican community in Tallaght had grown to 119 and the local congregation to almost 900. In the 1950s, the number of Sunday masses was increased from five to six to accommodate the growing numbers. Pressure grew on the Church throughout the 1950s and 1960s. The idea of extending it had first been mooted back in 1940 by Father John Houston, brother of 1916 Volunteer Sean Houston.

In 1966, Father Paul Hynes was elected Prior of the Dominican Priory. After almost 25 years of debate, within six months of his election, Father Hynes appointed an architect to draw up plans for an extension to the Church. The architect was Edward W Brady, a favourite with the Dominicans, who would go on to design St Aengus's Church in Glenview.

Dominican Priory with new 1901 East Wing. Note the front-facing lateral chimney stacks on the Priory building to the left, since removed.

Construction commenced in November 1968 and was completed twelve months later. During the construction of the extension, mass was held on the ground floor of the 'new' library building, from which the bookshelves had been temporarily removed. A young Galway-born architect, Raymond Hosty, was the Architect-in-Charge onsite for the duration of the build. On completion of the project, Ray Hosty would abandon his career as an architect and go on to pursue a greater love – as an artist and painter.

The builders on the project were Mssrs E Stone and Co. At a cost of £140,000, the new extension increased the capacity of the Church by 600. As part of the project, a portion of the old high wall on Tallaght Main Street was lowered to reveal the arcaded concrete façade, perhaps reflecting the new spirit of openness and inclusion after the Second Vatican Council. Visually, it diminished the demarcation between the Church and the village, eroding the visible boundary between the Church and its people. The community of Tallaght contributed generously toward the cost of the build.

A new tabernacle was installed in the extended St Mary's. It was designed by Richard Enda King, one of Ireland's foremost sculptors, perhaps best known and remembered for his 55-foot-high granite sculpture 'Spirit of the Air', resembling a tailfin and erected on the roundabout at Dublin Airport in 1992. Placed on a polished limestone pedestal, the tabernacle was positioned to one side, so as not to obstruct the view of the altar.

At the Centenary celebrations for St Mary's Priory, 1956.

Windows by George Campbell

The stained glass windows on the eastern and western aspects of the extension are the work of an Irish artist who, since 2006, has had a roundabout in Malaga, Spain, named after him.

George Campbell was born on the 29 July 1917, at St Patrick's Terrace in Arklow, Co. Wicklow. His family moved to Belfast when he was young, and there he spent much of his youth. George didn't start painting until 1944, and in 1951 he paid his first visit to Spain, to Malaga. The visit marked the beginning of an intense, 25-year relationship with the area, spending six months of the year in Malaga. Campbell is credited with founding the Irish Exhibition for Living Art in 1943. He was made a Knight Commander of Spain in 1978, in recognition of his contribution to the arts. The roundabout in Malaga town, named in his honour, is called *Glorieta Jorge Campbell*.

Campbell's art reflected his surroundings throughout his life, from the destruction of the Belfast Blitz to the Flamenco dancers of Spain. (When not painting Campbell liked to play Flamenco guitar.) A cubist influence is discernible in Campbell's windows in Tallaght. They were designed to create a mood, rather than tell a story. His work in stained glass can also been seen in Galway Cathedral.

He died in Dublin in 1979 and is buried in St Kevin's Church in Laragh, Co. Wicklow, alongside his wife Madge. A plaque was placed on his childhood home in Arklow in 2017, to mark the centenary of his birth.

In 1975, the extension was recognised with the Cembureau Award, a European architecture award, having been nominated by the Irish Concrete Society.

For many years in the reception of the Dominican Priory, on the wall to the right, the Confederacy Flag or Rinnuccini Flag of Kilkenny, dating from 1649, was displayed. It was brought to Tallaght from Kilkenny in 1874. In recent years, it has been sent for essential maintenance work to the National Museum, where it currently resides. In 1949, the flag was insured for the sum of £2000.

Another curiosity held on site for many decades was the crucifix of Marie Antoinette, she who lost her head in the French Revolution. A necklace, the 'Cross of Marie Antoinette', was a gift to Father Tom Burke from the Wyse family in Waterford, who had received it from her Irish confessor, Abbé Henry Essex Edgeworth (de Firmont).

In the grounds of the Priory, on the ground between the old tower house and the Retreat Centre, lay two substantial mill wheels. Originally brought to the site by John Lentaigne in the 1830s, they are believed to be from Clondalkin Gunpowder Mill, destroyed in an explosion in April 1787. The explosion was so great it was felt in the city of Dublin.

The arcaded concrete extension to St Mary's Church under construction, 1969.

The farms

The Dominican farm was a model of self-sufficiency, producing milk, meat, potatoes, vegetables and eggs. What wasn't consumed by the community was sold in the markets in Dublin, to fund the purchase of those items not produced in-house. At various times, the Priory had its own tailoring workshop for the production of habits, a laundry and a book-bindery, to maintain and repair the extensive array of volumes in the library.

About 1917, the Government requisitioned 5.5 acres of the Dominicans' land, north of the Priory, to extend the Aerodrome. They bought the Loughlin Meadows, 37 acres on the eastern side of the Greenhills Road, in 1919. Many years later in 1948, they purchased 89 acres – Healy's Farm – near Tymon.

The community held on to neighbouring land until 1961, when it was sold to the Government for £330. In 1964, they purchased 95 acres of land in Killinarden. Many years later, the Dominicans would sell 30 acres of the Loughlin Meadows on the Greenhills Road to the Council for a nominal £1000, on the condition that it would be used only for sport and recreational purposes. The area would be called Father Paul Hynes Park. (There is now an astro park and athletic track there.)

Thirty acres of the Killinarden land was later acquired under a Compulsory Purchase Order by the Council for the construction of the Tallaght Bypass. The remaining land in Killinarden was sold to the Council in 1989, at a favourable rate, for social housing and public recreational use. The Dominicans donated land on the Belgard Road for the provision of accommodation for the travelling community. Other lands there were lost with the widening of the Belgard Road.

In 1918, the Dominicans bought a motor car, one of the first in the village. In 1925, they installed the first telephone, in St Mary's. (The Foxes Covert pub and the Jobstown Inn each had a telephone installed some years earlier, as they were ticket offices for the Dublin to Blessington tram.)

The Dominican community have played a leading role in many social developments in Tallaght over many years. They have been instrumental in the establishment of Tallaght Choral Society (Father Donal Sweeney, 1967); the Credit Union (Father Pius Doherty, 1968); Tallaght Welfare Society (Father Paul Hynes, 1969), now called 'Trustus'; Tallaght Youth Band (Father Len

Perrem); Tallaght Rugby Club (Father Len Perrem); Tallaght Theatre Group and the Now and Then Production Company (Father Gerard Dunne); and Tallaght Boys' Choir (Father Thomas McCarthy, 1983). Their early engagement with Thomas Davis Football Club back in 1907 remains reflected in the crest of that club, which contains elements of the Dominican coat of arms.

They were, of course, at the forefront of the spiritual development of Tallaght New Town between 1969 and 1990. No other institution in Tallaght has played such a critical role in the development of the community over the past 175 years. Much of the recreational land in Killinarden estate was originally held as farm land by the Dominican Order. A Scout hall was erected on Dominican lands in 1973. They provided much of the land for Technological University Dublin's Tallaght Campus. The Dominicans have housed or accommodated services such as Alcoholics Anonymous, Tallaght Centre for the Unemployed, the Tallaght Homeless Advice Unit and St Catherine's Counselling Service. At a time when there was a dearth of such services or facilities in a rapidly growing suburb, the Dominican community assumed an unparalleled leadership role in community development.

With numbers of vocations near historical lows and an ageing clerical community, the Dominican influence has notably declined in recent years. But their legacy in Tallaght arguably remains greater than ever. Many of today's youth leaders, community organisers, volunteers and entrepreneurs were inspired, mentored or nurtured in their formative years by Dominican outreach in the 1970s, 1980s and 1990s.

The Dominican archivist Father Hugh Fenning (RIP), in the closing paragraph of his fine (privately published) work *The Dominicans of Tallaght 1855–2006*, from which I have extensively drawn, notes:

> There have been so many 'watchmen', hundreds of them, who trained or worked at St Mary's since 1855, and left it to preach the Gospel of God's grace throughout the world … Yet there is another and more important part of the story which can never be told: the inner religious life and efforts of so many Dominicans, their personal trials and achievements. One can only say of them, as St Paul said about himself, that they fought the good fight and finished the course.

A Ramble About Tallaght

St Maelruain's tree

In the grounds of the Dominican Priory stands one of the oldest walnut trees in Ireland. School children in Tallaght in the 1930s believed that 'St Maelruain's tree' was planted by the saint himself in the eighth century. The tree is old enough and large enough for a young person to believe that such a thing could be true. And it is old enough and large enough to keep educated adults wondering just how old it is. It is an impressive, mysterious and now sacred specimen. It is the type of tree that gave birth to other worlds – CS Lewis's Narnia, Tolkien's Middle Earth, and the faith of our fathers. It is a tree that nature has managed to split, but has yet failed to fell.

Juglans regia, or the Persian walnut, was introduced to the UK during the late 1600s and to the Americas by Spanish missionaries during the late 1700s, where it thrives in sub-tropical regions of Chile and California. Saint Maelruain's tree is thought to have been planted in the 1700s. Although the tree was struck by lightning in 1795 and split into several parts, it survives to the present day. In 2013, it was studied and its height recorded as exactly 10.4m. The girth of the tree, when measured at a height of 1.2m, was 4.12m.

The antiquarian WD Handcock speculated in 1876 that 'it must be many hundreds of years old'. 'Must', rather than 'could'. O'Curry, visiting the same tree forty years earlier in 1837, noted, 'It must be very old.' At that time, the tree, already split, occupied a quarter of an imperial acre.

In times past, the annual walnut crop was gathered by gardeners in the Dominican Priory and sold in the markets of Dublin. It is, perhaps, the oldest surviving walnut tree in Ireland.

They are rare in the district, but 'St Maelruain's tree' once had a great fellow. He was felled long before Handcock made his rounds. In August 1837, while exploring the townland, Eugene O'Curry also visited Allenton House, then occupied by Mr Cotton. Cotton had, just a few years earlier, 'cut down a very large ancient walnut tree in the garden as it occupied too much room'. Cotton got ten guineas for the trunk of the great tree. So we know that as early as the 1820s, there was at least one other ancient walnut tree in the district. The fact that these trees were so impressive, variously described as 'large', 'great' and 'ancient' as far back as the 1830s, suggests that these were among the first such walnut trees planted in Ireland.

Father Hugh Fenning, ruminating on St Maelruain's tree in 2009, observed:

> I'm no farmer but I think it's all one tree; it just seems to dislike the perpendicular. We used to harvest walnuts from it in the 1950s. A Spanish student with us at the time – his hands turned brown, and he was to be received by Archbishop John Charles McQuaid. There was no way to clean his hands. We had to write to the Archbishop and ask him not to kick up a fuss; we explained it was from picking the walnuts from Maelruain's tree.

Father Fenning speculated that the tree was likely planted between 1720 and 1730. His view was as well-informed as anyone else's.

The tree has borne witness to the arrival and departure of archbishops and majors, knights and preachers. From the 1798 Rebellion to the 1867 Battle of Tallaght, the birth of a nation and the fall of grace, the tree has endured, standing stoutly, proudly, broadly. For 170 years, it has provided shade and shelter for the friars as they wrestled, each in their own way, with vocation, temptation, the temporal and the incorporeal. A hundred types of bird have rested on its boughs – the corncrake and the owl, the heron and the wren, the magpie and the robin, some impatient and some watchful, some predatory and some serene.

The tree has survived lightning strikes and the Night of the Big Wind in 1839. It has survived pruning and picking, neglect and the elements. A substantial branch was lost in a storm in 1946. The tree still bears an annual crop. We will only know and appreciate its true age when it is felled.

A postcard image of St Maelruain's tree.

CHAPTER 9

On the Move – Planes, Trains and Automobiles

The Dublin and Blessington Steam Tramway

On Wednesday, 1 August 1888, the Dublin and Blessington Steam Tramway (DBST) opened for business. The first train was the 8:35am mail train, leaving Terenure and stopping at Templeogue, Balrothery, Tallaght, Jobstown and the Embankment. The tramway connected with the horse-drawn trams at Terenure, taking customers to Nelson's Pillar in the city centre. Citizens of Tallaght could buy a ticket at the stop in Balrothery, at Foxes Public House in the village or at the Jobstown Inn.

The Blessington and Poulaphouca Steam Tramway was incorporated as a separate company and the four-and-a-half-mile extension of the line to Poulaphouca was opened in April 1895, running all the way from Terenure to Poulaphouca the following year. It was envisaged that the line would eventually be extended to 'The Churches' at Glendalough, only twelve miles from

On the Move – Planes, Trains and Automobiles

Above: A tram passing through Tallaght village, around 1918.

Below: A locomotive of the Dublin and Blessington Steam Tramway.

Blessington. In 1911, a proposal was put forward for the electrification of the line as far as Crooksling, but the intervention of the First World War prevented it from being put into effect.

A proposal for a train line or tramway dated back to 1864, and it took almost 25 years for that vision to become a reality. Commencing in the winter of 1878, construction of the tramline provided a great deal of work for labouring classes in the decade it took to complete the line. A sum of £90,000 was invested in rolling stock, with six engines brought in from England. After only six years in operation, by 1894, 180,000 trips a year were being undertaken between Terenure and Blessington.

There were very many casualties of the line. From its earliest years, the DBST was known as a maker of widows and orphans, a service that cut down young men in their prime, that prematurely retired or worse many of its own servants. Whatever benefits and conveniences the tram brought to its stops between 1888 and 1932, it visited a litany of losses on families, losses that would still be felt many years after the tram's own demise.

William Lawson, a twenty-year-old labourer, had the unfortunate distinction of being the very first casualty of the Dublin to Blessington steam tram. A young man, he had in his brief life already acquired intemperate habits. Having staggered out of a pub in Blessington at 9.30 on a summer's evening, he walked 200 yards or so out of the town along the recently laid tram tracks. He was just in time to meet the 8.30 tram coming into Blessington from Terenure and was not seen alive again. The tragic incident occurred only one week after the first tram had arrived in Blessington.

At an inquest into his death, a solicitor representing the Dublin and Blessington Steam Tramway Company opined rather lyrically, 'Nothing of the sort could possibly have taken place if he had not been drunk.' This statement would be sorely tested in the years, indeed decades, following. The first casualty of the DBST may well have been drunk, but there would be dozens, perhaps hundreds of other victims of the line in the years ahead that would be perfectly sober – men, women, children, horses, even sheep!

Under the 1845 Coroner's Act, a coroner could direct that a dead body be taken to a tavern, public house or house licensed for the sale of spirits. The Act was unpopular with publicans, who feared the spread of disease from deteriorating corpses. Local lore holds that the Templeogue

Inn came to be known locally as 'the morgue', due to the frequency of inquests held there arising from tram-line fatalities. There is, however, little on the public record to suggest the Templeogue Inn was any more popular with coroners than other licenced establishments on the route. The line itself was sometimes referred to as 'the longest graveyard in Ireland', due to the practice of erecting wooden crosses at the side of the tracks where tragedies had occurred. The 1845 Coroner's Act remained on the statute books until 1961.

In April 1892, John Lawless, a labourer from Killininny, was driving his cart home from Terenure when, crossing the track, he was struck by the tram. His body was removed to Mr Smith's livery stables on Harold's Cross Road, where an inquest was held. He had not been drinking.

In January 1898, Michael Gaffney, a 40-year-old labourer and resident of Tallaght, fell from a tramcar. Two bones in his right leg were fractured and the flesh pulped. Gaffney had visited two public houses, one at Portobello and one in Terenure, before getting the 5pm tram to Tallaght. Along with seven or eight other passengers, he was riding on the outside of the first of two cars comprising the tram. He was merry and had been singing, but was not quarrelsome. Gaffney had a ticket for Tallaght. He stayed on the tram when others descended after the driver had called out the Tallaght stop.

About a quarter of a mile beyond Tallaght, Gaffney bid the remaining passengers a good evening and descended the steps of the tram. The passengers assumed that Gaffney would be getting off at the next stop. There was a slight 'jolt' as the tram proceeded along the track, as Gaffney had fallen between the two cars. He was later found lying on the track, having lost a lot of blood, and was brought to the Meath Hospital, in shock. When Mr Dennison, the driver of the tram, and Daniel Dunne, the tram guard, had approached him, he was 'insensible from the start'. A Mr Fox of Tallaght made his car available to bring Gaffney to hospital. Gaffney never rallied, and died within an hour of admittance.

In September 1900, 28-year-old John Connors was crossing the line near Tallaght when he was hit by the tram. He received a large scalp wound and a fracture to the skull. He was transported to the Meath Hospital, where he was declared dead by House Surgeon Patterson.

On 18 January 1909, Norah Barragry, the seven-year-old daughter of Sargeant Barragry of Tallaght Barracks, was run over by a tram. Peter Morgan, a guard on the tram, was charged with negligence, but was acquitted. Following the inquest, it was recommended to the company that a man should walk in front of the tram when 'shunting', and he should carry a red light at night-time. Sergeant Barragry was 'recommended to the company for consideration of his loss'.

John Hollander, a 21-year-old unmarried porter, worked in the Cairo Café on Grafton Street in Dublin. In September 1912, he spent a leisurely Sunday afternoon drinking porter on Camden Street with his good friend Corporal Sydney Drake of the Royal Fusiliers. Between 3pm and 4pm, Hollander had five drinks of porter, before heading to Tallaght for a few more. Corporal Drake left his friend, as he had to go back to Wellington Barracks for 8pm. Drake said he left Hollander sober.

Henry Sherrock, driving the tram to Tallaght later that evening, saw a figure on the tracks ahead. The tram was travelling at about eight miles an hour, around a blind bend in the track near Stubbs' Lane, Balrothery. Sherrock couldn't halt the tram quickly enough to avoid contact. The engine and two carriages passed over Hollander's body. He suffered a fracture to the skull, laceration of the brain, a fracture of the spinal column and laceration of the spinal cord, several deep cuts to the right and back of the head and a badly lacerated right foot. Extraordinarily, Hollander reportedly recovered full consciousness the next day, gave a detailed account of his drinking up to the point of Corporal Drake departing his company, and then promptly expired. He had had at least seven drinks.

The driver of the tram was exonerated of any charges and the Coroner recommended that the curve of the track should be better lit. The Dublin and Blessington Steam Tramway Company argued that lighting the district was the responsibility of the local authority. John Hollander had contributed everything he earned to his parents. The family of the deceased was recommended for consideration of the company.

At 9pm on a Tuesday in October 1924, fourteen-year-old Annie Atkinson from Tallaght Main Street was sent on a message by her father. Little Annie got distracted when she saw some playmates jaunting on the back of a stationary tram car in the village. Children were regularly chased away from boarding the tram while it was moving. Sergeant Nyhan noted that he regularly had to 'hunt children home' from playing near the tramline. The tram began to move and had gone about six yards when twelve-year-old Josephine Connor saw her friend Annie Atkinson slip down between the cars. Josephine tried to raise the alarm, but little Annie Atkinson was dragged along the tracks for approximately 92 yards before the tram was brought to a stop. Dr Lydon noted the girl's spine was broken and she was badly mangled. Death would, in his opinion, have been instantaneous.

In March 1926, forty-year-old Thomas Joyce, a fireman on the Dublin and Blessington Steam Tramway, got caught up in the wheels of the machine during shunting operations near Tallaght. His right leg was severely injured and he was taken to the surgery of Dr PJ Lydon in Tallaght village. Lydon provided emergency aid to Joyce, before having him transported by Rathmines ambulance to the Meath Hospital. There surgery was performed by Surgeon H Stokes. He was reported, rather optimistically, to be 'progressing favourably', before dying several days later.

And in September 1931, John Jones, a 40-year-old conductor from Templeogue, had just finished his shift and was going to visit his seriously ill wife in 'Our Lady's home of rest' in Harold's Cross, when he fell from a tramcar after the wagon 'jolted'. He died a short time later from his injuries, leaving behind four young children, the eldest of whom was fifteen. On being told of her husband's passing, his wife insisted on discharging herself from the hospice. She died at home one month later.

From 1929, the Paragon Omnibus Company began operating a bus service between Blessington and the city centre, eliminating the need for passengers to transfer between the DBST and the Dublin tram at Terenure. This struck a fatal blow to the DBST. The service had been operating at a loss for a number of years and, to make savings, the use of steam engines had been discontinued in favour of petrol engines. Last-ditch efforts were made in 1931 to have the DBST taken over either by the Dublin United Tramway Company or the Great Southern Railways. Neither came to pass. The Dublin and Blessington Steam Tramway (Abandonment) Act, 1932, was passed. Forty-five staff would be pensioned off.

On New Year's Eve 1932, a wet Saturday night, the last ever tram from Terenure to Blessington ran through Tallaght, stopping at Templeogue, Balrothery, Tallaght, Jobstown and the Embankment, just as it had for the previous 44 years. The last scheduled trams that evening were the 6:15pm from Terenure to Blessington and the 10:30pm from Terenure to Tallaght. The last tram would arrive back at its terminus at Terenure for the last time at 11.20pm.

A Ramble About Tallaght

A carriage of the Dublin and Blessington Steam Tram line.

The Drury railcar was the last to run on the night. A number of extra wagons, ordinarily used to transport sand and gravel from quarries along the route, were attached to the engine and filled with people. As the engine started on its final journey, there were salvoes of cheers from the back wagons and passengers in the carriages sang along to the music of melodeon players. The tram was driven by James Sweeney and the attendant guard was a Mr Taggart. During the run, a collection, a token of appreciation, was taken up for the two men. People had gathered at each tram stop along the route to cheer on the last tram back to Dublin. Earlier that evening, a crowd had gathered at the terminus in Blessington at 8.15 to cheer goodbye to the last tram to Dublin.

On arrival at the terminus in Terenure at 11.25pm, the last tram from Tallaght, its carriages and wagons, were locked up in the engine shed.

Everything would be sold off as scrap – rolling stock, equipment and almost sixteen miles of permanent way (tramline). The scrap was valued at £10,000. Once the tramline was removed, in the first and second quarter of 1933, the route would be reinstated as a public road.

A number of carriages were, according to oral history sources, purchased by Bobby (Robert) Douglas of Bohernabreena. These were set up along the banks of the river Dodder and during the summer months let as holiday homes to city dwellers. By the 1940s, due to a housing shortage in the district, they had become semi-permanent residences for a number of local families. Collectively, they became known as 'Tin Town'.

One of the last remaining reminders of the Dublin to Blessington tramline is the 'tram marker' that can still be seen at the side of the road, opposite the post office in Blessington village. On one side of the marker are the letters D&B (Dublin to Blessington) and on the other B&P (Blessington to Poulaphouca).

The RAF and the Aerodrome at Cookstown

In 1971, Army explosives experts were called in to the factory of Irish Biscuits (Jacobs) Ltd on the Belgard Road. Night watchman Bill Newman had discovered what was described as a 'ticking parcel', approximately a foot and a half long, behind an old heater in his office. Gardaí and Special Branch officers arrived on the scene and threw a security cordon around the perimeter of the factory, as the Army bomb disposal team secured the immediate environs of the device.

The Irish Biscuits factory was located close to the site of what had once been the Royal Air Force's Aerodrome in Tallaght, before it became Urney Chocolates. That site had also served as 'The Camp', a Free State military camp, between 1922 and 1927, during which time an explosives factory was situated there.

Harry and Eileen Gallagher had located their chocolate factory (Urney's) on one half of the site almost 50 years earlier, and they later reported that they had found unexploded bombs on a weekly basis in their first year in Tallaght. The story was still well known in the community in the 1960s.

After careful examination, the 'ticking parcel' was discovered to be an elaborate hoax – just a pair of alarm clocks taped together with gaffer tape, wrapped up in brown paper. One could never be too careful though! Fourteen years after this false alarm, in November 1985, the Dublin Gas Company was digging trenches to lay new gas pipes in the ground outside Tallaght's new fire station, several kilometres further down the Belgard Road, when workmen did unearth an old, unexploded bomb. This was most definitely not a hoax. It was a pre-Second World War incendiary bomb, at least 50 years old. The fire station and nearby houses were evacuated, and the ordnance was detonated by the Irish Army. Nobody was harmed in the incident. It most likely originated in the 1918–19 period, when the Royal Air Force (RAF) briefly operated in the area.

The RAF in Tallaght

At the height of the Great War and following the increasing number and growing effectiveness of aerial raids on London and the south of England, Britain needed to greatly ramp up its aerial capacity. At the time, there was no airfield in Ireland. Cookstown in Tallaght and Baldonnell, just outside Dublin city, along with several other locations around Dublin, benefited from being geographically out of range of the enemy, and also from having a well-developed transport infrastructure.

An aerial view of Tallaght Aerodrome under construction, 30 July 1918.

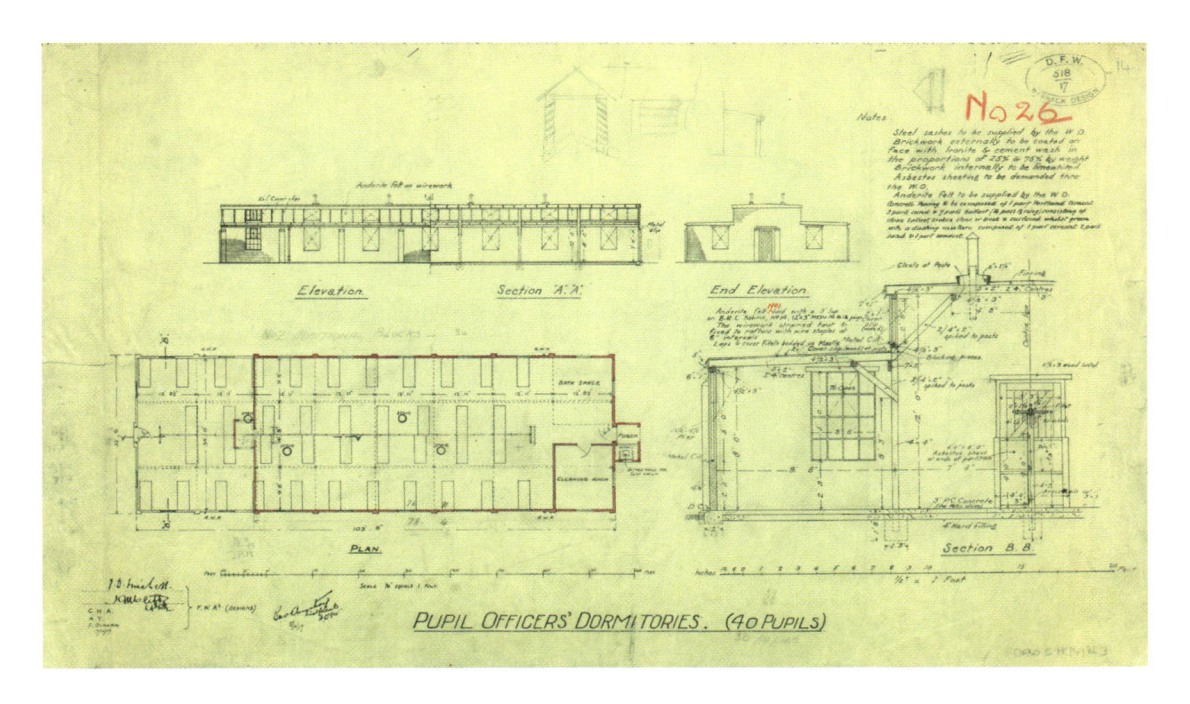

Architect's plans for Tallaght Aerodrome, 1918, showing (above) pupil officers' dormitories and (below) a more general view.

A Ramble About Tallaght

In 1917, a decision was taken, pragmatic and expedient, to commence the construction of a number of new airfields outside of Dublin, among them one at Cookstown in Tallaght and one at Baldonnell, west Dublin. They would support the Royal Flying Corps target of increasing capacity to 200 operational squadrons.

Construction commenced almost immediately, and the new Aerodrome, with an unpaved landing surface, was ready for operational service in August 1918. The Tallaght Aerodrome constituted Training Depot Station No. 25. The Dublin to Blessington tram line from Tallaght to Jobstown skirted south of the Aerodrome site and a narrow-gauge spur line was laid, connecting to the facility. According to military historian Michael Whelan, trams of up to eight carriages transported military personnel, plant and equipment to and from the base.

The Aerodrome was built on land previously owned by Andrew Cullen Tynan, father of the poet Katherine Tynan. The remains of the Tynan family home, Whitehall, are still standing.

A group of RAF officers in a hangar at Tallaght Aerodrome.

The Aerodrome – Katharine Tynan (died 1931)

So now the aerodrome goes up
Upon my father's fields,
And gone is all the golden crop
And all the pleasant yields.

They tare the trees up, branch and root,
They kill the hedges green,
As though some force, malign and brute,
Ravaged the peace serene.

There where he used to sit and gaze
With blue and quiet eyes,
Watching his comely cattle graze,
The walls begin to rise.

What place for robin or for wren,
For thrush and blackbird's call?
Now there shall be but flying men
Nor any bird at all.

'Twas well he did not stay to know,
Defaced and all defiled
The quiet fields of long ago,
Dear to him as a child.

But when the tale was told to me
I felt such piercing pain,
They tore my heart up with the tree
That will not leaf again.

A Ramble About Tallaght

Women's Royal Air Force (WRAF) group pictures at Tallaght Aerodrome.

Responsibility for Britain's aerial defence was split between the Admiralty and the War Office. In July 1914, the Royal Flying Corps' naval wing had been detached to form the Royal Naval Air Service (RNAS). On 1 April 1918, the two services were once again merged, to form the Royal Air Force (RAF). So by September 1918, Tallaght had its own Royal Air Force base.

The development of the facility made a significant, albeit brief, impact on the local economy and social scene. The population of Tallaght village was estimated at 360 people. In 1918, a newspaper headline declared that a labour strike at the Aerodrome saw 1500 people 'down tools' on the site. Its greatest lasting impact, however, was on the landscape of Cookstown. The 231-acre site was transformed in a twelve-month period, with 30 acres now under buildings, leaving a well-planned military base and state-of-the-art campus, for whatever was to come next.

Michael Whelan, who has studied the Aerodrome, noted:

There were many installations built … with well over a dozen airfields and aerodromes built in Ireland during this period with each of the main training bases being designated as a Training Depot Station and given a number. Each of the four Dublin area training installations (Gormanston No. 22, Baldonnel No. 23, Collinstown No. 24 and Tallaght/Cookstown No. 25) were built to exactly the same specifications, to house 72 based aircraft. The layout was to be the same in each: six aeroplane hangars, built in three pairs, sheds for workshops, lectures, gunnery, wireless, powerhouse, guard house, etc. Regimental buildings included Officers' Mess, Officers' Quarters, and facilities for Sergeants and enlisted men and a Women's Hostel. It is unlikely that much of the strength of the bases and infrastructure especially at Tallaght was ever fully realized but there is no doubt to its presence on the local landscape. One can only imagine what Tallaght would be like now if the Aerodrome had survived as a functioning entity … The old security hut at Urney's Chocolate Factory, used for many years after the military departed the site, had once served as the station morgue of Tallaght Airfield.

The facility was to be short-lived. Thirteen weeks after its opening, at 11am on the eleventh day of the eleventh month of 1918, the Armistice was signed, ending 'the war to end all wars'. While this was welcome news indeed for the whole of Europe, there may well have been some in Tallaght that heard the news with a heavy heart. The Aerodrome briefly brought new business to Tallaght, new prospects, plenty of new faces and a hint of glamour. The loss of its potential prospects to Tallaght would be the local price paid for peace in Europe. However long peace would endure in Europe though, it would not last long in Ireland or Tallaght.

The Camp at Tallaght

Immediately after the First World War, the recently constituted RAF faced a new challenge – what to do with what had very quickly become costly surplus capacity. Aerodromes in both Tallaght and Baldonnell were unnecessary. With the outbreak of the War of Independence in Ireland, only twelve weeks after the Armistice in Europe, such considerations were overtaken by events. However, by April 1920, unnecessary bases were not just an expense, but a military liability and a potential target for hostile local forces.

Consideration was given to allotting Tallaght Camp to the Department of Labour, to be deployed as a training and rehabilitation camp for disabled men – for the most part, war veterans and ex-service men. However, the Anglo-Irish Treaty of 1921 brought an end to the War of Independence, and military bases were handed over to the Free State Government in 1922. What now became known as 'The Camp' at Tallaght would very much become a target for hostile forces during Ireland's Civil War. (See Chapter 10)

The Leinster 200 and Leinster 100 Trophy motor races

At 3pm on Saturday, 20 July 1935, 21 cars lined up in Tallaght village for the first Leinster Trophy Motor Car Race in the district. The first Leinster Trophy Motor Car Race had been held in Skerries, Co. Dublin, the previous year. That race was won by Fay Taylour or 'Flying Fay', the only female competitor in the race, who drove a German-made, front wheel-drive Adler Trumpf coupé owned by Fianna Fáil TD Robert Briscoe. The thirteen-mile Skerries circuit had for some years been successfully used for the Leinster 200 International Motor

Cycle Race, but due to the narrowness of the roads, it proved unsuitable for motor cars. The Leinster Motor Cycle and Car Club, the organisers of the event, moved the race to Tallaght the following year. Official parking for the event was at the back of the grandstand, accessed from the Greenhills Road.

Brilliant sunshine glistened off the cars on the starting line, but scattered showers earlier in the day had made the road wet. The circuit started in Tallaght village and ran east down an incline towards Balrothery and further on to Templeogue, before swinging right towards Firhouse. From there it travelled west up to Oldbawn Bridge, right up the Oldbawn Road through Goose Park, returning to Tallaght village. The circuit was just short of six miles long (5.92 miles), and the race ran for 26 laps, bringing the total distance to 154 miles. In addition to the Leinster Trophy, the overall winner received a cash prize of £100, a sizable sum in the 1930s. A total of nine other trophies, cash prizes and minor awards were also presented.

In 1936 and 1937, both the Leinster 100 car race and the Leinster 200 motor cycle race were held on the Tallaght circuit.

The events attracted a sizable crowd of onlookers out to Tallaght, Templeogue and Firhouse. Up to 25,000 spectators lined the route. With both the starting flag and finish line located in Tallaght village, space for spectators there was in great demand and every wall and lamppost was utilised as a viewing point. Government ministers, camera crews from Pathé news, radio commentators and newspaper men jockeyed for premium vantage points.

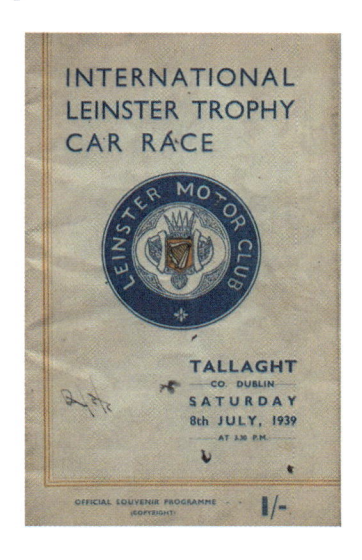

Programmes for the Leinster Trophy Car Race.

A Ramble About Tallaght

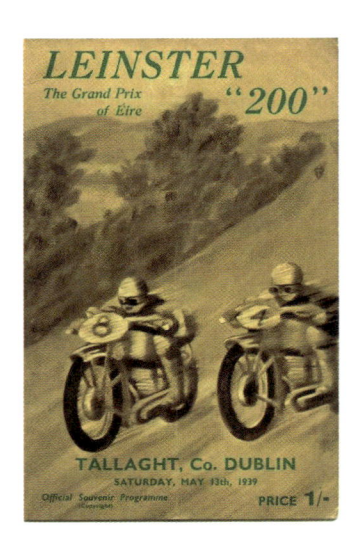

Leinster 200 motor cycle race programmes from the 1930s.

In 1936, local man Redmond Gallagher, son and heir of Urney Chocolates, competed against Adrian Conan Doyle, the youngest son of Sir Arthur, the famous author and creator of Sherlock Holmes. Conan Doyle drove a Bugatti in 1936 and again in 1937, competing against cars such as MG, Alfa Romeo, Ford and 'Leprechaun', a bespoke car made in Tallaght by Redmond Gallagher and his chief engineer in Urney.

By 1939, with the clouds of war gathering over Europe, a much-depleted field competed for the Leinster Trophy. The competition would be put in abeyance for the duration of the War, or the Emergency. It returned to Tallaght in 1948 for one last time. The growth and development of Tallaght, Templeogue and Firhouse in the years between 1938 and 1948, and the increase in suburban motor traffic after the War, meant the Tallaght circuit was no longer suitable for road racing. There was no race in 1949 and the Leinster 200 moved to Wicklow in 1950. It would never return to Tallaght.

It may have been held for only six years in Tallaght, but for many citizens of Dublin, the Leinster Trophy race was the only occasion they had to visit the village of Tallaght. The area would, in the popular imagination, be strongly associated with the event for many years after. In the following decades, the people of Tallaght would recall the anticipation, the excitement and the thrills of the Leinster 200 coming to their small, sleepy village.

The Nicholson Memorial Scramble

In 1932, Robert Nicholson, a native of Tallaght and a member of Tallaght Motor Cycle Racing Club, acting as a race marshal at the 1932 Leinster 200 Motor Cycle Race in Skerries, died as a result of fatal injuries received when he was struck by a motorcycle. Nicholson had gone to render first aid to another official who had already been struck by a motorcycle, when he received a violent blow to the back from another machine coming around a corner.

Robert's brother Alfred Nicholson, Hon Secretary of Tallaght Motor Cycle Club, was acting as a time keeper for the race. Unaware that his brother had been struck, he continued to clock each lap while Robert was being transported to the Mater Hospital. Robert Nicholson died *en route* to the hospital, and Alfred only learned of his death after the race. It was the first fatality in ten years of events organised by the Club. Robert was laid to rest in St Maelruain's burial ground in Tallaght village.

In his memory, the Dublin and District Motor Cycle Club instituted the annual Nicholson Memorial Scramble motorcycle race. The last Nicholson Memorial Scramble, a fourteen-lap race, took place at the Slade, near Crooksling, in October 1972. (The 1958 Nicholson Memorial Scramble, due to take place on 1 November that year, was postponed until the following year due to the death of Pope Pius XII.)

In 1933, the moribund Dublin and District Motor Cycle Club, the oldest such club in the Free State at the time, was on the verge of disbanding. Instead, it amalgamated with the more recently formed and energetic Tallaght and District Motor Cycle Club, giving the former body an injection of energy and a new lease of life. The combined entity decided to retain the name of Dublin and District Motor Cycle Club. This explains in part how the Leinster 200 Motor Cycle Race came to move from Skerries to Tallaght in 1935. It also explains why the 'Dublin' club continued to mark the untimely passing of Tallaght native Robert Nicholson for 40 years.

The first motor car in Tallaght perhaps!

On the second Saturday of January 1907, seventy-four-year-old Pat Rogers was lying in his sickbed in his house up in Ballymorefin, near the Brakes of Ballinascorney, when there was a knock on the door of his farmhouse. He had been unwell for some time, having suffered a heart attack six weeks earlier. He had remained in bed for much of the Christmas. Several months earlier, Pat Rogers had bought a raffle ticket for the Knocknagow Bazaar Prize Draw.

On opening the door, his wife Bridget was informed that Pat Rogers's ticket had been drawn for the first prize – a £300 motor car from Mr Burke's Motor Company in Clonmel, Co. Tipperary. Pat Rogers heard the news with a degree of disbelief. His health deteriorated throughout the day, and he died that night. He was buried in the local burial ground in St Anne's three days later, with need for neither car nor cart. It is unclear whether the car was ever delivered to Ballymorefin!

CHAPTER 10

Tallaght in Times of Strife

For much of its history, Tallaght has had a reputation as being a kingdom of ruffians, rebels and banditti. From the tribal raids of the O'Tooles and the O'Byrnes, rampaging down from the hills to wreak havoc on the settlers in the seventeenth century, right up to the Civil War, authorities have often been wary of the town. The community of Tallaght could never fully be depended upon to adhere to the laws of the land. From the 1798 Rebellion, the Tithe War of the 1830s, the Rising in 1867 and up to the War of Independence, the people of Tallaght, or certainly some of them, demonstrated an inclination to throw their lot in with the rebels' cause.

For most of its history, Tallaght was not just on the periphery of the city. It was on the periphery of civilisation, or at least of civilised society as it was understood by those in administrative authority. Up to the 1980s, some argued, it still was. A small number of very high-profile incidents have kept Tallaght's reputation as a volatile district alive.

Many of the young men who participated in the 1867 Rising were sons of those who had played an active part in the Tithe War in the 1830s. The burning of properties in Whitestown, Ballymana and Killinarden during the Tithe War was well remembered. It was remembered too that the collection of tithes was suspended and eventually abolished by the Disestablishment Act. Their actions had had some effect.

The tradition has been kept alive and transmitted to the present generation. Of anywhere in Ireland, the 'Anti-Water Charges Campaign' reached its most militant in Jobstown in Tallaght on 15 November 2014, when local protesters falsely imprisoned the Tánaiste, Joan Burton, and an advisor.

Jobstown lies in the midday shadow of Tallaght Hill. A generation of Tallaght's new citizens in the 1970s, 1980s and 1990s grew up looking at a plaque on Tallaght's Main Street commemorating 'The Bold Fenian Men of 1867'. For over twenty years, it was the only plaque of its kind in Tallaght village.

There appeared to be little else to celebrate. In order to rectify that, in 1988, a plaque was installed celebrating the Clondalkin writer of middling talent, Katherine Tynan, and claiming her as Tallaght's own. It was, in its own subtle way, a rebellious installation, appropriating for Tallaght something that wasn't rightfully ours (Tynan was born in Dublin city, lived in the parish of Clondalkin and died in England). The plaque was unveiled by President Mary Robinson.

Robinson had built her own professional reputation defending rebels and those on the periphery of society. She had represented the Wood Quay Nine, including Leo Swan, the Principal of Loreto Boys' National School, who illegally occupied the Wood Quay site, then being developed, in 1979. She also represented Traveller families who set up camp, obstructing the Tallaght Bypass, in 1984. It has always been possible to stand with the rebel, rise to power and retain an air of the respectable, the civilised. Perhaps the O'Byrnes and the O'Tooles were simply the precursors to todays 'SJWs' – social justice warriors.

> Hurrah then hurrah, For remember oh remember
> that the fate of Ireland now depends on her own exertions.
> Hereditary bondsmen, I believe you know the rest.
> Very faithfully, yours
> Daniel O'Connell

On Thursday, 22 March 1832, a party of up to thirty 'armed ruffians' made a nocturnal visit to the pound in Tallaght with the intention of reclaiming cattle that had been distrained – held in lieu of tithes due in the district. The pound was located only several hundred metres from the police barracks and the police were roused by the uncharacteristic sound of mooing in the moonlight.

Two officers, half asleep, sallied out of the barracks to ascertain the cause of the disturbance, wearing nothing but pistols in their hands. The men were more fully awoken by a short gun or carbine being placed at the head of one of the officers. He was informed that if he took one more step, his brains would be blown out. Without a thought, the officer reflexively shot his own loaded pistol into the body of his assailant. One of the thirty fired a weapon at the officers from a distance, grazing the wrist of one of them. None too gingerly, they retreated into the barracks to get heavier arms and their rudely awoken colleagues.

Shortly after, the officers returned to the pound to find it littered with arms and bludgeons, but not a ruffian in sight. The cattle had done what cattle do, their degree of disinterest characteristic of their breed. The only thing the ruffians had gained custody of was the profusely bleeding body of their fallen comrade.

The following month, the house of Mr Trant in the Brakes of Ballinscorney was burnt down. The fire was discovered in the early hours of Sunday morning when a tenant, Simon Doyle, returned to find his own thatched dwelling, attached to the house, in flames.

At a meeting of local rate payers in the district, it was noted, 'Their Lordships must be aware of the disturbed state of that part of the country for many years back.' The Tithe War had only just begun.

The Emancipation Act of 1829 had been passed by Parliament three years earlier and Daniel O'Connell's Repeal Association, agitating to repeal the 1801 Act of Union, was gaining some momentum. The people of Tallaght and district would not be found wanting when it came to involvement in the Tithe War. The tithe burden lay directly on the shoulders of farmers, whether tenants or owner-occupiers. More often than not, tithes were paid in kind, in the form of produce or livestock.

On 1 July 1832, over 5000 people gathered in Bohernabreena to listen to impassioned speeches arguing that tithes should no longer be payable, or indeed paid. The gathering was principally made up of small farmers, cottiers and, importantly, labourers. Those who held land were requested to withhold tithes due. Labourers were asked to support the effort by withholding labour from those who paid or collected tithes. And all were asked to refrain from having any business dealings with the payers or collectors of tithes. It was essentially a call for a 'boycott', almost 50 years before that word was coined.

John McGrane, a large farmer from Oldcourt, acted as Secretary to the meeting and William Poole, a landowner from Ballyroan, chaired the gathering. Speakers included Marcus Costello and Thomas Reynolds, neither of whom held land in the district or were required to actually pay tithes. They were there in support of the campaign nationally.

Chief Baron Joy, who presided at a Special Commission in response to the meeting, reported that the men

> unlawfully incited the Kings liege subjects, to a spirit of hostility and resistance to the laws on the 1st July 1832, at Bohernabreena where different liege subjects of the King were assembled together and they did, there and then unlawfully incite the liege subjects of the King, to confederate together, for the purpose of opposing the receipt and the collection of tithes and all sums payable as composition for the same and rendering ineffectual the means for collecting the same; And for then and there unlawfully inciting said liege subjects to carry into effect and in a combination for that purpose, and not to deal with such persons as would either pay or collect tithes.

He continued with concern:

> The assemblage of 5000 persons of the lower order, a people naturally violent in their passions, infuriate in their temper, easily roused to vengeance and barbarous in the execution of that vengeance, addressed in language calculated to rouse every bad passion of the human heart, and to incite to the commission of acts of vengeance against the respectable class of society, to the destruction of their rights and life.

Addressing Reynolds and Costello specifically, Chief Baron Joy suggested:

> It was your gratuitous love of mischief that solely actuated you ... With the Parish of Tallaght you had no concern. You were not called on to pay Tithes. Nothing but mischief was to be achieved – and where mischief was to be achieved, that was your proper element.

A total of 25 charges were presented at the Commission against the organisers of the rally. They were found guilty of only one. In August 1832, William Poole, Marcus Costello, John McGrane and Thomas Reynolds were found guilty of being 'agitators who engaged in their active resistance to tithes'.

Poole, Costello and Reynolds were each given a six-month sentence. John McGrane of Oldcourt was sentenced to three months in Kilmainham Gaol.

When McGrane was released from prison in January 1833, a welcome-home reception was organised in Bohernabreena, chaired by Ben Bradley of Marlfield, who had been active in the district in the 1798 rebellion.

Marcus Costello would go on, less than ten years later, to become Attorney General of Gibraltar, for HM Government, a post he would hold from 1841 to 1856. He wouldn't be the last person to build a lucrative career on the back of local excitement and the passions of the hoi polloi, and progress to enjoy the bountiful privileges of the old order.

The meeting of 'the Bohernabreena Boys' held in July 1832 had been, in all ways, satisfactory. By the summer of 1834, the Tithe campaign was at its height, nationally and locally. The campaign burned brightly in the townland of Tallaght.

In March 1834, a Mr Hastings and his family were asleep in their home in Killinarden, close to Tallaght Hill. Hastings had recently taken an action against a tenant, serving him notice to quit his cabin as he was in rent arrears. The tenant had resided in the cabin for five years. As Hastings and his family slept, persons unknown stuffed the gable ends of his home with combustible material. The Hastings family were awoken by the sound of a shot being fired. A ball perforated a window shutter and lodged in the ceiling of their dwelling house.

On arising, they found the gable ends of their home smouldering. An adjoining thatched outhouse was in flames, and another outhouse, at a distance that no accidental fire could have spread to, was also burning brightly in the dark, crisp night. Fleeing their home, they discovered their haggard of hay and oats blazing, and stooks of hay left in the field also ablaze.

George Mansergh, a police officer from Tallaght barracks, arrived with a party of police to hear shots being fired in the distance.

After that night, Hastings's tenant was never seen again. The Lord Lieutenant offered a reward of £50 for the apprehension and conviction of any person concerned in the outrage.

Eight weeks later, on Monday, 12 May 1834, a cabin in Whitestown was set ablaze. The cabin was the property of James Byrne and was home to a poor labourer, John Martin, and his family. Stones were thrown at police officers working to extinguish the flames.

In August 1835, four tons of hay, the property of a Mr Bentley, were maliciously burnt in Ballymana.

The rise in agrarian discontent and militancy was proving a challenge for the body politic. The growing mayhem created public outrage and placed an increasing strain on police relations. The government suspended the collection of tithes, one official lamenting that it now 'cost a shilling to collect tuppence'.

Civil disobedience and direct action were not confined only to the anti-tithe campaign. In 1832, a toll gate was placed on the Blessington Road near the recently reconstructed Church of St Maelruain in the village. Persons unknown tore up the five-mile stone marker and flung it into a ditch. They littered the newly tolled road with obstructions.

The War of Independence in Tallaght

The great Gaels of Ireland are the men that God made mad,

For all their wars are merry, and all their songs are sad.

GK Chesterton, 'The Ballad of the White Horse'

Unlike the Civil War, which would give rise to much armed conflict in the district, the war of Independence in Tallaght was principally characterised by republican raids on farms and houses, in their quest for arms. These raids were very often carried out by local republicans on local farmers. They knew the neighbourhood well. They knew each other well.

On Sunday, 10 February 1919, only one month into the war, Robert Jones was about to retire for the night in his farmhouse in Ballinascorney Lower, when he heard a loud thumping noise on his back gate. It was almost 10.30. He left the house to investigate. 'Who is there?' he shouted. A voice called out in the darkness, from beyond the gate, 'I have an urgent telegram for you.' It could not be good news.

Jones opened the gate to find six masked and armed men. Three of the men seized Jones and held him at bay in the yard. They carried revolvers and let Jones know that they would be happy to use them. The other men entered the house and spent 30 minutes ransacking it, searching for arms and ammunition. All they found was a fowling piece and six cartridges.

The next day, the six young men were seized in raids around Tallaght. When Patrick Winders, Joseph Bulger, James Mansfield, James Holden, Michael Grimes and Patrick O'Shea were being brought by car from Tallaght village to Dublin, they were cheered by a crowd of local Tallaght people. The six men were charged on remand with unlawful assembly. They all pleaded guilty.

Sergeant O'Driscoll of Tallaght, who had charge of the case, said the six men were of excellent character and he asked the magistrate to deal leniently with them. The Magistrate granted bail of £20 each and a surety of £10, and bound them to keep the peace for twelve months.

Later that summer, a similar raid was carried out on Larry Dunne's farmhouse in Greenhills. At midnight on Wednesday, 6 August 1919, ten armed and masked men forced their way into Dunne's home. They searched the farmhouse and took a firearm away.

Watkins' Country

By November 1920, the country's prisons were bursting at the seams and the authorities, both civil and military, were struggling to contain the growing number of detainees. A decision was formally taken to bring the old disused aerodromes in Tallaght and Collinstown into commission as temporary prison camps. Untried political prisoners were detained in the wooden huts and structures formerly occupied by the Royal Air Force. In reality, the military had already started using the camp for detaining prisoners before it was officially sanctioned, for lack of anywhere else to bring them.

Facilities in the old Aerodrome at Tallaght were poor. Much of the stock, plant and buildings of the Aerodrome had been auctioned off the previous year. The nearby Baldonnell was also used, making it a target for republicans. £600 worth of damage was inflicted on the pumping station serving Baldonnell and Tallaght aerodromes by 'ill disposed persons' – republicans.

The incident would cause a fracture in relations between the military authorities and South Dublin Rural District Council (RDC). The military sought to hold South Dublin RDC responsible for repairs to the pumping station. A letter received by the RDC noted: 'The competent

Military Authorities also wished you to understand that they will hold the Council responsible for any further interference with the water supply to the forces of the Crown within the area administered by South Dublin Rural District Council.' The Council repudiated any responsibility for the cost of repairs to the station, or costs associated with any further interference to the supply.

The 'ill disposed persons' responsible for disabling the pumping station were almost certainly local men the Watkins brothers and their comrades.

The Watkins brothers of Tallaght Main Street were respected, red-hot republicans. John Watkins, better known to his friends as Jack, was considered a dangerous man. They were wanted in Tallaght by the Royal Irish Constabulary for subversive activity.

Jack Watkins had worked in ICI, a chemical plant in Swansea, Wales, where he learned about the making of explosives. Tom had worked in a quarry in Wales, where he learned how to use them. Tom had joined the Irish Volunteers in 1915.

Jack Watkins became an officer in the IRA, 7th Battalion, and took part in many operations during the War of Independence. Tom Watkins, a 'crack shot', was appointed Captain of the Saggart Company from 1919. He regularly drilled republican forces in Mount Seskin and would spend some time with Michael Collins in Athlone.

Jack was arrested in Tallaght by the RIC and imprisoned in Beggars Bush Barracks. He was later transferred, chained to Father Burbage, a Catholic priest, on a destroyer from Dublin to Belfast. He was held at Ballykinlar Camp. His politics remained unchanged.

Another person of interest was Richard Mullally. Mullally was charged before field-general court martial for possession, on 16 January 1921, of four rounds of .45 ammunition for a revolver. In a raid on his home, ammunition was found in a pot and another round on the floor, among old papers. It was not securely held, in a house with children present.

In court, Mullally claimed the ammunition wasn't his and had been 'planted' in his home by one of the officers. He also claimed he had been ill-treated during the raid and was struck by an officer and called a 'bloody swine'. Mullally was found not guilty of the charge, but as soon as he left the precinct of the court, he was again taken into custody. Mullally was a member of A Company, 7th Dublin Battalion, of the IRA. He would go on, in the late 1930s, to be Honorary Secretary of the association of Old IRA for the 7th Battalion.

MS 20,643/3/3

Óglaic na h-Éireann,
Longport: 206 Sráid an Stáin,
Át Cliat.

Hon. Secs. { Eoin MacNeill, B.A.
Laurence J. Kettle, M.I.E.E.

THE IRISH VOLUNTEERS,

Telephone..............
Headquarters: 206 GT. BRUNSWICK ST.,
DUBLIN.

To Company Commanders
DUBLIN COMPANIES.
TRAINING CAMP FOR DUBLIN VOLUNTEERS.

A site has been selected on the banks of the River Dodder at Old Bawn, Tallaght. Full facilities are afforded for field work, scouting over mountains, close order drill, rifle ranges, swimming etc. The camp which is easy of access by steam tram, or cycle will be conducted on military lines by an experienced camp staff for instruction of Dublin Volunteers. Certificates will be awarded to those who pass the necessary tests.

The charge made for each volunteer will be at the extremely modest rate of 11/- per man, per week. For this ridiculously low sum men will get excellent active service training, good camp accomodation and good food.

The camp will open on Saturday 1st. August. Volunteers joining should make _immediate_ application to Headquarters, Irish Volunteers, 206, Great Brunswick St. Dublin, stating how many weeks they will stay in camp, the dates on which they will join. All applications to be marked on the left corner of the envelope "Training Camp". Those who make first application will be accomodated first, as the number to be taken is limited. A reply giving full information will be sent to all such applications.

In particular every man who has taken up the position of officer is expected to join the camp for training.

Notice of Irish Volunteers training camp in Oldbawn.

Thick as thieves

On 28 January 1921, a house in Kiltalown belonging to one John Kenny was raided for arms. Three young Tallaght men – Francis O'Reilly from Ballymount, James Connolly from Tymon North and Arthur Gilsenan from Kilnamanagh – were later charged with robbery and having attempted to murder Mr Kenny and his stepdaughter, Miss Mary Quinn. On the evening in question, the three young men entered the property and demanded arms. They searched the house and, failing to find any, they left.

A short time later, the three men returned to the house, and ordered Mr Kenny, his wife and Mary Quinn into the parlour. One of the men demanded to know if any harm had been done during their previous visit. Kenny's wife inspected their bedroom and found two broken boxes and two wristwatches missing. A sum of £8.15s had also been taken.

Mr Kenny went to move towards the bedroom to see, and O'Reilly drew a revolver. Mary Quinn threw her arms around O'Reilly, catching hold of the revolver. A brief scuffle ensued. Kenny went to restrain O'Reilly, who was attempting to reclaim the revolver from Mary Quinn. The trigger was pulled. A bullet struck Mary Quinn's wrist, passing through the palm of her hand. John Kenny managed to restrain Francis O'Reilly until the police were summoned. Connolly and Gilsenan fled the scene.

Guards arrived from Rathcoole and arrested O'Reilly, who protested, 'I did not fire the revolver. It went off by accident.' According to later testimony from Connolly, the raid had been planned several nights earlier. Mary Quinn recovered from her injuries, but required a skin graft to her hand.

It would appear that Connolly and Gilsenan had suspected O'Reilly of having stolen the watches and cash during the earlier raid. This had not been the intended purpose of the raid. Gilsenan and Connolly each received a four-month suspended sentence, while O'Reilly was sentenced to three years in a borstal.

Not long after his release in 1923, Francis O'Reilly of Ballymount and his older brother John were charged with an armed raid and attempted murder in Celbridge. When their names were called out in court, John O'Reilly replied, 'Anseo.'

Four months after the incident in Kiltalown, the post office in Tallaght was raided. On 14 May 1921, a lone armed man coolly walked into the premises, pointed a revolver at the assistant postmistress and demanded the contents of the till. He casually left and departed the village in a motorcar. He got away with £10. It is not known if the raid was connected with republican forces.

The last shots fired in Tallaght

On 10 June 1921, a young officer in the Camp at Tallaght told his colleague, 21-year-old Gunner Joseph Hoare, that he could have all of his belongings – his mess set, his kit and his few personal effects. Loading a round into his rifle, still standing in a rack, he told Hoare his parents had disowned him and he was going to do himself in. It was clearly a cry for help. 'Don't be a fool,' Hoare advised his colleague. The officer went to unrack the loaded rifle. Hoare attempted to seize the rifle from his troubled young friend. The strap of the rifle became entangled with the trigger and, in the scuffle, the rifle was accidentally discharged. A single bullet passed through the brain of Gunner Joseph Hoare. He died instantly.

It was one of the last shots fired in Tallaght, in Ireland's War of Independence.

Many men who had served during the War of Independence took the Anti-Treaty side during the Civil War. According to Military Service Pensions Collection files (1936) held in the Military Archives, the following units and personnel were among those active in the district through 1921 and 1922:

7th Battalion, Dublin Brigade, Active Service Unit

OC: Gerard (Gerry) Boland; Vice OC: Patrick Kavanagh (Russborough, Blessington); Ad jt: James Fox- Banba , (Clondalkin); Quarter Master: Thomas Byrne (Rathdrum).

Gerald Boland would later go on to become Minister of Posts and Telegraphs in the Free State Government. He was a personal friend of Jack and Tom Watkins.

'A Company' (Tallaght and Firhouse area)

Captain: William Coombs; 1st Lieutenant: Thomas Rice; 2nd Lieutenant: Michael Mullally (died), later replaced with Patrick Winders.

'B Company (Clondalkin area)

Captain: James McNulty (Saggart).

'C' Company (Ballinascorney area)

Captain: Christopher Nolen (from Crumlin); 1st Lieutenant: Thomas Downes (Ballinascorney); 2nd Lieutenant: Thomas Devine (Ballinascorney Upper).

'H' Company (Rathcoole and Saggart)

Captain: Thomas Watkins.

Active Service Unit

John (Jack) Watkins (Tallaght); Paddy Carroll (Naas).

Civil War in Tallaght

The brief period between the War of Independence and the Civil War was no less eventful or more peaceful in Tallaght. The country was awash with arms, emotions were running high, and those opposed to the Anglo-Irish Treaty had little regard for the prevailing governing authority.

Those serving the national army (still called the IRA) in Tallaght had time to kill as they awaited mobilisation. The devil finds work for idle hands.

On 1 May 1922, officers of the national army who had recently been deployed to the Tallaght Camp were 'messing about', when one accidentally shot one of his fellows dead and injured two more. An inquest into the death of Private Gerald Kinsella, of the IRA Tallaght Camp, heard that Private T McGuinness was tricking with three or four of the guards when his rifle accidently fell. In his attempt to catch the falling firearm, he fired the gun, discharging a bullet through the hand and into the thigh of twenty-year-old Private Kinsella. Lieutenant Hegarty managed to stop the flow of blood pumping from Kinsella's thigh.

The mortally wounded young officer was conveyed to the Meath Hospital, where he later died. Two other officers, Browne and Quinlan, were also wounded in the incident. Private McGuinness was exonerated of all charges and Kinsella's demise was recorded as an 'accidental death'. The men had been on the best of terms. It was the friendliest of fire.

While the IRA were tricking about in Tallaght Camp in the lull between the wars, the neighbouring Airfield Cottage, home to Mary Tynan O'Mahony at the time, was raided and ransacked. The family were not at home at the time. Groups of armed men were traipsing around the townland, looking to have their immediate needs met, as they awaited orders.

On 3 June 1922, William Coombs, Thomas Lee, John Clifford, Edward Boyd and Jeremiah Connolly, armed with revolvers, entered James McDonnell's public house, the Cuckoo's Nest in Greenhills. Between 2am and 3am, they terrorised the assistant, Ms Delany, and demanded drink. The men were all later remanded on bail of £8 each. William Coombs was Captain of A Company (Tallaght and Firhouse area), 7th Battalion, Dublin Brigade.

McDonnell, the gentleman in whose establishment they toasted the Republic, was a retired servant of the Dublin Metropolitan Police (DMP).

On 11 April 1922, the 2nd Eastern Division of the Irish Republican Army took over Tallaght Aerodrome, Wellington Barracks and Howth Coastguard Station from Crown Forces. There was little ceremony. Ten weeks later, on 28 June, the Civil War in Ireland broke out with the shelling of anti-treaty forces occupying the Four Courts in Dublin. The presence of National Army troops at the old Aerodrome – the Camp in Tallaght – made it a key and immediate target for anti-treaty forces. Within hours of the Civil War commencing, the first shots were heard in Tallaght village. That evening, National Army troops were seen digging trenches along the tram tracks from Templeogue to Tallaght.

The familiar *kerrx-kerrx* that usually drifted over the village in the summer – the corncrake's cry from Newhall and Cookstown – was interrupted by the faint rap of machine gun fire. As the hours passed and the sun descended, the gunfire grew louder. Between 8pm and 9pm on that warm summer night, shots were fired at the main guard on the Tallaght Camp. Civil War had come to town. The Dominican Fathers in the Father Tom Burke Memorial Chapel in the College honoured their timeless ritual of an 8.30pm procession after compline or evening prayer. To Caesar what is Caesar's and to God what is God's.

Later that night, between 11pm and 4am, shots were fired into the Camp from several directions. The garrison replied in kind, with a Lewis gun. A sergeant of the Free State forces received a bullet wound to the arm. It would be the first of many sustained Irregular attacks on the Camp at Tallaght throughout the following eleven months.

A Ramble About Tallaght

On one of the first nights of the war, in the Camp at Tallaght, a Free State brigadier and his staff prepared their plans for the following day, seated at a table in the yellow glare of an oil lamp. Save for half a dozen beds, there was little furniture in the room. Crown forces had auctioned off anything of value in the preceding years. But revolvers and rifles were everywhere close at hand.

Eager young staff officers traced probable routes on survey maps. Places where mines were said to have been laid, and the houses of suspected Irregulars, were marked and noted by subordinate officers. These men knew the politics, the habits and the habitats of their opponents. And their opponents knew theirs. Many had, until recently, fought together as brothers in arms against the Crown forces.

At 11.15pm, the troops turned in for the night, some in beds and some in sleeping bags on the floor. They would need to be well rested in preparation for their engagements the following day. The Brigadier lay on his bed, smoking a cigarette. He didn't sleep. After midnight, more troops arrived from the city and were brought into the quarters. The Brigadier promptly gave up his own bed to one of the new arrivals.

After 1am, five or six shots were heard in quick succession, ringing out in the still night air. A machine gun outside the men's sleeping quarters returned fire. The men lay in their quarters listening to the sporadic exchanges. An armoured vehicle was heard revving up, preparing to leave the compound and patrol the surrounding country roads of Jobstown, Fortunestown and Greenhills. This was followed by a period of relative silence.

After about fifteen minutes, the men heard what sounded like a rifle firing, off in the distance. The men, in silence, studied the tone, the rhythm and the volume. It sounded like it was coming from above the Aerodrome. It was suggested that the sound was too regular to be rifle fire. The men listened intently until it was discovered that it was a staff officer in the corner, who had taken to snoring in short snaps. The sleeping quarters erupted in a nervous, giddy laughter.

The next morning, heavy clouds hung over the hills around Tallaght, providing cover to whatever Irregular troops were camping out there. A long and noisy convoy of Free State lorries and Crossley tenders left Tallaght Camp. In Saggart, a woman ran out into the street to warn the troops that Irregulars had placed a landmine on the road near the Embankment. At Rathcoole, it was found that Irregulars had abandoned the barracks there. A large force of national troops kept a presence in Rathcoole and Saggart. A body of Irregulars were believed to be stationed between Brittas and Blessington.

Tram services between Dublin and Blessington were suspended for a period, for the first time in their history. It would have been all too convenient for Irregular forces to move about quickly on the line.

This was Watkins country. During the War of Independence, Jack and Tom Watkins had distinguished themselves as brave, reliable and uncompromising republicans.

At the time of the attack on the Four Courts, Tom Watkins was in charge of the IRA garrison in Kilbride Camp. Both brothers, taking the anti-treaty side, were now considered enemies of the State. These two men, natives of Tallaght, knew the hills of Saggart, of Rathcoole and Kilbride. They knew the terrain, the people and their politics. They had the experience, the character and the respect of anti-treaty officers, and probably some pro-treaty officers too. If mayhem was to be prevented, these men could not be left at large.

Tom Watkins was captured in August 1922, only eight weeks into the Civil War. He was safely interned out of harm's way in the Curragh until December 1923. He was in prison with George Gilmore, who had a reputation as an escapologist.

A Volunteer Reserve Recruiting Office was established in the Camp at Tallaght. Local men of military service age were asked to serve their country and were offered a per diem rate of two shillings and six pence per day, with an additional allowance for those married with dependents.

In the opening weeks of the Civil War, a number of armed raids were carried out by anti-treaty forces on private property in Tallaght. Nine sheep and four bullocks were confiscated from Samuel Boothman in Kiltipper. The Boothmans, a prominent Church of Ireland family in the district, had a particularly hard time during the Civil War. They were targeted repeatedly by anti-treaty forces, being subjected to five armed raids in the first four months of the War.

Military checkpoints were set up at strategic locations. On Sunday night, 2 July, a Government patrol stopped a vehicle in Tallaght containing six men. Only five of them had passes. The sixth man was found to be an Irregular who had evacuated Bray Barracks.

In those first weeks, Kennedy's public house (the Old Mill) was raided for foodstuffs by Irregular forces, as was Conaty's Embankment House.

Everyone in the country was on heightened alert and those with guns kept them close at hand. On Saturday, 22 July, newspapers reported that Lord Massy in Killakee had shot a raider the previous Wednesday (19 July). Killakee was an isolated outpost and the land around Massy's estate had a storied history during times of strife. Killakee had been a rendezvous point for the Fenians in 1867. More recently, forest land around the estate had been used for drilling by republican forces.

Massy and his wife were about to retire that evening when a knock was heard at the door. Anthony Walsh, a man from Piperstown, demanded money from Massy. The impecunious Lord offered him a meagre £5. There was a scuffle and Massy accidentally discharged a revolver at Walsh, fatally wounding him. The Rathmines ambulance removed Walsh's remains to the morgue. Curiously, the death certificate for Anthony Walsh states he died on 10 July, seven days earlier. Information and newspaper reports were censored by the Free State government.

Innocent civilians could, and often did, find themselves caught up in local 'operations'. In the early hours of the morning on 22 August 1922, four employees of Purvey Dairy of Kimmage were milking cows in a field in Jobstown when they came under heavy machine gun fire from the direction of Tallaght. They found themselves under a hail of bullets. A 24-year-old dairyman, Edward Morrissey, was seriously wounded. A number of cows were also hit. Morrissey was removed to the Meath Hospital. The cows were milked no more.

Attack on Tallaght Camp

On Saturday, 9 September, four young men, all Irregulars, were killed in a fierce onslaught on Tallaght Camp. Two others were seriously wounded in the all-night battle. A flying column of Irregulars arrived in two lorries shortly before 11pm. They brought with them two Thompson, or 'Tommy', guns and positioned one at each end of the camp. At 11pm, a first attack was made on the northern end of the camp. A Tommy gun opened fire from a vacant house about 300 yards from the camp buildings. Prior to the attack, the telephone wires to the camp had been cut.

By midnight, the camp was being attacked from all sides. A second Tommy gun had commenced firing from the southern end. The relentless attack lasted seven hours. One machine gun post on the northern end came in for particular attention. A grenade was thrown at the post and an attempt was made to rush it. It was defended by a handful of men with a Lewis gun. In the early hours of the morning, when the attack was at its most intense, a Lancia armoured car dashed out of the main gate of the camp and managed to silence the attackers. It was the heaviest attack in the Camp's history.

After the battle, bloodstained bandages, lint and other dressings were found in the surrounding fields. Two seriously wounded Irregulars were brought to a Dublin hospital. Rifles and ammunition left in the field by irregulars bore the US Army mark.

Ten days later, on Tuesday, 19 September, another attack was made on the Camp. At one o'clock in the morning, revolver fire was opened on the southern end. National troops replied with a Lewis gun and rifle fire. The battle lasted for only twenty minutes before the Irregulars withdrew, continuing to fire as they retreated, believing they were being pursued. There were no National troop casualties.

Amid repeated armed attacks on the Camp at Tallaght, the ordinary citizens of the village attempted to carry on their business as usual. On 4 October 1922, O'Neill's public house (The Dragon) was held up by a number of armed men. They were met by the formidable 72-year-old Mary O'Neill and her daughter Gertie. Whatever took place, the raiders fled with little more than loose change. (The O'Neills were cousins of prominent anti-treaty Sinn Féin TD Austin Stack. They would be among the chief mourners at his funeral when he died in 1929.) When the case was later brought to trial, the O'Neills, perhaps shrewdly, could not identify any of the raiders.

Embankment House.

Four months into the War, the most shocking incident of the conflict in the district occurred. On Friday, 6 October, three very young men gathered in one of their houses in Drumcondra. They were little more than boys, aged sixteen and seventeen. They had acquired a typewriter and an old printing press. At about 11pm, they left the house with a bucket of paste, some paintbrushes and a neat pile of leaflets, what the authorities would consider anti-treaty propaganda. They intended to post them on lamp standards and notice boards. Shortly after, the boys were seen in Drumcondra, not far from their houses. They were stopped and searched by Free State troops and brought off in a lorry.

At 5am on 7 October, two milkmen were leaving the village of Clondalkin on foot when they made a most gruesome discovery. The bodies of two young, respectably dressed men had been dumped on the grass bank of Monastery Road, some distance outside the village. One body was in a sitting position, the other lying on the grass. The moon was still high in the sky on that cold October morning. The spot was a wild and open piece of country with little but quarries, sand hills and limekilns. A postman arrived on a bicycle and was given the grim news. The three men stood for a moment in silence. The postman cycled to the Camp at Tallaght to inform them of the find. At 8.30am, troops from the Camp arrived at the scene and removed the two bodies to the mortuary in the Camp hospital.

One was about 5'10", and wearing a brown suit and a trench coat. He had a bullet wound in the right lung. The other man was younger and had a bullet wound in his right cheek. There was very little blood about and no sign of a struggle. It was supposed that they had been killed elsewhere and their bodies dumped.

Two hours after the bodies were removed from the roadside, another shocking discovery was made. A third victim was found in a quarry, beside a bed of nettles, about 50 yards from the road. He was still alive, but unconscious and fading fast. By the time Father Clune, the Chaplain from St Joseph's Monastery, arrived to give him the Last Rites, he had expired. He had been wounded over the heart and in the thigh. From smeared bloodstains on the face of the quarry, the man appeared to have spent some time trying to climb out of it. His had been a slow, painful and terrifying death. In his coat pocket was found a small paintbrush. It had not been used.

The three young men were named as Edwin Hughes (seventeen), an Engineering student; Brendan Holohan (seventeen); and Joseph Rogers (sixteen). Sixteen different wounds were found on the body of Joseph Rogers. He was described by his mother as 'a lame boy'. Edwin Hughes was a member of the Neptune Club and the Irish National Blind Home Workers' Association.

An inquest into the death of the boys returned a finding that the three had died of gunshot wounds, inflicted by persons unknown. Several witnesses had testified that they had seen the boys being put into a military tender at about 11.20 on the Friday night, under the direction of Lieutenant Charlie Dalton. Dalton had grown up in the same neighbourhood as the three boys. At nineteen years of age, he was already a seasoned killer and a member of 'the Squad' assembled by Michael Collins. Charlie's brother, Emmet Dalton, had only six weeks earlier cradled the head of a dying Collins, at Béal na mBláth. No one would ever be charged with the summary execution of the three young men, dumped on the road outside Clondalkin.

Out on foot patrol the following night, walking along the steam-tram track, a group of troops from Tallaght Camp spotted a large party of Irregulars walking toward them. From about 100 yards, the troops saw the Irregulars rush for cover in hedgerows at the side of the road. The Irregulars opened fire. The troops returned fire and pursued the men across a ploughed field towards Jobstown. A Thompson gun opened fire on the small patrol, and they were compelled to fall back to the Camp. The firing lasted an hour. One of the Irregulars was heard crying out, 'I am hit.' During the exchanges, Sergeant Rossiter of the Free State troops had a narrow escape, a bullet grazing the shoulder-band of his overcoat.

Men from Tallaght fought on both sides of the War. Twenty-two-year-old Private Michael Forde from Oldbawn fought with the Free State army. Sadly, he would not see the end of the War. In January 1923, he was buried in St Maelruain's graveyard. Captain JP Stafford of Portobello Barracks had charge of the funeral arrangements, and a firing party from the Tallaght Camp played 'The Last Post' as his remains were lowered into the family plot. He had not died in battle, but of pulmonary tuberculosis, in Jervis Street Hospital. Barrack living was conducive to such contagion at the time.

The Civil War set Tallaght men against Tallaght men, Saggart men against Saggart men and Firhouse men against Firhouse men. These soldiers, twelve months earlier, would have died with each other, even for each other, as countrymen. Their respective mothers and fathers, for the most part, sat in the same churches, on the same pews. Their memories would be as long as their prayers. On the grounds of Bohernabreena Church, where once neighbours loitered after mass on a Sunday to get the gossip of the week, now families departed promptly after the final blessing: 'Let us go in peace, to love and to serve the Lord.'

In St Maelruain's, the Church of Ireland congregation – the Jolleys of Jobstown and Boothmans of Kiltipper, the Nicholsons and Longs from the village and the Foxes of Whitestown – discreetly coalesced around concerns for their future.

In November 1922, Foxes public house was raided, armed men entering the premises just as Mrs Fox was locking up for the night. She ran upstairs to the counting table to hide the night's takings. A revolver was pointed at her, and she was obliged to hand over the cash, a sum of £22. The men departed on foot. That same month, Kennedy's public house (Old Mill) was raided by armed men. They made off with 50 shillings' worth of cigarettes and tobacco.

On 26 January 1923, a lorry containing a patrol of National Army troops was returning from Milltown, Co. Dublin, to the Camp in Tallaght. At 11.15pm, passing Terenure College, it drove over a landmine that had been placed in the middle of the road. The mine exploded with a reverberating roar that shook the entire neighbourhood. The windows of nearby houses were shattered. The explosion was heard in Dublin city centre and with some alarm in Portobello Barracks. The lorry was lifted completely off the ground by the force of the explosion, and its occupants thrown onto the pavement. Four of the men were seriously injured.

Quartermaster Sergeant Berney had several teeth blown out of his head and received a number of shrapnel wounds. His brother was driving the lorry and received wounds to his head and face. Two other brothers, Lieutenant and Sergeant Confrey, were also injured. Private Matthews was blown over the wall of Terenure College into the playing fields. Extraordinarily, he was uninjured.

A large crater was blasted into the road. One of the wheels of the tender was found 250 yards away. The radiator and parts of the engine were later found inside the boundary wall of Bushy Park. A void was blown into the roof of the gate lodge to the college. It was frightening to the world.

Two little sisters, Annie and Lily Vaughan from Templeogue, were walking about 50 yards away from the lorry at the time and were badly injured. A lamplighter doing his rounds had his leg broken by the explosion. Amazingly, nobody was killed. The explosion caused a terrific concussion – those who escaped injury were so dazed that it took some time before they realised what had happened.

They were initially unable to render assistance to the victims. The little Vaughan girls, the Berney brothers and Lieutenant Confrey were all transferred to the Meath Hospital.

On 22 February 1923, Captain Michael Dowling, a native of Clondalkin, was leaving that village, cycling to report for duty at Tallaght Camp. He was approached by two men on the road, who shouted at him to halt. The men produced pistols and Dowling, abandoning his bike, rushed for cover in a hedgerow. The men opened fire on the young Captain. Dowling returned fire with his revolver and the two men retreated. After a short time, Dowling emerged from the hedge and remounted his bicycle. In the distance he spied a third man. He heard a shot, and then felt a bullet pierce his left shoulder. He tumbled from his bicycle. With the last round in his chamber he returned fire. The man fled. Dowling ran frantically, eventually taking refuge in the home of a local man, Bernard Daly, who kindly dressed his wound.

It was the second time that Dowling had almost met his end on the road between Clondalkin and the Tallaght Camp. Three months earlier, on 13 November, he had been accompanying a nineteen-year-old sergeant, John Devoy from Clondalkin, back to the Camp. Devoy was unarmed when they were caught in a similar roadside ambush. Devoy died from the wounds he received. Dowling was brought to hospital, were he recuperated from his wound.

Explosives Factory

During its operations in the Camp in Tallaght, the Chemical Corps of the Irish Army established the only explosives factory in the Irish Free State. It was primarily involved in the production and manufacture of 'Irish cheddite', an industrial explosive similar to gelignite. A factory was erected for the manufacture of cheddite in cartridges, ready for use in industrial applications.

By July 1923, the explosives factory at Tallaght Camp was turning out 3,500 lbs of Cheddite a week and claimed to have the capacity to double that output at short notice if needed. The explosive was principally intended for use in quarrying, repairing damaged roads and construction work. Under the supervision of the Director of Chemicals, Colonel Joseph Dunne, and his second in command, Captain Daniel Stapleton, the factory also manufactured detonators. Many of the 40 officers and staff working in the factory were highly skilled and educated.

The Church of Ireland St Maelruain's Church.

A retreat at the Camp

On Whit Weekend in May 1923, a short religious retreat was held by the Command Chaplain, Reverend Francis A Gleeson, for the officers and men of the 24th battalion. The retreat ran from Saturday evening until Monday morning. Reverend Gleeson heartily congratulated all present for responding to God's call and reminded the participants to take the sacrament of confession monthly. In concluding remarks on the Monday morning, he said the best advice he could give the Irish people and the Army was, 'Fear not a Bolshevism or a barbarism that destroys the body, but intemperance and sensuality that destroys both body and soul into hell.' A great weekend was had by all.

Two days later, one of the last operations of the Civil War in Tallaght took place. Troops stationed at the Camp raided a house in Glenasmole looking for men and arms. They didn't find any. But they did find a gramophone and gramophone records of opera and classical music. These had been stolen from the house of James Brady, the Superintendent of the Waterworks in Glenasmole, two weeks earlier. A civilian was arrested and charged with possession of stolen goods.

The next day, Frank Aiken ordered anti-treaty forces to dump their arms and return to their homes. The call was supported by Eamon De Valera, who issued a statement directed at anti-treaty forces: 'Further sacrifice on your part would now be in vain and the continuance of the struggle in arms unwise in the national interest. Military victory must be allowed to rest for the moment with those who have destroyed the Republic.'

As the news came through, the officers in Tallaght Camp sat around listening to Mr Brady's gramophone records. The opening strains of Puccini's 'Un bel di, vedremo' echoed around the mess hall. The Civil War was over.

After the War, in 1926, Jack Watkins became a founding President of the Tallaght Cumann of Fianna Fáil, of which he remained a member for 40 years. He went on to serve in the LDF during the Emergency. Tom and Jack Watkins established a gravel business. For many years, they had a contract to provide stone to the County Council for road construction. Tom Watkins died in 1969. His brother Jack Watkins died in 1970.

The burning of Tallaght Court House

On 26 October 1904, at a meeting of the South Dublin Rural District Council, discussion centred on a proposal from Dublin County Council to construct a courthouse in Tallaght. The County Council would give £450 toward construction of the building and for equipment. The proposal was passed by a majority of only one vote.

In addition to housing a courthouse, it was anticipated that the new municipal facility could also be used for technical education, talks and public lectures and occasional concerts. There was concern in some quarters that the building could be used for political purposes. A resolution of the County Council was passed that the vesting of the building would be with the Rural District Council (RDC).

Several sites were examined by members of the County and Rural District Councils and the magistrates. In November 1904, a site near the National School on the Greenhills Road was chosen and recommended by a committee to the Council for approval. Over the following eighteen months, a substantial one-storey brick building was erected. In September 1906, a surveyor's report was received by the Rural District Council stating that the courthouse was now complete, and on 20 September 1906, the keys to the new courthouse were handed over to the Clerk of the Petty Sessions.

The first sitting of the Petty Sessions in the new Tallaght Courthouse was held on 1 October 1906. In January 1915, £50 each was allocated for the erection of sheds on the sites of both Tallaght Courthouse and Rathfarnham Courthouse.

Tallaght Courthouse was used for a variety of purposes, most notably during the war years from 1914 to 1918, when a series of 'war effort' events were held. In July 1915, the City and County of Dublin Recruitment Committee held a 'Rally for Recruits' in the Courthouse, which was addressed by, among others, Sir John Erwin. In the previous months, also as part of the war effort, grand concerts were held 'in aid of our refugees' and in aid of the 'Soldiers and Sailors Help Society (Men's Clothing Guild)'. A special tram was laid on from Terenure to Tallaght for the event.

On Thursday, 30 March 1916, Mrs Max Green's play They Also Serve was staged in Tallaght Courthouse, by the Ladies' Recreation Committee of the South Dublin RDC. It was, according to reviews, enthusiastically received by a large and appreciative audience. The entertainment started somewhat late, so that it didn't clash with a mission held in the Church of the Dominican Fathers that evening. The play had been performed in Ballyboden the night before.

One Sunday morning during the Civil War, on 4 February 1923, the Courthouse was discovered to be in flames. A window at the rear of the building had been forced open and an empty petrol tin was found in the debris. The outbreak was first discovered by a young lady going to 6am mass in the Priory. The interior of the building was already a raging mass of flames, and the fire appeared to have been in progress for some time.

She raised the alarm with the caretaker who lived in a neighbouring cottage (Court Cottage!), and he sought the assistance of personnel from the Camp in Tallaght. All efforts to save the building proved futile. The building was completely gutted and all that could be saved from the inferno were a couple of tables.

A number of courts had sat regularly 'under the new regime' in the building. The last court to sit in Tallaght Courthouse was a monthly meeting of the District Court on 16 January 1923, three weeks earlier. All of the court records and valuable legal volumes were destroyed in the blaze.

CHAPTER 11

Industry and Commerce

Any time is Urney time – Urney Chocolates Ltd

Eileen Gallagher (*nee* Cullen) was from a prosperous family from outside New Ross, Co. Wexford. In her youth, her family experienced an unusual setback. Her father developed an unhealthy obsession with playing the organ and as a consequence the family's fortunes diminished considerably. Eileen moved with her mother to Kenilworth Square in Dublin, where her mother started taking in stitching and sewing to help make ends meet. From her mother, Eileen learned the values of both industry and frugality.

Harry T Gallagher, her husband, was the son of a Donegal magistrate and successful businessman. He was sent to Castleknock College in Dublin to be educated. On finishing school and returning to Donegal, he was deemed by his father to be 'too stupid for business', and so was sent back down to Dublin to study Law. He qualified as a solicitor, returned to Donegal and was later appointed Crown Solicitor for the county.

In 1918, Harry and Eileen moved with their three children from Dunwiley House in Stranorlar, Donegal, to the townland of Urney, between Strabane and Clady in Co. Tyrone.

There they had acquired an old Church of Ireland rectory set on five acres, in which to rear their young family.

On the five acres of gardens, Eileen Gallagher began to cultivate flowers for cutting, and vegetables and fruit for the local market. Unemployment was high and poverty widespread in the district, with many of the girls of Strabane, Clady and Urney packing their bags for America. Eileen and Harry Gallagher thought, wouldn't it be wonderful if something could be established in the district to provide employment for the local girls?

Eileen started to make jams with fruit from their garden. After the First World War, sugar for jam-making was strictly rationed and Eileen Gallagher was denied a quota. Sugar traded for £150 a ton on the open market, but if you were granted a quota, you could purchase it for £50.

Eileen and Harry travelled to Dublin to plead their case with the Controller of Sugar, Rodney O'Donnell. As luck would have it, Rodney was a Derry man and had grown up not far from Strabane. After much discussion of local connections and an hour of familiar banter, O'Donnell expressed great regret that he couldn't grant the Gallaghers a sugar quota for jam-making. He could, however, give them a quota if they wanted to make sweets! Not knowing the first thing about sweet-making, the Gallaghers nevertheless promptly accepted the offer.

Eileen started to experiment, making toffee in a pan on the hob in her kitchen in Urney. She would sometimes get her housekeeper to help, and if it was a particularly large batch, she would ask the children's nurse to lend a hand. She tried making fudge, with limited success. In 1919, she established a small cottage industry, employing half a dozen girls.

In 1920, she visited the Glasgow Confectionary Exhibition in Scotland, and by chance met an old school acquaintance, now married to a man who had established a sweet factory in Scotland. The couple introduced the Gallaghers to an advisor, a Dutch chocolate maker. From Glasgow they travelled to Dundee, where they purchased the necessary equipment to establish a sweet factory.

Within four years, Eileen and Harry Gallagher's company, Urney Chocolates, was employing 40 people and was already distributing its produce commercially throughout the island of Ireland. The enterprise was principally Eileen's initiative – the vision, the plan and the execution. But Harry Gallagher was quick to recognise the potential first spotted by his wife.

Eileen Gallagher was a niece of Father James Cullen, founder of the Total Abstinence Pioneer Association, and her mother was a cousin of the Irish nationalist politician John Redmond. During the Great War, Harry Gallagher had thrown himself into the campaign to help recruit young men to fight on behalf of the Crown in Europe. Like his father and grandfather before him, Harry was politically active.

After partition, in 1923, his role as Crown Solicitor for Donegal was gone. The new border ran by the River Finn at the bottom of the Gallaghers' garden. As a Catholic and ardent nationalist, now living in the six counties, he was without position. In Donegal, in what was now the Free State, he had been Crown Solicitor and a recruiter for the Great War. He had been responsible for prosecuting cases against Sinn Féin members in the years following 1916. His professional standing and perhaps social standing was now somewhat diminished.

Commercially, they were also now cut off from their main market in the new Free State. In later life, Harry Gallagher recalled, 'When Urney goods were sent to Belfast, they were often returned marked "We want no Pope here!"'

On Monday, 11 February 1924, shortly after the workers of Urney Chocolates stopped work for their dinner break, a fire was discovered in the Gallaghers' factory. The RUC and Beechmount Special Constabulary arrived on the scene before Derry Fire Brigade was summoned. The Brigade arrived and managed to save the engine room, which contained some of the company's most valuable plant and machinery. The rest of the factory was completely gutted, the cost of damage estimated at £20,000. The factory would need to be entirely rebuilt, at considerable cost. Around the same time, the Free State Government imposed six shillings a pound duty on chocolate manufactured outside the Free State. The twenty-six counties were the primary market for Urney's products.

Given the new tariffs in the Free State, it made little sense to rebuild the factory in the six counties. The Gallaghers considered all their options: rebuild in Urney; move down south; or emigrate to Canada! Harry Gallagher opened discussions with senior politicians in Dublin, WT Cosgrave among them. Cosgrave served as President of the Executive Council of the Irish Free State from 1922 to 1934. Cosgrave suggested that the Gallaghers should consider a move to Co. Dublin.

Within four months of the fire, a decision was taken to relocate to the Free State. A site was offered for lease in Tallaght, Co. Dublin, from the Free State Government. It was part of an old Royal Air Force aerodrome and more recently a military camp. On a warm June day in 1924, Harry and Eileen Gallagher visited Tallaght to inspect the partially decommissioned military site they were being offered. A cool, gentle breeze was blowing down from the hills around Tallaght. Harry and Eileen Gallagher looked each other in the eye. They decided there and then that they needed to investigate no other sites. They accepted the Free State Government's offer, promising to bring their industry to Tallaght.

Urney Chocolates Ltd agreed to take the southern end of the Camp, while the remaining northern half would be retained by the military authorities. The 7th Infantry Battalion of the National Army was still stationed there and operated an explosives factory. When Harry Gallagher called into the Dominican Priory in Tallaght village and told a priest that he intended to establish a chocolate factory at the camp, he was told, 'It's [work] boots that people need around here, not chocolates!'

The company initially secured ten acres of the site, containing 30 buildings, including the Camp hospital, tennis courts and a recreation hall. The Gallaghers lived in what had been the Camp hospital. Huts that had provided accommodation for troops were repurposed to provide dwelling houses for workers. Unexploded bombs were occasionally discovered on the site.

Approximately 30 staff members would relocate to Tallaght from Strabane. Willie McElwee joined the firm at fourteen years of age and came to Tallaght from Strabane with the Gallaghers. He would remain with the company for the following 45 years, eventually becoming Head of the Chocolate Coating Department. William McCauley, also from Strabane, joined the firm at thirteen years of age and came to Tallaght. He would in time become Head of the Confectionary Department.

The enterprise was to be run as a 'model factory' and Eileen Gallagher's vision was to develop the area into a 'garden city'. The Gallaghers anticipated employing up to 300 girls and 50 men. They initially recruited less than 30 new staff, mostly drawn from the neighbourhood of the Camp.

The Urney Chocolates factory was blessed on 1 December 1924 and a mass was held in the main factory building. In addition to staff, the service was attended by a large number of officers and men from the infantry battalion still garrisoned next door.

The following year, Harry Gallagher put a written notice on the gate of the factory stating that five workmen were needed for an immediate start. Those interested should present themselves at the gate for 8.30am the next morning. It was the last time Harry would post such a notice. The next day Gallagher came down to the gate at 8.20 to find 300 men gathered outside the factory, looking for work. It was a challenging time for the workers of Tallaght and district.

Harry Gallagher quickly established himself among Dublin's business and political classes. In September 1928, he became a founding Director of what would become the Irish Press newspaper, along with Eamon de Valera and others.

In 1927, a rumour circulated to the effect that Urney Chocolates Ltd was controlled or financed by cross-channel or 'non-Irish' interests. As an entirely Irish chocolate manufacturer, based solely in the Free State and serving almost exclusively an Irish market, given the political sensitivities after the War of Independence and the Civil War, the rumour had the potential to significantly dent the emerging Urney brand. The company published a statement unequivocally declaring, 'Urney Chocolates are made in Ireland, and the company is financed and controlled by Irishmen.'

The statement wasn't entirely true. From the foundation of the company, Irish identity was central to the branding of its products. 'Colleen Kisses', 'Leprechaun Toffee' and 'Nora Chocolates' were among the company's earliest offerings. The statement was signed by the four shareholders, two of whom were women, one of which was Mrs Eileen Gallagher – founder, visionary and director. A reward of £100 was offered for information leading to the discovery of the person or persons responsible for the vexatious rumour.

In March 1933, the factory was broken into and a sum of almost £700 taken. The Civic Guards in Tallaght and Rathfarnham, under Superintendent O'Reilly, investigated. The office had been ransacked, a safe broken open and three cash boxes removed and the room left in complete disorder. £380 in cash belonging to the company was taken, along with £250 of personal property belonging to a director, Mrs Nora Callinan (after whom the 'Nora' chocolates were named!), along with between £30 and £40 and a gold denture, the property of Harry Gallagher. The burglars had been well acquainted with the premises and had entered the office through a fanlight in the roof. Six weeks later, one of three defendants – a Mr Halligan – in admitting his role in the burglary, shouted from the dock, 'We only got £161 each. That's all we got.' He denied ever having seen Mr Gallagher's tooth.

Eileen Gallagher was generally considered to be Ireland's first female commercial traveller, roaming around Ireland in the early days of the company, promoting and selling Urney produce. Later in life, when Urney Chocolates was well-established, Eileen Gallagher sought to diversify the family's business interests. She introduced the first American broad breasted white turkeys into Ireland in 1951, smuggling a half-dozen fertilised turkey eggs through customs.

White turkeys lay almost as many eggs as a hen. Within five years, Eileen Gallagher's hatchery contained almost 1000 turkeys. Eileen had ambitions to scale the operation up to develop a poultry export business to rival her growing chocolate business.

A number of spin-off businesses were explored. The under-feathers of each dead and oven-bound bird could be used to make marabout trimming (a type of down-feather trimming, originally from the marabou stork, whose under-tail down once provided the feathers). Turkey droppings, mixed with compost, could make a valuable fertiliser.

Industry and Commerce

Left: Workers on the grounds of Urney Chocolates.
Above and below left: Work on the factory floor.
Below middle and right: Statements to Urney customers.

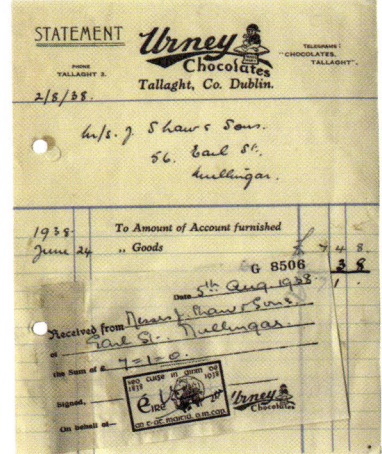

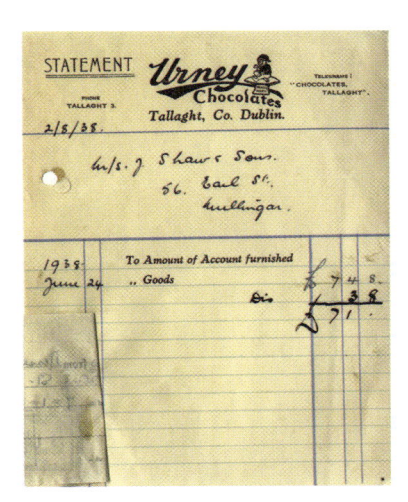

Eileen Gallagher travelled several times to America to research American turkey production and breeds. In 1956, she visited farms in America and came to appreciate the scale of the competition. In the US, commercially run turkey farms typically had around 37,000 turkeys and were organised so that one or two workers could run the entire enterprise. After this research in the United States, she decided to discontinue the enterprise. The days for Tallaght's white turkeys were numbered.

The chocolate factory children

Harry and Eileen had three children. Their eldest son, Edward, became a surgeon in England.

Their only daughter, Helen, was educated in Dublin and France, before training as a nurse in St Vincent's Hospital, Dublin. She married a civil engineer, Dermot O'Clery, in Bohernabreena Parish Church in April 1936. Though trained as a nurse, Helen O'Clery devoted much of her married life to writing children's books, and she became a respected children's author. Her husband Dermot was, for a time, President of the Irish Inland Waterways Association, and both Helen and Dermot were passionate advocates for the inland waterways.

The newly married couple initially lived on the Urney factory campus, before moving in 1945 into St Maelruain's, the old glebe house beside the factory. In later life, they acquired Knocklyon Castle, before moving to Thornfield, a substantial three-bed bungalow in Jobstown. Their daughter Ann married Chris Shouldice of an old Palatine family, and they continued to live in Knocklyon Castle.

The Gallaghers' youngest son, Redmond or 'Red', was initially sent to England to be educated as a boarder, but returned to Belvedere College in Dublin, where he enjoyed a reputation for playing rugby to a high standard.

As a young man, Redmond Gallagher developed a passion for driving and motor car racing. In the early 1930s, he attended Irish Motor Club races in the Phoenix Park and, at fifteen years of age, acted as a race steward. He was due to compete in a junior race there in 1933, but shortly before the race, he broke the crank on his Austin car and so was unable to compete.

In 1934, Red Gallagher left Tallaght to undertake a six-month tour of Germany, studying chocolate manufacturing methods in factories in Dresden and Halle. While in Germany, he was introduced to Adolf Hitler. Gallagher found him to be almost comical. Almost.

Industry and Commerce

In March 1937, Redmond Gallagher, driving his car on the Merrion Road in Dublin, knocked down a male pedestrian. The pedestrian died several days later. While negligence was admitted, Gallagher's counsel argued in the High Court that the pedestrian's death was not due to injuries suffered as a result of the accident. The High Court found otherwise and the victim's wife was awarded £700 damages for the loss of her husband. £275 was awarded to the man's son and £300 to his daughter in damages for the loss of their father.

Red Gallagher married a Welsh lady, Audrey Kewley, in September 1938. The newly betrothed couple briefly lived in Griffeen Lodge in Lucan before purchasing a residence on land in Cappaghmore, Clondalkin. Audrey Redmond paid sums totalling £3000 to Albert W Briscoe, a solicitor, to complete the purchase of the house. Briscoe, however, failed to pass on £2250 of this to the vendor, giving rise to the Law Society of Ireland seeking to have Briscoe struck off the Roll of Solicitors for professional malpractice. The purchase was, after some time, completed and Briscoe was duly struck off.

Audrey and Red later lived in a fine eighteenth-century Georgian residence in Cypress Grove, Templeogue. The house had previously been home to the Walsh family. Dr Tom Walsh had been Keeper of the Botanic Gardens, and Ella Walsh was one of the only female professional gardeners in the country. In their gardens stood a 200-year-old cork tree that had been visited by the Royal Horticultural Society of London on their excursion to Dublin in 1825. The Gallaghers often hosted up to 70 guests in their lavish drawing room for musical recitals and social evenings.

In 1945, Urney Chocolates Ltd experienced one of its few industrial disputes. A ten-day strike occurred in response to workers refusing to work with four union members who were

Harry and Eileen's daughter, Helen O'Clery.

A Ramble About Tallaght

The glebe house, St Maelruain's.

Industry and Commerce

in arrears with the union and with two non-union members. Urney refused to collect arrears on behalf of the union, the ATGWU, or to concern itself with workers' union membership.

By 1951, Redmond Gallagher had succeeded his father as Managing Director of the Company. Harry stayed on as Chairman of the firm, which now employed almost 400 people, making it the largest single employer in Tallaght's history.

As an aside from the day job, between 1953 and 1958, Redmond Gallagher became a familiar face and name as a race car owner and driver in Irish motor racing circles. Driving a 1500cc French-made Gordini, Gallagher took first place in the Irish Motor Racing Club's International Wakefield Trophy in the Curragh in 1954.

It was a bitter-sweet win. Two spectators and a driver were killed and fifteen other spectators seriously injured when a competing car ran off the road during the race. Gallagher would compete against such notable competition as Stirling Moss in Belfast over 94 laps of the Dundrod Circuit. Gallagher took first place in races there in 1953 and 1954.

With the Chief Engineer of Urney Chocolates, Nicholas Flynn, Redmond Gallagher built his own series of racing cars – Leprechaun, Leprechaun II and Leprechaun III ('Leprechaun' sweets were a popular choice in Urney's product line). Gallagher's bespoke racing car, Leprechaun III, was the most successful.

While motor racing provided a thrilling diversion for Redmond Gallagher, Urney's primary export market, the UK, was presenting growing challenges. In the early 1950s, Urney switched their export focus from Britain to North America. After years of rationing in the UK throughout the 1940s, the new decade was seeing a boom in domestic chocolate and confectionary production in Britain, which Urney struggled to compete with.

Redmond Gallagher.

In 1958, Redmond Gallagher embarked on a two-month tour of Canada to drum up support for Urney's trans-Atlantic business. A visit to the USA the previous year had resulted in an increase in orders from $1 million to $1.5 million, a 50% increase in one year.

It was two months well spent. He returned to Tallaght with orders valued at $2 million (Can). One order alone was valued at $250,000 (Can). This was good news indeed for Urney Chocolates and for the workers of Tallaght. It was also good news for Ireland's farmers, with Irish milk and Irish sugar (from beet) being the primary ingredients. One million gallons of milk and 1000 tons of sugar would be required to fulfil the order. Urney Chocolates was one of the Irish Sugar Company's largest customers.

Everything in Urney's chocolate, with the exception of cocoa beans, was locally produced. Redmond Gallagher liked to joke that if the Irish climate had been more benign, they would have produced them locally too. Ireland's production of 'chocolate crumb' accounted for 23 million gallons of milk, and annual export sales were valued at £5 million. The packaging for Urney Chocolates was also manufactured in Ireland.

The scramble was now on in Tallaght to ramp up production to meet the extraordinary demand from foreign markets. The company recruited another 100 staff members, bringing the total workforce to almost 500. Ireland's shipping facilities were one of the greatest constraints for Irish industry attempting to reach the North American market – its capacity, frequency and speed of delivery. The development of the port of Cobh offered the greatest promise of progress in that regard.

In 1958, on his father's retirement, Red Gallagher assumed the chairmanship of the company. He sought to beef up the executive management team, appointing Mr Thomas (Tommy) Headon as joint Managing Director. A graduate of UCD with first-class honours in both Chemistry and Maths, Headon had, as a young man, played rugby for Ireland in 1938–39. After qualifying as a chemist in 1942, he worked briefly for Urney, before going to London where he worked as a Production Manager for a chocolate firm. He went on to become Technical Director of a firm in Surrey. On re-joining Urney as joint Managing Director with Redmond Gallagher in 1958, Tommy Headon, his wife Elisabeth and their young family took up residence almost onsite, in St Maelruains, the old glebe house occupied some years earlier by Redmond's sister.

Industry and Commerce

With Headon's appointment, Redmond Gallagher wasn't just looking to strengthen the management team. He was looking for a way out – he was preparing to exit the company. Headon quickly took the reins of the old family enterprise. Redmond Gallagher was keen to see Headon assert his executive leadership. Keener, perhaps, than old Harry Gallagher. Headon's arrival marked the beginning of a decline in the Gallagher family's control of the business. Headon was granted a substantial shareholding in the company, as Redmond Gallagher prepared to relinquish his own and his family's interest.

A number of corporate acquisitions were made to bolster Urney's production capacity. In 1959, Urney acquired the assets of Dungarvan Milk Products Ltd and set about reopening a chocolate crumb factory in Dromkeen, Co. Limerick, that had closed the previous year. In September 1960, Liam Devlin Ltd and Old Dutch Confections Ltd, both operating in Cork Street in Dublin, were acquired in full by Urney Chocolates Ltd. The following year, Urney bought Murch Company Ltd in Burnley in the UK to bolster supply to the UK market. Urney's British market was still worth around £250,000 a year.

The early 1960s saw the frenetic expansion of Urney's market, its market share, its capacity and its acquisitions. The company's rapid expansion brought opportunities and risks. The pace of its growth demanded capital investment on a scale few families could shoulder. In

Below left: Tommy Headon
Below right: Betty and Tommy Headon with Eamon de Valera.

A group at an Urney dinner dance.

addition to numerous international acquisitions, if Urney was to meet the growing international demand for its produce, it would need to expand the production capacity of its primary factory in Tallaght.

In 1961, Urney Chocolates Ltd exported £1m worth of product. The factory was processing 3 million gallons of milk, 3000 tons of sugar and 1500 tons of glucose annually. Three hundred tons of cardboard and 150 tons of paper was consumed by Urney's Cardboard Box Department as they turned out five million fancy boxes annually. At peak times of the year, from May to November, up to 850 people were employed by Urney Chocolates in Tallaght and another 200 staff in associated companies. Over 400 staff enjoyed subsidised lunches provided in the canteen in Tallaght every day. General production staff, mostly women, were paid around £5 a week.

A quality-control panel of ten staff was responsible for tasting 110 different products, and a five-person committee met weekly to review marketing and packaging ideas.

The year 1962 would prove transformative for the company. The ageing Tallaght plant saw £100,000 invested in new technology and an extension of the factory. A complete refit of the Chocolate Section to automate chocolate production was the first phase in its expansion. Machinery and plant was brought in from Italy, Switzerland, England and Germany. It would ordinarily take ten to twelve weeks to bring such machinery into operation, but within twenty days of delivery, the machinery was up and running on Urney's production line. 'We survive or we die and we are determined that not alone shall we survive, but that we will continue to grow. This plant is an expression of our faith in the future,' Redmond Gallagher stated at the opening of the 'Extension' by An Taoiseach Seán Lemass.

Always an astute political operator, the ageing Harry Gallagher, while acknowledging that WT Cosgrave had played an important role in Urney's decision to relocate to Tallaght 38 years earlier, also noted the central role the economic policies of Lemass had played in the business ecosystem of Urney Chocolates in the intervening decades.

Their international expansion was advanced with a number of acquisitions in Capetown and Johannesburg in South Africa. These included Chapalot Industries Ltd, Humphries Ltd, Bensdrop Ltd, Wicks Ltd and Seasonal Products Ltd. Thomas Headon became Chairman of all of them.

Several new appointments were made to the Board of Urney Chocolates Ltd. Arthur Behan was appointed Assistant Managing Director. Behan had been with the company since 1931 and had been appointed Works Director only four years earlier. Charles D Kelly was appointed Sales Director. He had joined the company as General Sales Manager two years earlier.

If Eileen and Harry Gallagher had successfully developed an indigenous Irish enterprise of national importance, Red Gallagher had matched their success in transforming the company into an international exporter of chocolate crumb.

Redmond Gallagher, as head of a leading Irish export company that underpinned the export of Irish agricultural produce, was lauded as a visionary, a leader in Ireland's industrial aspirations. It must have weighed heavily on the shoulders of one who had merely inherited his parents' enterprise. Gallagher had many other interests – including in motor racing, horse breeding and farming. As a young man, he had wanted to pursue a career in engineering. His father had prevailed upon him to commit to the family business.

Eileen and Harry Gallagher still lived on the grounds of the factory in 1962. However, their lavish ornamental gardens, which they had spent 40 years cultivating and nurturing, were incrementally being eaten up by the relentless expansion of the factory. The gardens had been so well tended and developed that they had, over the decades, become something of an attraction for day-trippers. City dwellers would come out to Tallaght just to see 'the gardens of Urney'.

It wasn't only the gardens that were changing. The business world had changed in the 40 years since Eileen Gallagher first made fudge in her kitchen in Urney. And Ireland's economic policy had also changed. Urney Chocolates had largely enjoyed and benefitted from Ireland's isolationist and protectionist economic stance.

Red Gallagher and Thomas Headon both recognised the need to scale up and align with a larger international partner, if they were to compete and thrive in an open international market. It was something Harry and Eileen were perhaps less convinced of.

With Grace

In November 1963, Urney announced that an American firm, WR Grace, had taken a 49% stake in the company. WR Grace was the 88th-largest company in the world at the time. The founder of the Grace business empire, an Irishman, had emigrated from Ireland to Peru in 1850, after the Famine, and established a fertiliser and shipping business. He later moved to New York, where he became Mayor.

WR Grace had recently acquired another confectionary firm in the UK, Van Houten. They promptly closed Van Houten's factory at Chesham in the UK. Urney of Tallaght, it was thought, might now have to rise to the mammoth task of supplying the British Commonwealth and the entire British home market. It was a time of irrational exuberance and unprecedented optimism. Much was made of Grace's Irish family history and the Grace family's affection for the old sod. There was talk of the wheel of history turning, of how William Pitt had closed factories in Ireland in 1800, so that British factories could supply the Irish market. Few, however, anticipated the speed with which such wheels can turn.

By 1964, Urney were exporting $4 million worth of produce. That year marked peak production and peak employment for the company. Redmond Gallagher stepped back from the company to focus on other interests. He had now largely relinquished his and his family's share in the company – it was now in the hands of WR Grace and Tommy Headon.

In 1965, Redmond Gallagher was the principal behind the development of a new 100-acre industrial estate situated between the Greenhills Road and Belgard Road. Working with Collen Brothers builders of East Wall Road, the laying of water mains, sewer pipes and electricity commenced in October of that year, and plans were made for the laying of roads and the building of factory bays – capable of extension and adaptation.

It is worth noting that this vision and ambitious plan predated Myles Wright's plan for the expansion of Dublin, published four years later and often credited with the development of Tallaght New Town. Progress and development was happening, with or without a regional framework in place. Planning permission for the industrial estate had been granted by Dublin City Council.

In 1966, 49-year-old Thomas Headon died suddenly. WR Grace acquired his shareholding, taking full ownership of Urney Chocolates. Forty-two years after its establishment, the company was now in the hands of an international conglomerate. The American firm had bought out Hughes Brothers (HB) in 1964, and acquired Lucan Dairies the following year. In 1969, they exchanged the dairy interest of Hughes Brothers with the ice cream interest of Premier Dairies and opened a new £1 million ice cream factory in Rathfarnham. They went on to rationalise the ice cream industry in Ireland.

Only seven years after acquiring Urney Chocolates in full, and renaming it HB Chocolate, WR Grace hived off or sold the chocolate business, along with the rest of HB, to Anglo-Dutch industry giant Unilever. The 'HB' factories now being acquired by Unilever employed almost 900 people. Only two months later, in May 1973, Unilever were reported to be in talks to sell the Tallaght plant, giving rise to a temporary work stoppage by disgruntled workers, rightly concerned for their futures.

Still living on the grounds of the factory, at 93 years of age, Harry Gallagher would stay in bed reading until noon. Honey, a lively Chihuahua, scampered by his bedside. His wife Eileen, a creature of discipline and habit, was up at 7.30 most mornings, but would retire for an afternoon nap. Old Harry Gallagher, by his own admission, would drink anything out of a bottle – anything, that is, but ginger ale. He drank neat brandy at race meetings, and liked to go to race meetings as often as possible, often driving himself there and back. With advancing age, among his most pressing concerns was whether he would have his driving licence renewed.

Harry Gallagher died in 1975, at 95 years of age. Eileen died the following year, aged 89. They lived their last years in Urney House, on the grounds of the factory. The remains of Harry and Eileen Gallagher were laid to rest in the shade of an ancient tree in St Maelruain's graveyard in Tallaght village. Their grave is marked by a simple stone.

Following Ireland joining the European Economic Community in 1973, the flooding of the Irish market with foreign confectionary in the mid-1970s contributed to a declining trading environment for Irish producers generally. On 25 April 1980, workers were called in and told the Tallaght plant was to close in the coming months. HB Chocolate was to be no more. The Unilever subsidiary had lost £1.6 million in the previous twelve months and was projected to lose another £1m in the following twelve months.

The closure would see 300 jobs lost. Many of the workers were second- or indeed third-generation employees. Some were the children or grandchildren of those who had come to Tallaght with the Gallaghers back in 1924.

The factory hadn't just provided jobs. The Urney Social Club, along with the Glen Abbey Social Club, provided an important focal point in the social life of the community. For over 50 years, Urney Chocolates had provided an economic backbone to Tallaght and district. From the foundation of the State, the people of Tallaght had set their watch to the sound of 'the Hooter', the Urney Horn, calling workers to their labour. In the 1930s and 1940s, children from the outskirts of Tallaght knew it was time to set out for school when the Hooter sounded. The Hooter was long gone. And now so were the jobs.

In July 1980, the factory gates were closed for the last time. A chink of light had been given to the community the previous month, with the announcement by Telectron Ltd of a deal with CIT Alcatel, promising the creation of hundreds of jobs for Tallaght. The deal, however, would ultimately not go ahead. Hundreds of jobs were not created.

Many of the redundant workers were angry. And some were desperate. Later in the year, a raid on the old Urney Social Club yielded £800 for the thieves. They appeared to have been familiar with the premises and the routine of the club. They had known of the bar–grill's weak points and appeared to have known that the previous three days' takings had not been banked. It was believed to have been an inside job.

In December 1980, 15.5 acres of the Urney site on the Belgard Road was sold to Monarch Properties. The following year, Dockrells' Builders' Providers moved their operations from Ballymount to the old Urney Chocolates site.

Horses in west Tallaght

Saint Maelruain's (originally the old glebe house, now the site of Exchange Hall), once home to the Headon Family, was leased as a headquarters by Redmond Gallagher to the newly established Bord na gCapall in 1971. Plans were emerging that would make the adjoining land and estate a site for the breeding and training of purebred horses. The plans would come to nought and in 1981, the fallow land was occupied by members of the Travelling community and unbridled horses.

In the year of his father's passing, Redmond Gallagher bought Athgarvan Stud in Co. Kildare, for a sum believed to be in the region of £125,000. The residence, built about 1800 by the Prince Regent, was set on 88 acres with 409 loose boxes and staff quarters. England's George IV had once stayed there on a visit to the Curragh races. Gallagher sold it on three years later for £490,000.

Oranges in Spain

When Thomas Headon, Managing Director of Urney Chocolates, died at 49 years of age in 1966, Redmond Gallagher, who himself had been widowed the previous year, married Headon's widow, Elizabeth. Gallagher employed an attractive young lady, Máirín McGrath, to act as chaperone to his second wife. In 1977, Redmond Gallagher eloped with Máirín McGrath. She was 37 years his junior. They travelled throughout Europe, spending time in France and Andorra before settling in the town of Sagra in tax-friendly Spain in 1980. Redmond Gallagher was advancing plans to develop an orange plantation in Sagra when news came through of the closure of Urney in Tallaght.

Following the death of his second wife Elizabeth in 1982, Redmond and Máirín were married.

Redmond Gallaher died on 31 October 2006 in his villa in Sagra, Spain, where he had lived his last years with his third wife. He was buried in the town on 3 November 2006. He was 94 years old. His sister Helen O'Clery died in the same year, aged 96.

The reminiscences of Redmond's third wife, Máirín McGrath Gallagher, were recorded by Irish Life and Lore oral history archive in 2006. She died in 2020.

The success of Urney Chocolates was not just a combination of vision, industry and hard work. Economic protectionism had played some role in both the rise and the fall of the Tallaght firm.

But its role in the history of Tallaght should not be forgotten. From 1924 until its eventual closure in 1980, several thousand workers from several hundred families enjoyed relative prosperity and a degree of security in an era of uncertainty and scarcity. For several decades, the wages from Urney Chocolates helped to underpin the entire local economy of Tallaght. For a small country village on the outskirts of Dublin, the Gallaghers' enterprise for 50 years provided an economic boon as the recently established State struggled to establish and assert its economic and political independence.

The Gallagher family are fondly remembered as decent and industrious people who treated their workers fairly and fully appreciated the social responsibility that accompanied their economic success.

And the products manufactured in the factory at Tallaght are remembered with equal affection, from back when any time was Urney time!

Lucky Joe Griffin and Red Breast Preserving Co.

When Joe Griffin was nine years old, living on Montague Street in Dublin, he bought two raffle tickets. With those two tickets he won two Christmas hampers. His mother told him, 'Joe, it is better to be born lucky than to be born rich!' He never forgot those words and, from then on, Joe Griffin believed he was born lucky – a belief that would remain with him for many years.

Joe didn't know much about business. He didn't know much about horses either. But for a brief period between 1952 and 1955, he was considered by many to be a titan of both business and horse racing in Ireland. At his peak, Griffin boasted of having personal credit of £1.8 million.

He rapidly built up a multi-million-pound export business, employing over 300 people in Tallaght in 1954. He bought eighteen racehorses, and won the Aintree Grand National in two consecutive years, 1953 and 1954 – the first racehorse owner ever to do so.

In the early 1950s, the largest factory and employer in Tallaght was Urney Chocolates, located on the appropriately named Urney Road, or as many called it, the New Lane (later to become the Belgard Road). But the second largest was a company called Red Breast Preserving Co. (Ireland) Ltd. Registered as a company in 1947, it was founded by Joe Griffin and his brother James. Red Breast produced salad cream, mincemeat (dried fruit), sauces and lemon curd. By 1953, the company was reportedly making up to £1000 in profit a day!

In 1949, Red Breast Preserving Co. employed 130 staff in Tallaght, mostly 'factory girls', and exported almost 3 million bottles of salad cream to Britain. The company was fined £200 in the UK for being 12.5% short, when 250 bottles were sampled by the Weights and Measures Office. Joe Griffin unsuccessfully appealed the fine, suggesting that thieves had helped themselves to the contents of the bottles in transit.

Unbeknownst to most, Griffin's earliest forays into the business world had already rewarded him with a twelve-month prison sentence. Back in 1944, Griffin had been convicted of selling adulterated sulphate of ammonia. Tests showed the 'sulphate of ammonia' was, in fact, 98% common salt. To cover his tracks, he later claimed to have spent time in the Carmelite Abbey in Loughrea, Co. Galway.

Fidgety Joe

Barely five feet tall, florid-faced and fidgety, Joe Griffin liked to tell of how he had borrowed £16 to set up Red Breast Preserving Co.

Food shortages and rationing, still in place in the UK after the Second World War, meant a booming export market for Irish companies exporting dried and preserved foodstuffs. In the late 1940s, Griffin bought a £100,000 shipload of dried fruit on credit from the Greek Government – a consignment that had been exported from Greece, and had arrived in the UK just after the order for it had been cancelled by a British supermarket. Griffin brought the consignment to Red Breast Preserving Co. in Tallaght, where they made mince pies from the dried fruit. A rare

A Ramble About Tallaght

'goodie' in the UK in the post-war years, Red Breast then sold the mince pies for £200,000 to the same British supermarket chain that had cancelled the original consignment. Joe Griffin was on his way to the bigtime!

Red Breast Preserving Co. quickly established a lucrative trade across the Irish Sea, selling tinned 'mincemeat' – sweetened dried fruit – to the UK market. Within five years of being established, the company's annual turnover was almost £2 million. It appeared to be an overnight success, making its founder Joe Griffin one of the richest men in the Tallaght district and a prominent Irish businessman.

As his business boomed, in 1951, Joe moved his family – his wife Peggy and their three young children – from their comfortable house on half an acre, Woodlands in Ballyboden, down to the more salubrious country residence of Knocklyon House, set on 24 acres of orchards, paddocks, pleasure grounds and gardens. The house had four reception rooms, eight family bedrooms, a ballroom and a billiards room. Griffin bought the house for £6000 in 1951 and promptly set about

Knocklyon House, home to 'Lucky Joe' Griffin.

spending £30,000 renovating, extending and upgrading it over the following two years. A new billiards table was installed in the billiards room and the ballroom got a new floor.

In the mornings, before Joe set off in his imported American Buick motorcar on the short drive to Urney Road, he had to bid good morning not just to Betty and the children, but also to the cook, the nanny and the gardener.

Befitting a man of his newfound wealth and status, Joe Griffin bought eighteen of the finest racehorses in the country. He had many of them picked and trained by a man who was to become arguably the greatest horse trainer in Irish racing history, Vincent O'Brien of Cashel, Co. Tipperary. Griffin's success in the coming years was unlike anything seen in Tallaght or Ireland before, earning him several monikers, among them 'Mincemeat Joe' and 'Lucky Joe Griffin'. And his downfall would be just as swift and spectacular.

On 15 February 1953, a vehicle driven by a Mr William Harris crashed into Joe Griffin's car at the junction of the Knocklyon and Firhouse roads. Harris was drunk and failed to stop. Griffin's Buick was lightly damaged and the accident was little more than an inconvenience. Griffin had more important matters on his mind. His racehorse Royal Tan had finished in second place the previous March in the 1952 Aintree Grand National. This year, he was hoping to do just as well with Early Mist, a horse he had bought for 5300 guineas.

The finances of Red Breast Preserving Co., one of the largest employers in Tallaght, were not up to date. A list of legal actions relating to unpaid debts against the company was growing. It will be okay, he thought. The company was clearing up to £1000 profit a day. On 21 March, a week before the Grand National, Griffin popped down to the Rathfarnham Courthouse to see Harris charged with drunk driving and leaving the scene of an accident. Harris was found guilty and was fined £15 and had his licence suspended for twelve months. Griffin could get back to work, to put things in order, before heading off to Liverpool for race week.

Lucky Joe's first National

On 18 March 1953, in a field of 31 horses, the rank chaser Early Mist romped home at twenty lengths, at 20/1, in a convincing victory, in what was then considered to be the greatest steeplechase in the world. Early Mist had fallen at the first fence in the same race the previous year.

When news of the win came through from Liverpool to Tallaght, the 300 workers of Red Breast Preserving Co. downed tools to celebrate. Mr McCosh, the Works Manager, phoned Griffin in Liverpool to congratulate him and the staff on duty gave three cheers in unison down the telephone to Lucky Joe Griffin. While Joe was on the phone, his wife Peggy, a vivacious brunette, paraded around the winners' enclosure at Aintree in a mink stole, diamonds and pearls. This was arguably Griffin's finest moment. He was only three years in the horse racing business and had eighteen horses in training across two stables.

Griffin spent £1,500 throwing an after-party in the Adelphi hotel in Liverpool (a celebration he would repeat the following year). The champagne flowed like water. A formal meal preceded the party, to which Griffin had invited Minister for Agriculture Thomas Walsh and Senator Quirke to join himself and other local dignitaries, among them, the Mayor of Liverpool. Flush with the exuberance of this great Irish victory in the British coronation year – an Irish owner, an Irish horse and an Irish trainer taking the Queen's Gold Cup – Minister Walsh slurred over flutes of free champagne.

At midnight, as formal proceedings were coming to a close, the band struck up 'God Save the Queen'. The Irish Minister for Agriculture, in a fit of unrestrained nationalism or outright intoxication, refused, or was unable, to stand for the British anthem. 'I'm not standing up for any fucking English queen,' he is purported to have yelled. 'Purported' rather than 'reported', for Lucky Joe Griffin later confessed to having paid off several journalists in attendance to have the story hushed up, as the Minister was being carried up to bed.

It was open house, all the way, on the boat back to Dublin. The horse, on its return to the capital, was honoured with a civic reception and Lucky Joe Griffin was the toast of the town. A reception laid on in Dublin's Mansion House was followed by a party in the Gresham hotel.

On the day of Early Mist's Grand National win in 1953, Griffin let it be known that he would pick up the tab for the celebrations in every pub in Cashel, to celebrate the champion horse's victory parade through the town, on its return to Tipperary from England. Publicans were wary, but took Lucky Joe at his word. And true to his word, every tab was settled the following week.

Most of the staff of Red Breast Preserving Co. in Tallaght had taken a punt on their flamboyant employer and had backed Early Mist on-the-nose. The extraordinary celebrations in the community were not just heartfelt joy for Lucky Joe Griffin. Hundreds of workers from Red Breast Preserving Co. in Tallaght were given the day off work, to greet Griffin at the pier head in Dún Laoghaire, as he returned in triumph on the mail boat from Liverpool. Griffin was carried on the shoulders of workers and a car was waiting to bring him to O'Connell Street in the city. Early Mist was paraded from the Parnell Monument to the Mansion House. Tallaght Girls' Pipe Band led the procession down Dublin's main thoroughfare.

To mark and celebrate the coronation year, the Grand National Cup of 1953 was valued at £500. Cups in previous years had been valued at £350. Newspapers celebrated that the cup would become Griffin's 'permanent property'. Little did they know of Griffin's precarious business position and financial situation!

Back in Tallaght, to celebrate the extraordinary victory, Griffin introduced the new 'Early Mist Jockey Bar' to its range of products. A national competition was launched offering a £500 prize, if customers could predict the first three horses to pass the winning post in the 1954 Aintree Grand National. Entries needed to be accompanied with four 'Early Mist Jockey Bar' wrappers. It is unclear if the aim was to entice racing enthusiasts to eat more chocolate, or to encourage children to take a greater interest in steeplechasing. The winner would likely be at the very end of a long line of creditors.

The second National

The earliest indication of Lucky Joe's financial difficulties came on the eve of the 1954 Grand National. On the night before jockey Bryan Marshall was to ride Griffin's horse Royal Tan in the race, he accosted Joe Griffin in the Palm Tree Lounge in the hotel where they were both staying. He demanded the payment of £500 he was still owed by Griffin for riding Early Mist to victory the previous year. Earlier in the day, Marshall had ridden a horse Stroller to victory in the Griffin colours, bagging £515 for Griffin in prize money.

Lucky Joe promptly retrieved £450 from under the bed in his hotel bedroom, promising to settle the outstanding money later. Marshall was enraged and threatened to assault Griffin. Only after Dermot O'Brien, brother of the horse's trainer Vincent, borrowed £50 from the hotel manager on Griffin's behalf to settle the debt was the issue resolved. It was 4.30am when Marshall finally agreed to retire to bed, only hours before he was to ride Royal Tan in a second Grand National for Joe Griffin.

Royal Tan won by a neck, beating Tudor Line, coming in at 8/1. But Joe Griffin's luck was fading fast.

After Joe's unprecedented second consecutive Grand National win, publicans in Cashel wasted little time in getting the celebrations started, assuming the same arrangement as the previous year would be honoured. People came from far and wide to Kilcoran Lodge hotel outside Cashel, close to Vincent O'Brien's stables, drinking and singing to the early hours. But this year, publicans in Tipperary would be left high and dry.

Betty Griffin said she had had a dream about four weeks before the race, in which the horse won by 30 lengths. Betty Griffin's foresight was sadly confined to horseracing.

Lucky Joe Griffin was on the verge of bankruptcy. He had personally guaranteed all the company's creditors and a £20,000 mortgage on the Tallaght factory he had taken out from a London finance company. By July 1954, the company was in receivership. Over 300 people working in the Tallaght factory lost their jobs, including a new Production Manager who had just joined the company in June 1953, after 22 years with Denny's. It was an unfortunate move.

During Griffin's bankruptcy hearing, Bryan Marshall would be one of many creditors owed money, a sum of £2781. It took three and a half days for a court stenographer to read the record of his bankruptcy proceedings in a subsequent trial in the District Court. Griffin had paid £5565 for Early Mist, paying with a cheque drawn on the Red Breast Preserving Co. account. The expense was lodged in the company ledger as a business cost, under 'raw materials'. Griffin's increasingly lavish lifestyle was almost entirely paid for with money drawn from the company's account – before bills were settled.

Between 1952 and 1955, Griffin won at least £65K in stake money alone, and a multiple of that in gambling coups. He won £78K, having backed Early Mist in a number of bets at odds between 66/1 and 20/1. The following year, he owed £65,000 to British bookmaker Jack Swift, and was unable to get credit in 1954, the year of his second win. Lucky Joe, in a moment of irrational exuberance immediately after his first Grand National win in 1953, had bought Teapot II for £10,000.

Two days after his bankruptcy was declared, an English business associate, Fred Pontin of Pontin's holiday parks, arrived at his house in Knocklyon with a box of champagne to cheer him up. The following Monday morning, another friend, Paddy Prendergast, sent an envelope addressed to his wife, with five £100 notes in it as a gift. The gestures and kindness were never forgotten.

Hundreds of punters and spectators thronged the RDS in Dublin for the subsequent sale of Griffin's horses, in what was described in one newspaper as 'the greatest show in town'. Three years after Vincent O'Brien had bought Early Mist on behalf of Griffin for 5300 guineas, the horse was sold to O'Brien for 2000 guineas. A representative of Prince Aly Khan bought Royal Tan for 3900 guineas. Teapot II, a horse Griffin had paid £10,000 for, was sold for 40 guineas. His two Grand National trophies, gold cups each weighing 50 ounces, would be auctioned off in Dublin, along with his racing binoculars. All he was left with from his historic racing victories were the eight horseshoes and the racing silks from Early Mist and Royal Tan.

Vincent O'Brien would go on to win a third consecutive Aintree Grand National in 1955 with Quare Times, a horse that had been offered to Joe Griffin.

Knocklyon House

By March 1955, Joe Griffin's wife hadn't enough assets to feed their ten pigs. The pigs were sold to pay creditors. Leaving Knocklyon House, Joe's daughter, when asked by her mother how she felt about leaving the house, replied, 'Mammy. Sure, I would never get a boyfriend if we stayed way out here!'

In September 1956, Knocklyon House was sold for £15,300 under a sealed tender process in the High Court, after an auction of the premises proved abortive. It was less than half of what Griffin had invested in it over the previous five years. It was bought by an equally colourful, wealthy and charismatic character – Captain Spencer Freeman, founder of the Irish Hospital Sweepstake.

The Red Breast Preserving Co. factory, on the Urney Road in Tallaght, was bought out by Johnson and Johnson in 1955.

Lucky Joe's later years

By 1957, 38-year-old Joe Griffin was living in a borrowed house in Killiney, Co. Dublin, on a salary of £15 a week, on which he supported his wife and family. In June 1960, he received a sentence of twelve months with hard labour, suspended for two years, for knowingly receiving a stolen cheque for £20 and cashing it in a bar. He had six children and was in poor circumstances.

Griffin left Ireland in 1965 and lived from 1967 to 1977 in Orbington in Kent in the UK, running a small dried fruit business. In the late 1970s, after ten years in England, Lucky Joe was gearing up to return to the bigtime. He announced a plan to become 'King of the Pickled Lemon' business, hoping to rebuild his business empire by selling jars of sliced lemon to hotels, bars and restaurants serving new and fashionable cocktails. Lucky Joe's business plan was, well, a bit of a lemon. He died in London in 1992, at the age of 75.

The Father, Son and Holy Ghost – Dr Otto Glaser and Telectron of Tallaght

One night in 1938 in Vienna, Austria, a twelve-year-old boy lay in his bed listening to his parents talking in hushed tones downstairs. The country had recently been annexed by Adolf Hitler's Germany. His father was telling his mother that because he was of Jewish heritage and was a Minister in the Austrian Government, it was no longer safe for the family to stay together in Vienna. The boy's mother wondered whether, if it was discovered that she was a Catholic, that would make any difference. It didn't.

Shortly afterwards, that little boy, Otto Glaser (Jr), was put on one of the last 'children's trains' out of Austria. With the assistance of a network of Catholic family friends, he was spirited out of mainland Europe for the duration of the War. He was sent to Ireland, to board with the Holy Ghost Fathers in one of Dublin's most prestigious Catholic boarding schools, Blackrock College.

Arriving in Blackrock in July 1939, Otto had little English but had a strong foundation in Latin, which he had studied in the Real-Gymnasium XIV back in Vienna. As the masters in Blackrock College had little German, for the first year of Otto's stay, they communicated with each other largely through Latin. The motto of Blackrock College was 'Fides et Robur' – Faith and Fortitude – and Otto Glaser would demonstrate both in the years ahead.

Back in Vienna, his father, Otto Glaser Sr, was arrested and sent to Dachau concentration camp as a political prisoner. He would be one of the few detained there to survive the war.

Industry and Commerce

Once a year, the German Embassy in Ireland would contact Blackrock College to inquire as to how their young 'German' student was progressing, and would request a meeting with their young charge. Each year, after agreeing to an emissary from the Embassy coming to Blackrock to visit the boy, the college would 'accidentally' schedule the meeting to clash with a time when the young student was away for the day in Bray, 'on retreat'. The College authorities believed that young Otto Glaser, as the son of an Austrian Minister, was at risk of being kidnapped.

Glaser distinguished himself as a student in Blackrock, quickly gaining proficiency in the English language. In 1943, he was awarded a scholarship to study at University College Dublin, where he successfully completed a Science degree, before advancing to a Master's degree in Physics and Chemistry. After the War, Otto returned to Vienna to pursue further studies, successfully taking a Doctorate in Atomic Physics.

On graduating with his Doctorate, he returned to Ireland. In 1952, Otto married a student he had met in UCD – Patricia Delamer, the daughter of a First World War pilot and notable Irish aviator.

Otto's father-in-law was an impressive, if not a somewhat imposing, figure. Colonel William Percy Delamer had fought in the First World War with the Royal Flying Corps and Royal Air Force and was awarded the Cavaliere, Order of the Crown of Italy. He had been shot down over Ypres, 'Yippers', in France. After demobilisation, he travelled to London, where he completed a course in engineering. On his return to Ireland, he became Commander of the Irish Air Corps in 1922 and was Officer-in-Charge of the Air Corps School between 1932 and 1939.

Following the outbreak of World War Two, when young Otto Glaser was exchanging Latin phrases with the Holy Ghost Fathers, Delamer was charged with organising and operating the Irish Air Defence Command. In 1941, he was appointed Chief Technical Officer of the Irish Air Corps and, the following year, Director of Military Aviation. After the War, in 1946, Delamer took up the role of Manager of Dublin Airport, a post he would hold until his retirement in 1966.

When Otto was courting Patricia, William Percy Delamer was impressed with his knowledge, his industriousness and his ambition. Otto was pursuing a career in telecommunications, something William Percy Delamer know a thing or two about.

Among Glaser's contemporaries at UCD had been Garret FitzGerald and Charles J Haughey, who would both go on to achieve the highest political office in the land. FitzGerald, early in his career, worked in Aer Lingus, inhabiting the same orbit as Delamer.

On returning to Ireland, Dr Otto Glaser secured a post in the Department of Posts and Telegraphs, designing and installing radio navigational aids for Dublin Airport and the much larger traffic control centre at Shannon Airport. Advanced telecommunications were in an early stage of development in Ireland, and Glaser was quick to spot opportunities for growth and development in the sector.

In the mid-1950s, he joined a small research company in Dublin, Technico Communications Ltd, which imported and installed telecommunications systems. They installed public automatic telephone exchanges for the Department of Posts and Telegraphs and 1100 extensions for the ESB in their Head Office – the largest network in Ireland and one of the largest in Europe. They also installed equipment for Aer Lingus, with 40 exchange lines and 400 extensions. Technico Communications Ltd provided the bulk of VHF equipment to Cork, Shannon and Dublin airports, supplied the radar at Shannon and was about to provide the same for Dublin Airport.

Technico, as an Irish associate of the German giant Telefunken Ltd, was established in 1954 with £10,000 capital investment by Dr Kurt Ticher and Caeser Beckmann, both naturalised Irish citizens. Beckmann had come to Ireland in 1932. Dr Kurt Ticher, a Bavarian-born Jew, was a wool merchant, antique dealer and the author of *Irish Silver in the Rococo Period*. Ticher was an experienced, erudite and internationally connected company director with import and export experience. In 1948, Ticher had started exporting tweed to British forces on the Rhine in Germany, before selling in bulk into the West German market. The export trade quickly grew to other European markets. By 1963, Ticher's Irish Wool Weavers Cooperative were showcasing the best of Irish tweed at Leipzig Autumn Fair. Ticher had converted to Protestantism when he arrived in Ireland.

He was a founder, Director and Chairman of Fuji Ireland and would go on to become a Director of a company in Tallaght, FL O'Dywer (Trimmings), in the Hibernian Industrial Estate, Greenhills, Tallaght.

Dr Otto Glaser, Dr Kurt Ticher, Caeser Beckmann and William Percy Delamer soon realised that equipment could be manufactured, or at least assembled, in Ireland. In late 1960, the four men established Telectron Ltd., holding 100,000 ordinary £1 shares between them. The firm was established as a manufacturing partner of Technico Ltd.

Telectron Ltd

Telectron were 'manufacturers and assemblers of, and wholesaler and retailers in, television and radio transmitting and receiving apparatus and component parts'. The first directors were listed as Caeser Beckmann, of the Orchard, Bray Road, Bray; Dr Otto Glaser, 28 Glenomena Park, Stillorgan Road, Dublin; William Percy Delamer, Ardvullen, Ailesbury Road, Dublin; and Dr Kurt Ticher, Grasmere, Zion Road, Rathgar, Dublin.

Telectron Ltd initially operated out of an office at 15 Herbert Street in Dublin, while it commenced negotiation for a site with the IDA. Having been a Commander in the Irish Air Corps in 1922, William Percy Delamer was very familiar with the remarkable success of Urney Chocolates, on the old Aerodrome site. If a chocolate factory in Tallaght could achieve huge international success, there was no reason why a cutting-edge telecommunications company could not do the same.

After some negotiation, the firm secured a three-acre site on Main Road, Tallaght, in 1962, and extended it further two years later. The company employed principally 'draughtsmen' and 'female assembly workers' and, by the end of 1962, between Telectron and Technico they were employing 100 staff. CJ Bradley was appointed Director of Telectron Ltd.

By 1963, the company was already providing audio equipment to Raidió Éireann and Telefís Éireann, and was directly associated with the technical expansion of Telefís Éireann. That the soon-to-retire manager of Dublin Airport, William Percy Delamer, was now a partner and substantial shareholder in the manufacturing partner of Technico, which provided technical services to the Airport, appeared to bother no one.

Otto Glaser Jr had once declared his ambition to establish factories 'where he could see cows from the windows', and by the mid-1960s, he had achieved it.

In 1968, the private bank Guinness and Mahon Ltd and the Industrial Credit Company (ICC) took a share in Telectron Ltd, and the company received £23,000 in State grants and subsidies. A major expansion was announced in 1969, with the creation of 300 new jobs, bringing the workforce in Tallaght to 450. The jobs entailed a 40-hour, five-day week, with the promise of three weeks' holidays. The staff were mostly female, involved in light assembly work. Staff were in such demand that they were being bussed from Lucan to Tallaght by the company. The firm continued to grow, peaking in 1974 at almost 600 staff in Tallaght and exporting to 50 countries. The company even had its own football club, Telectron Athletic, which regularly played against local side Newtown Rangers.

In early 1980, Telectron announced a deal with French firm CIT Alcatel. The two companies had jointly tendered for a £40 million contract with the Irish Government to overhaul Ireland's telecommunications network, and the partnership was the preferred bidder. The £40m order was to be shared between the two companies.

It was announced that a joint enterprise – a factory – would be established in Bandon in County Cork. Telectron planned to increase its workforce nationally from 800 to 1,800. HB (Urney) Chocolates closed its factory gates in Tallaght for the last time that summer, and the workers of Tallaght hoped that the expansion of Telectron might help offset the job losses arising from Urney's demise.

CIT Alcatel had significantly more modern and advanced technological capability than Telectron. But Telectron had an established Irish presence and local production, distribution and installation capacity. It also had established relationships and a track record with Irish public sector utilities and bodies. This was the logic behind bringing CIT Alcatel and Telectron into a joint venture. There would be a transfer of technology from the French into Telectron and a build-up of the company into new-era technology.

The deal, however, was never progressed. Alcatel opened its own factory in Bandon in Cork to manufacture electronic exchanges, gaining a foothold in the Irish market in competition with the Irish firm.

Telectron had a turnover of £10 million and a workforce of 800 staff, with 600 in its Tallaght plant and another 200 across smaller factories in Donegal and the Aran Islands. Up to 60% of Telectron's products were bought by the Department of Posts and Telegraphs, with the remaining 40% exported to foreign markets and the Middle East.

The following year, Guinness Ireland Ltd took a 24% stake in the company, investing an undisclosed sum into the firm, with an option to acquire a further 6%. Guinness and Mahon Bank, an unrelated firm and one of the earliest investors in the firm, already held over 10%.

Guinness Ireland Ltd Chairman Mark Hely Hutchinson was a member of Bord Telecom Éireann. He promptly left the State board to join the Board of Telectron. Guinness Ireland Ltd had in recent years been keen to diversify its interests and, by 1980, up to 25% of the company's profits were coming from non-brewing-related activity.

Hely Hutchinson was one of Ireland's most respected and successful executives. An amateur jockey who rode for pleasure, he twice rode the racehorse Arkle in competitive races, losing on both occasions. The son of the Earl of Donoughmore, his parents had been kidnapped by the IRA back in 1974. He was educated at Eton and Oxford, before serving in the British Army. Hely Hutchinson was widely considered an honourable and effective executive of the highest ethical standards, at a time in Irish business when such standards could not be assumed. (Many years later, while still Chair of Guinness Ireland, when asked what he thought of the taste of the new 'Guinness Light', he paused and reflected before replying, 'Ghastly.')

In January 1982, ATTI, a subsidiary of American Telegraph & Telephone (AT&T) – one of the largest companies in the world and owner of Bell Communication and Western Electric – took a 45% stake in Telectron. Less than 21% of shares in the company were now held by the families of the original founding directors. Their shareholdings had, over time, been traded for significant capital injections to enable the company to expand and prosper.

ATTI were now the largest single shareholder. In the first three months after the deal, three sections of the Tallaght plant were closed by Bob Egan, the newly installed American executive director – the PBX division, the control systems division and the instrument division.

Telectron was meant to benefit from access to AT&T's international sales and marketing expertise. Logic suggested that demand for their products would surge. Instead, product lines were discontinued. As roles in the factory became vacant, they were not backfilled. Recruitment and promotions were frozen.

Frustration among the workforce grew and morale rapidly declined. By early 1983, almost 150 staff, mostly professional engineers and other skilled roles, had left the company. The remaining staff felt a dark foreboding.

In March 1983, only fourteen months after taking control of the company, Bob Egan issued a handout to all staff, informing them that the company intended to make 197 people redundant – almost a third of the total staff. It was all at odds with the announcement and fanfare declaring the partnership only fourteen months earlier, about how the two companies would be stronger together.

Dr Otto Glaser, who had his sold his entire share to ATTI, confident that it would strengthen and secure the Tallaght factory for many years to come, was utterly dismayed. But his views no longer had any bearing on the company's future. It was an annus horribilis for the Glaser family. William Percy Delamer, Glaser's father-in-law and fellow founding director of Telectron, died later that year, aged 83.

In April 1983, while talks were ongoing in Dublin between the ITGWU and local management, directors in America made a decision to wind up the company. On a Monday morning, 500 Telectron staff were told they were to be laid off the following Friday. A company that had successfully traded from Tallaght for twenty years, and one of the largest employers in the district, was wiped out in fifteen months.

In Dáil Éireann on Tuesday, 3 May 1983, standing orders were suspended by agreement between 6pm and 7pm, to allow statements to be made by members on the situation in relation to Telectron Limited. Deputies Sean Walsh TD (after whom Sean Walsh Park is named) and Mervyn Taylor TD were among those who made statements on the matter. Sean Walsh TD said:

> The Minister [John Bruton TD] assured us that the manufacture of the product would continue in Ireland, but unfortunately the Minister did not say where. I should like to know if the product will continue to be manufactured in Tallaght. Today the 500 workers of the factory turned out in a protest march. The position is very depressing for them and they are disillusioned about the whole situation. Tallaght has been described as a new town with a projected population of 175,000 people. When it was planned Telectron was one of the industries in the area which offered the prospects of secure employment for some of the population. Unfortunately, a number of the other firms have gone out of business due to the recession. As a local representative I was disappointed to hear last week of the decision to close the Telectron plant …

Tallaght had many old native industries over the years, but many of these have now disappeared. Successive governments down the years have told us of great strides in industry and advised that the time had come to concentrate on the technological side. This firm of Telectron showed great promise and offered a great future. What has happened here and what went wrong? Successive governments have injected large amounts of capital into this development by way of grants and this company have secured a major Government contract. Things appeared to be going well, but suddenly something went wrong. It is the duty of the Government to ensure a proper investigation, from the point of view of the workers.

Mervyn Taylor TD noted:

The level of unemployment in Tallaght is one of the highest in the country from the percentage point of view. It would be nothing short of a disaster if the new town of Tallaght were stricken by 500 job losses in one fell swoop at Telectron. Such an eventuality would cause tremendously increased depression in this town. It would have an effect far beyond the jobs actually lost, in that the loss of purchasing power of the workers and their families would work its way through the entire business system of this major, growing new town.

It is a matter of the utmost importance that those jobs be preserved. The Minister has suggested that nothing should be said here which might prejudice negotiations which are taking place. Of course, he is quite right there, up to a point. Nonetheless, we have responsibilities here, in particular those of us who represent the constituency of Dublin South-West, to raise a number of questions as to what went on in the matter of Telectron and its acquisition by the AT&T multinational company of the United States.

It has been pointed out here that Telectron were losing substantial amounts of money in recent years, yet it is only within the last year or so that AT&T, one of the major industrial complexes in the world, saw fit to buy and take over the Telectron company. Is it suggested that they did not do their homework, their sums and investigate what exactly was going on in Telectron before they parted with an appreciable sum of money, running into some millions of pounds? I doubt that. I think that they knew, as a result of investigations and examinations, exactly what the position was in Telectron, exactly what the prospects were and what the cash flow would be. I have no doubt that, if they wished, AT&T

could make a very viable company of Telectron and could import new research and development. That was denied to that company for many years past. Let us hope that the efforts of the Minister and the IDA will change that. The indications at present are that AT&T will not do that but that, on the contrary, they callously intend to close down that operation and put 500 unfortunate people and their families on to the dole.

… apart from any other consideration, very appreciable sums of money, which have been paid for by the taxpayers, have already gone into Telectron. The Irish people are entitled to expect that they will in the fullness of time reap the reward from that investment. We were told before, when some other industries fell down, that we cannot complain about that, that we must look forward and get into the new technologies. What newer or more beneficial technology can there be than electronics? The electronics industry has become a part of the life blood of this country and it is exemplified at Telectron at Tallaght.

I call on the Minister to ensure by every means, with the cooperation of AT&T or without it, even to the extent of taking over and nationalising that factory and running it as a State operation, that the vital and essential manufacturing capacity of the country is maintained and expanded. This industry has an essential key role to play in the future of the country and, given the opportunity and research and development, which has hitherto been denied it, I believe that henceforth it will prove itself not only to the satisfaction of its workers and of Tallaght but to the benefit of the entire country.

A number of stark facts were set out in relation to the closure of Telectron. The company had lost £10 million over the previous three years. There had, over a long period, been a lack of investment into modern plant and machinery. Research and development had not taken place. Telectron had retained a well-developed capacity to deliver and install old technology.

Telectron Ltd closed its Tallaght plant the following Friday. The social and economic consequences of the closure for the town of Tallaght was profound, coming as it did only three years after the closure of Urney. Young couples had met in Telectron, married, and taken mortgages based on two incomes from the long-established factory. The economic ripples of 500 jobs obliterated in one fell swoop would be felt throughout the community – in shops, in schools, in pubs and, not least, in homes.

Dr Otto Glaser lived in Howth, and remained active in the Irish telecommunications sector after the demise of Telectron. In the 1970s, his father, Otto Glaser Sr, by then widowed, left Austria and came to live his last years with his son and daughter-in-law in Howth.

In later life, Dr Glaser Jr became a Director of Coras Trachtála (the Irish Export Board), and of Dublin City University, and a Board member of the Dublin Institute for Advanced Studies. In retirement, he distinguished himself in sailing circles, sailing yachts competitively out of Howth. He was a fan of classical music and called his boat after a Polka by Johann Strauss II: *Tritsch-Tratsch*. He liked to tell an anecdote about Mozart, who he claimed was fond of an old Irish drinking song, 'Cruiskeen Lawn' ('little brimming jug'), and worked it into one of his own larger pieces – his Mass, where the song is now embedded.

In 1997, Dr Glaser, then President of the Irish Austrian Society, desired to support young Irish students to learn the German language. Having been educated in Ireland, he was looking for a way to give back and foster education of his native language. He founded the German Language Essay competition, which has been run every year since.

The company Technico, founded in 1953, continues to operate in Dublin. Since 1989, it has provided a range of optic fibre installation and test solutions to the Irish market.

Dr Kurt Ticher died on 2 November 1989. He was 91 years old. He left an estate of over £1.3m. In his lifetime, he donated almost £250,000 worth of silver antiques to the National Museum of Ireland. When Charles J Haughey presented a teapot to British Prime Minister Margaret Thatcher in 1980, the teapot had been part of Dr Kurt Ticher's silverware collection.

Dr Otto Glaser Jr died in his ninetieth year, in 2017. His wife Patricia died one month later. He is remembered fondly.

CHAPTER 12

The Best Laid Plans

In the early 1900s, many longstanding and substantial landholding families divested themselves of their holdings in Tallaght. Andrew Cullen (AC) Tynan, retiring from farming, sold almost 400 acres around Whitehall and Cookstown in 1901. Tynan, the father of writer Katharine Tynan, had inherited much of the land from an uncle. Tynan offered for sale over 260 acres at Cookstown, 71 acres at Cheeverstown, 66 acres at Newhall, 27 acres at Whitehall and fifteen acres at Ballymount. He did not relinquish his entire holding; members of the Tynan-O'Mahony family, notably Barry Tynan O'Mahony (an uncle of the comedian Dave Allen), would reside in Airfield into the early 1930s.

Some of this 'Tynan' land would later become an aerodrome, briefly the RAF base in Tallaght and, later still, Urney Chocolates. The Department of Defence would continue to hold over 50 acres up to the 1960s, letting the land for tillage.

The Lentaigne family of Tallaght House, despite not having lived in the area for over 60 years, only relinquished their remaining substantial interests in Tallaght in January 1919. Among the lands put up for auction was the site on which Tallaght Courthouse was built (held on a 99-year lease from Lentaigne, by Dublin County Council) and the RIC barracks. The auction was to take place in the actual Courthouse itself. They were quite literally selling the ground from under them.

Among the nineteen lots offered for sale were several houses and cottages with gardens, shops and yards in the village, including the house and yard adjoining Barrett's on Main Street, and Rose Ville cottage, which would be subject to a Compulsory Purchase Order 50 years later. Like a portion of Tynan's land, some of Lentaigne's land was let and occupied by HM Air Council, for the Aerodrome.

The Lentaignes had retained over 103 acres of land around the town, having disposed of only a portion of their holding to the Dominican Order 65 years earlier. Almost all of this land had once constituted the estate of the Archbishop of Dublin, which Lentaigne had secured with the acquisition of Major Palmer's interest in it. The auction of Lentaigne's land took place only two weeks before the outbreak of the War of Independence in Ireland. It was perhaps a timely departure. Captain EC Lentaigne, on whose behalf the auction was held, was serving overseas with British forces in the 4th Gurkas.

The Tynans and Lentaignes had been two of the most prominent Catholic families in Tallaght in the nineteenth century, holding substantial estates. Many of the principal landholding families in the district were related to each other through marriage – for the most part, Roman Catholic to Roman Catholic and Church of Ireland to Church of Ireland.

Some of the larger farms had been held by families belonging to the Church of Ireland and many of the finest headstones in Tallaght graveyard, casting their long shadows over untended plots, continue to serve as reminders of the families that once held large tracts and great sway in this small agricultural village. The Church of Ireland community was tight-knit, and many of the families were intermarried over several generations. In the late 1800s, it was still not uncommon for first or second cousins to marry. Through this process, at least six of the most notable families – the Foxes of Whitestown, Boothmans of Kiltipper, the Browns of Brookfield, Boardmans of Bolbrook, Stubbs of Newtown and the Flanagans of Walkinstown/Greenhills – were all interconnected through marriage. Of this list, only the Boardmans were not farmers and only the Stubbs and Flanagans not Church of Ireland.

In 1876, Richard Boothman of Kiltipper House married Mary Fox, Daughter of William Fox of Whitestown. James Fox of Whitestown was listed as a next of Kin of Robert Browne of Jobstown (Brookfield) in 1900. The Stubbs and Boardmans had both married into the Browns of Brookfield and Jobstown.

Vast tracts of Tallaght's prime agricultural land, stretching from the Dodder at Kiltipper across Whitestown to Jobstown, Fettercairn and Brookfield, were farmed by families inter-related through marriage, along with lands at Newtown and Bolbrook, Stubb's Lane and at

A Ramble About Tallaght

Greenhills and Walkinstown. By the 1950s, many of these families had either died out or had relinquished their holdings.

But not all large farms were held by those who attended Sunday worship. A small number of notable Catholic families also held substantial farms – the Bagnalls (Killininny, Ellenboro and Ballinscorney), Dunnes (Greenhills), Jordans (Oldbawn), Kennedys (Spawell), Mooneys (Fortunestown), Muldoons (Allenton and Millbrook), Poyntons (Bancroft) and Rafters (Tymon Lane) among them. Those families, sometimes large Catholic families in a small agricultural community, also married into each other.

The Muldoons of Allenton House and later Harlem House (Millbrook Lawns) and the Jordans of Oldbawn, for example, inter-married in 1867, when Michael Jordan of Oldbawn married Catherine Muldoon of Allenton. Three years later, Timothy Muldoon of Allenton House married Mary Jordan of Oldbawn. The Muldoons had substantial holdings south of the Dodder at Allenton, while Jordans held land on the north at Oldbawn. For several generations, those families played an active part not just in the farming life, but also in the political life of the community.

Main Street, Tallaght.

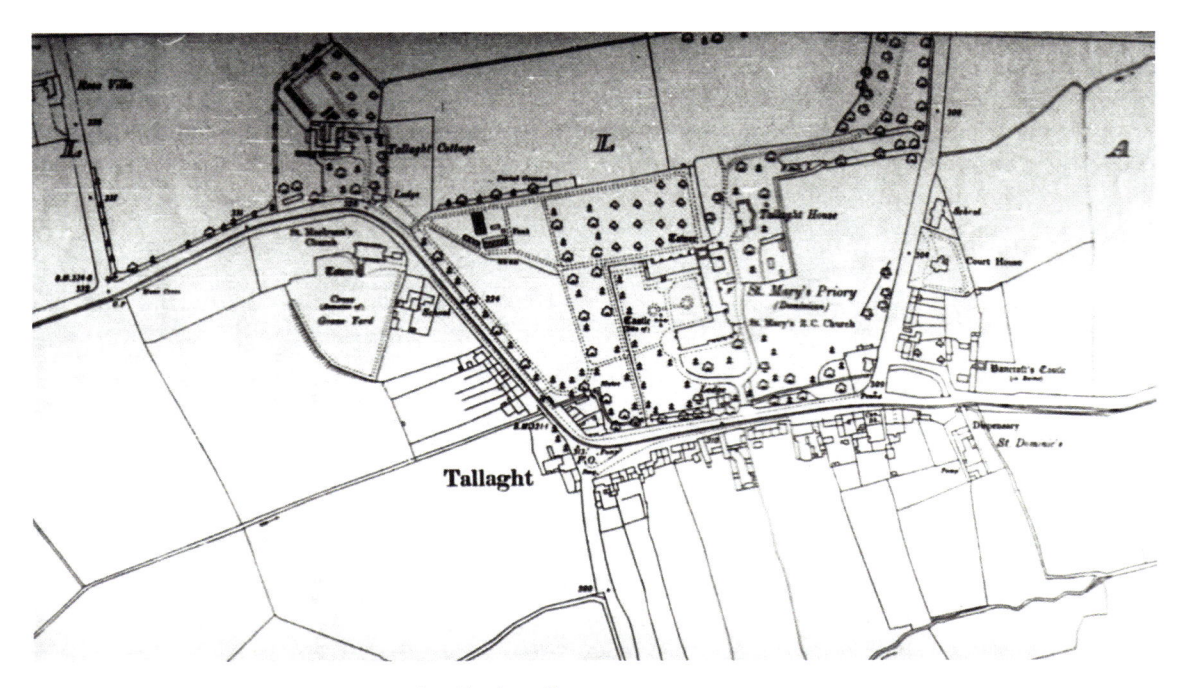

Ordnance Survey 25-inch map of Tallaght village, 1901.

The Bagnalls (of Ballinascorney) and Kennedys (of Spawell's and Mount Pelier) were connected through the marriage of Peter Kennedy and Greta Bagnall in 1930. Their familial connections were further consolidated ten years later in 1940, when John Kennedy married Mary Anne Bagnall. Tallaght was typical of many tight-knit, small farming communities in Ireland of that time.

Some large holdings had been split over successive generations and were ultimately disposed of incrementally. Some farmers, such as Austin Muldoon at Milbrook Lawns and Brendan Poynton in Bancroft, simply retired from the business in the 1960s and the lands were sold. Some farmers died 'without issue', and their land was disposed of by executors' sales.

Herbert 'Herbie' Steen of Kilnamanagh died in 1984 at 91 years of age. He had retired decades earlier and had disposed of 125 acres around Kilnamanagh Castle that had been farmed by his maternal family (Farrells) since the 1780s.

Some farmers sold up or divested their holdings as land values increased on the city's hinterland, and bought large holdings elsewhere. Some held on to the land into the 1980s, until they were made offers they simply could no longer refuse. They found themselves sitting on properties of such value that it simply made no sense to leave it undeveloped.

From the development of housing at 'Poynton's Estate' at Bancroft in the 1950s, the development potential of land around Tallaght began to get greater attention. By the time Myles Wright's The Dublin Region: Advisory Regional Plan and Final Report was published in 1967, developers and speculators had already acquainted themselves with the district and had begun to acquire potential development land. A draft of Wright's final Plan had earlier been circulated and that was enough to give confidence to both private and public interests to embark on a scramble for development land in the area.

Glenview and Bolbrook Lodge

In 1961, a number of parcels of farm land around Tallaght were bought by an industrious, educated and ambitious young communist. The land in Bolbrook and in Whitestown had, earlier in the century, been farmed by the Foxes, Boothmans and Stubbs.

This young man was Justin Keating, son of Irish romantic artist Sean Keating and Mary Walsh Keating, a socialist and feminist. Keating built a modern and comfortable home, Bolbrook Lodge, close to a declining farmhouse (near what is now Glenview Roundabout), in which to raise his three young children and to farm the small holding of 30 acres.

Keating had been educated at Sandford Park School in Dublin and then at University College Dublin, where he qualified in Veterinary Medicine. He went on to study Animal Physiology in the University of London. From 1955 to 1960, he lectured in Anatomy at UCD Veterinary College, before securing a position in 1960 as Senior Lecturer in Trinity College, Dublin. After this appointment, the 30-year-old Keating set about acquiring a hobby farm in Tallaght.

In the years following his move to Tallaght, Keating enjoyed considerable professional success, accepting a prestigious role with RTÉ in 1965 as editor of agricultural programmes. He scripted and presented a 48-part series, *Telefís Feirme*, for which he won a Jacob's Award in 1966. Keating was a busy man and Bolbrook Lodge was one of the few homes in Tallaght to have a telephone installed at the time.

On his farm, he confined himself to growing grain: 'Growing of grain does not take up as much time as other aspects of farming and requires less labour,' the nationally recognised figure noted.

Allenton House, home to the Muldoon family.

Only six years after acquiring the land, Keating sought to reduce his holding. His land at Bolbrook was put up for auction in March 1967 by estate agents Murphy, Buckley and Keogh. The land advertised had 'valuable development potential'. On 5 February 1968, Justin Keating accepted an offer from Dublin Corporation to purchase his land at Tallaght. He had held the land for seven years.

Keating had purchased the land at agricultural prices and sold it to Dublin Corporation for over £2000 per acre. It was reportedly the highest price ever paid for land in Tallaght at the time. As a private citizen, his business dealings were a private matter. But the following year, Justin Keating made his first attempt at running for a seat in Dáil Éireann, as a Labour Party candidate for North Dublin. It was noted that he 'first became a member of the Labour Party in 1946'. That may well have been true. In the interim, however, he had been a member of the communist Irish Worker's Party.

Justin Keating was elected on his first political outing. The private business dealings of a very public socialist would now become a matter of public record, and Keating's land deal in

A Ramble About Tallaght

Tallaght was the subject of regular and acrimonious exchanges in Dáil Éireann.

It was one of the first, but not the last, land purchases by a local authority in the area that would raise issues of legitimate public interest and become grist for the political mill. The character, ethics and reputation of people holding positions of influence or land in Tallaght would be as tested as the patience and fortitude of those families soon to inhabit the 'new town'.

In 1956, five years before Keating bought his land in Bolbrook, Rafter's 136-acre farm at Tymon Lane had been sold for £14,300. It gives some indication of the price of agricultural land in the area in that period.

CPO city

The first wave of Compulsory Purchase Orders (CPOs) under the 1966 Housing Act were announced for Tallaght in April 1971. The compulsory purchasing of land was a time-consuming process, and could take a number of years to complete, from announcement of the order to closing the title.

Lands listed for compulsory purchase in April 1971 were finally confirmed in 1974. They included: 248 acres attached to Fettercairn House; 277 acres on the Blessington road; 89 acres attached to Brookfield House; 51 acres on Fortunestown Lane; 24 acres attached to Virginia House; fifteen acres attached to Newhall; seventeen acres at Rosevilla; 97 acres at Killinarden (in four holdings) and eighteen acres at Kiltipper; twenty acres on the Oldbawn Road; and eighteen acres at Westpark, nearer the village.

George Nolan's farmhouse at Glenview.

Dozens of other smaller and marginal holdings were included in that first list. The Dominican Order had acquired 95 acres of agricultural farmland in Killinarden in 1964. Thirty of those acres were now to be acquired by the Local Authority under a CPO, for the building of the Tallaght Bypass. The Dominicans would hold on to the remaining 65 acres in Killinarden until 1989, before finally selling them 'at a low rate' to the Local Authority for social housing and public recreational use.

In addition to the publicly declared list of holdings subject to CPOs, the Corporation and County Council also bought land directly from farmers, negotiated through agents. In the spring of 1967, the City Manager of Dublin City Council confirmed he had already purchased 100 acres of land in Tallaght for development. He reported that speculators and private developers were already buying sites in Tallaght with a view to holding on to them for inflated values. (This was twelve months before the Corporation acquired the Keating land.)

There was nothing preventing farmers from disposing of their land privately, even after it had been listed for compulsory purchase. Some of the lands listed for compulsory purchase in 1971 were sold privately, before the CPO process could be executed. Nor was there anything to prevent the local authority from selling on land that had been acquired by them under a CPO. The very earliest transactions in Tallaght, and later ones too, were mired in rumour, innuendo and suspicion.

Jim Guinan, Chair of the Finance and General Purpose Committee of Dublin County Council, was reportedly outraged when he learned that 240 acres of land at Fettercairn – land listed for compulsory purchase in 1971 – had been sold on by the farmer, Pa Mooney, to a private developer. Dublin Corporation proceeded to buy the land off the developer for an 'enhanced price', only five months after the developer had purchased it.

The Chair was apoplectic when he further discovered that the Corporation had given an undertaking that it would give 100 acres of the 240-acre development site back to the developer for building on – after roads, pipes and drains had been laid.

In May 1975, space for a shopping centre was 'reserved' on the site. The following November, Dublin Corporation announced it was to undertake £609,000 worth of groundworks, with the installation of distributor roads, pipes and drains on the site. In December 1977, the layout plan for 182 houses for the Fettercairn estate was approved.

A Ramble About Tallaght

Guinan, as Chair of the Committee, also expressed concern about another site close to Fettercairn. A seventeen-acre site at the junction of the Belgard Road and Blessington Road, zoned industrial and also subject to a CPO fifteen months earlier, had in the previous month been bought privately by a developer. Guinan accused Dublin Corporation of effectively 'collaborating with developers'. It was perhaps a forerunner of what in later decades would come to be known as 'public/private partnerships', with public investment virtually guaranteeing private profit – dressed with a veneer of respectability.

Mooney's farm at Fettercairn House was one of the largest farms in the district, farmed by Patrick 'Pa' Mooney and his family for much of the twentieth century. Mooney was a prominent and active member of the Farmers Protection Association, along with some of Tallaght's other largest farmers – the Jordans of Oldbawn, Muldoons of Allenton, Kennedys of Spawell and Larry Dunne of Greenhills. Patrick Mooney died in 1971. He was remembered as having had the first mechanised threshing mill in South County Dublin.

Greenhills Road in the 1960s.

The acquisition of Mooney's farm was not entirely unrepresentative of the process by which Tallaght – the village, townland and outskirts – was about to be transformed. A lack of transparency, accountability and cohesion appeared to be the defining characteristic of the process through which the new *Outline Development Plan for Tallaght 1971* was to be advanced.

Millbrook Lawns

After the demise of Harlem Mills, the land at Harlem House (Millbrook Lawns), came into the Muldoon family, historically associated with Allenton House. For much of the 1930s, 1940s and 1950s, it was farmed by Austin Muldoon. Austin ran a dancehall and at times in the 1930s a shebeen here, occasionally running afoul of Garda Nyhan. Harlem had been farmed by, and had been home to, John and Belinda Muldoon in the 1920s, before Belinda died tragically at the hands of her husband John. The notable Irish writer Alice Furlong was resident in the house on the night, and was called as a witness in the case.

When Austin Muldoon retired from farming, the land was acquired for development. The public 'green space' leading east from the Oldbawn Road, parallel and to the north of Seskin View Road, is the original avenue to Harlem House and Mills. A small bungalow was built by widower Austin Muldoon for himself and his housekeeper (and sister-in-law) Bridie Brady, in what came to be known as Brady's Field, the field at the junction of Seskin View Road and Oldbawn Road.

After Bridie's death, Austin Muldoon lived in the bungalow he named St Colman's. He died in 1969, leaving an impressive estate of £77,548. St Colman's and the land was acquired by the Local Authority and became home to a municipal park ranger. Brady's Field became playing fields for the local soccer club. The bungalow was damaged by fire in 2021, having been vacant for a number of years. It was levelled in 2021 to make way for social housing for older people, the construction of which is presently underway (spring 2023).

A Ramble About Tallaght

Bancroft Estate – Poynton's Farm and Bancroft's Castle

The Poynton family had farmed around Tallaght since at least the 1840s and around Bancroft's Castle since before the late John Poynton died in 1873. John Poynton died intestate, later giving rise to a fracture in the Poynton family in 1918 between his sons, Frank and Joseph. A third brother, John Jr, had left the place. John Poynton Sr had left an interest in three farms – the Stonehouse, the Upper Commons and Castle Bancroft.

Frank Poynton died childless in 1919, very shortly after the legal wrangle with his brother. In 1948, Joseph Poynton put 61 acres of his land up for sale. He was ageing and in poor health and died only eight months later, aged 77 years.

Quirk and Towey builders completed the first houses in Poynton's Estate, 'four-bed Grant-type houses', in 1953. One notable resident of the area was Din Joe (Denis) Fitzgibbons, the RTÉ broadcaster and national celebrity, best known for his radio programme 'Take the Floor', in which people danced on national radio. We are, no doubt, a poorer country for having lost such shows. Din Joe's house, Green Gables, was burgled in June 1960, along with two of his neighbours. A wristwatch and a packet of tea appeared to be all that was taken.

The opening years of the 1960s saw residential development at Bancroft Estate get into full swing, with the proposed developed of up to 180 private houses. It was the largest single housing development and first substantial private housing scheme in Tallaght's history at the time. The main contractor on the estate was Patrick Flynn. On 22 February 1963, Minister for Social Welfare Kevin Boland opened the first 'all electric show-house'. The ground-floor living area had electric warm flooring or 'underfloor heating', while the rest of the house had wall-installed electric convector heaters. The bathroom benefitted from an infra-red heater. Houses in Bancroft were offered for between £3000 and £4000, depending on the number of bedrooms, heating options and specifications.

These were fine houses, aimed at the educated, skilled and upwardly mobile – those enjoying the fruits or the expectations of Lemass's First Programme for Economic Expansion. The substantial residential development would underwrite the social and economic life of the village, without putting too great a strain on local infrastructure. The continued growth and success of Urney Chocolates and the opening of Telectron the previous year, on a three-acre site close to

The Best Laid Plans

The Glen Abbey (left) and Gallaher (right) facilities in the late 1960s.

the estate, brought an economic optimism to the town, underpinned by longterm local employment in Glen Abbey Textiles (Barnes Brothers) since 1946, Gallahers Tobacco, and Johnson and Johnson, which had taken the old Redbreast factory in 1955. Tallaght in 1962 was a beautiful, prosperous and rapidly industrialising town. Optimism was high in the district.

That spring, Brendan Poynton announced he was retiring from dairy farming. He put an advert in the paper announcing the sale of his agricultural machinery at Bancroft. He still held at least eleven acres of 'old meadow'. The building of Bancroft estate had marked in dramatic fashion the beginning of the transition of Tallaght from a small, tight-knit agricultural community, to a growing suburb. But it was only a hint of what was to follow.

Killinarden House

In August 1947, a fine Georgian residence, set on 32 acres with a walled vegetable garden, was put up for auction. The estate, held by the Irish Land Commission, included over 4000 apple trees (mostly dessert apples), planted over 26 acres, and 2.5 acres of plum trees. All had been planted in the previous twelve years and were in full production. Killinarden House, a 'non-basement Georgian type', was in a good state of repair, a considerable sum having been expended on it in recent years. It included a hall, cloak-cupboard, scullery, pantries, WC, four family bedrooms, bathroom, drawing room and dining room. It benefitted from electric light and power from the Shannon Scheme.

A hundred years earlier, in the 1850s, Killinarden House had been occupied for a time by William Ebbs. Ebbs was the land agent for Dominick Trant, Esq., nephew and heir to Henry Dillan Trant of Belgard. Trant held extensive estates in the district.

Killinarden House had most recently been occupied by the McGarry Family, into whose possession it had come through the marriage of James B Toomey and Elisabeth Clare McGarry in 1917. On the death of Toomey, a widower and owner of the Jobstown House, it passed to his wife's family, the McGarrys. McGarry had previously held McGarry's public house in Firhouse (more recently known as Morton's) before she married Toomey.

Killinarden House and much of the land attached to it was taken by Tom Harty, a notable Tipperary hurler back in the 1930s and by the 1960s one of the most successful greyhound trainers in the country. He kept up to 40 dogs in his kennels at Killinarden House – dogs such as Killinarden Tornado and Killinarden Lady. In 1962, Harty, along with James 'The Jingler' McDermott, attempted to establish a south Dublin course club at lands in Jobstown. The Jingler briefly held the Jobstown House at the time, while Harty had Killinarden House.

When the land came to be acquired under CPO for the construction of the Tallaght Bypass and Local Authority housing in the 1970s, Harty built a new house for himself on the Blessington Road in Saggart, with a commanding view of the city. He called his home Montana. He salvaged the ancient iron gates of Killinarden House, and took them with him to his new home. In 1992, Tom Harty was inducted into the 'Hall of Fame' at the National Greyhound Awards. Knockmore National School now stands close to the original site of Killinarden House and its orchards.

The Jordans of Oldbawn

By the 1970s, the Jordan family had farmed in Oldbawn for 130 years, since the 1840s. Jordan family lore transmitted down through the generations tells a tale from the 1798 Rebellion, in which four of the Jordan men were killed and a fifth captured and executed on 'Billy's Bridge' (Edmonstown Bridge). On the night of his hanging, the story goes, their father died of a broken heart.

In the early 1840s, the Jordans occupied a modest cottage in Oldbawn, close to Tallaght village, from which they were evicted. They briefly decamped to Rockbrook (Mount Venus), before

An advert for Old Bawn Dairy, Irish Independent, *13 July 1937.*

Mick Jordan secured a lease on Angler's Cottage in 1845, from the Tynte's of Dunlavin, into whose possession the original Oldbawn House had come.

Angler's Cottage was a short distance northwest of the Oldbawn Bridge, over the River Dodder. As the original Oldbawn House fell into disrepair, Angler's Cottage acquired the title of Oldbawn House, and the name was, for many years, painted on the entrance piers to the house. The Jordans later acquired Park House, another substantial residence – the old keeper's lodge beside the ancient Oldbawn House.

At the turn of the century, Michael Jordan, an ambitious and progressive farmer, endorsed what was then the latest farming technology – the Universal Cultivator.

In the following years, Michael's youngest son, Patrick, married Mary Leavy of Castle Nugent House, Granard, Co. Longford. They put a £300 extension onto Angler's Cottage, including three large bedrooms, a pantry, a breakfast room and an exterior bathroom mounted on four concrete pillars with a 2000-gallon steel water tank sitting overhead on its roof. A hay-shed was erected a couple of years later in the haggard.

The lean years following the First World War proved a challenging time for dairy farmers and all available measures were taken to manage costs and maximise income. In 1923, Patrick Jordan was fined fifteen shillings for selling new milk from which fifteen percent of its original fats had been extracted. Jordan could not account for the deficiency. He explained the milk was sold as it came from the cow!

Jordan's farm went from strength to strength and in 1952, Patrick Jordan of Oldbawn bought a 194-acre farm in Trim, Co. Meath, for £9,700. Jordan was one of 200 bidders for the farm. His son Vincent continued to farm in Oldbawn and became a prominent member of the Dublin Farmers' Association. In 1962, Vincent Jordan hosted demonstrations of the latest agricultural technology, a 'Rivierre Casalis Variable Density Baler', on his farm in Oldbawn. An advert for the new machinery was reminiscent of the 'Universal Cultivator' endorsed by his grandfather over sixty years earlier.

A Ramble About Tallaght

Two years later, David Jordan, Vincent's son, won the Hughes' Trophy for best minor Dublin ploughman. He was seventeen years old and was well on his way to keeping the Jordan family tradition of farming alive in Oldbawn.

On Monday, 24 April 1967, at 6.30am, there was a knock on the door of Oldbawn House – the Jordans' farmhouse. It was the Gardaí, with a warrant for the arrest of David Jordan. Similar raids were taking place on farms throughout the country, involving 350 Gardaí and several hundred soldiers.

Vincent Jordan was President of the Lucan Branch of the National Farmers' Association and he and his son David were active in National Farmers' Association protests. Earlier that year, young David Jordan had taken part in a road blockade, as part of an NFA national protest. Young Jordan had been arrested and was fined £21 or faced three months in prison in default. The fine had not been paid.

Over 40 other farmers from around the country were rounded up throughout the day and locked up for non-payment of similar fines in relation to the earlier protest, or for not paying rates. One such farmer was Sean Collier, a farmer from Kilmessan in Co. Meath and a panel member of the Meath senior hurling team, who was due to play Kerry in Croke Park that weekend. Many farmers had goods and property seized in the raids for non-payment of rates, including Michael Gibbons, the brother of Jim Gibbons, Parliamentary Secretary for Finance. A meeting of the National Executive of the NFA had been scheduled for that night.

Oldbawn Bridge over the River Dodder.

It was, according to the National Farmers' Association, a 'declaration of war'. NFA pickets were placed outside Mountjoy Prison, where the farmers were held. Vincent Jordan held a placard stating 'Farmers Jailed For Farmers' Rights'. Nineteen of the farmers were transferred to Portlaoise from Mountjoy that evening.

Throughout the 1960s, the Jordans of Oldbawn played an active part in the farming community, nationally, regionally and locally. In 1968, Jordans' farm in Oldbawn hosted the All-Ireland National Sheep Shearing Championships, sponsored by Macra na Feirme. Close to 50 competitors from around the country would demonstrate their shearing prowess, and 35 Macra members from eighteen counties contested the sheep judging championships.

Vincent continued to farm in Oldbawn into the 1970s, but incrementally sold the land, parcel by parcel. He eventually moved out and sold the house in the late 1980s, having been tormented by numerous break-ins. Oldbawn House (or Angler's Cottage), the old Jordan family homestead, was finally demolished and cleared in 1998 to make way for a new housing development, Riverview. All that remains is a portion of the old farmyard wall.

In August 1970, the summer before the publication of the Outline Development Plan for Tallaght, Vincent Jordan, one of perhaps the last generation of Tallaght's large farmers on the low lands, hosted the South County Dublin Games Association and Bohernabreena Branch of Macra Na Feirme's 7th Annual Field Day on his farm in Oldbawn. On Vincent Jordan's land that day, the people of Tallaght and further afield gathered to enjoy sheepdog trials, a gymkhana, a tractor-backing contest, an exhibition of ornamental birds, a donkey derby, a treasure hunt for children and a bonny baby contest.

A few modest housing developments had been constructed in Tallaght in the previous three decades. The building of Newtown and the development of Maelruain's Park – or 'Mellors' to those who grew up there in the 1950s – preceded the development of the new Poynton's Estate and Bancroft, the first large private development in Tallaght in the 1960s. More recently, Westpark estate had been under construction to the southwest of the old village. (The first 49 houses of Westpark were completed in September 1969 and, in February 1970, Westpark Residents' Association was formed.)

The Field Day in Oldbawn, unbeknownst to those in attendance, perhaps marked the end of an era. It brought to a close the agricultural era in Oldbawn and Tallaght and marked the beginning of a suburban revolution.

Ballycullen farm

In September 1981, it was reported that two brothers, Chris and Gerry Jones, were set to make a profit of £15 million following a decision by Dublin County Council to ignore planning and engineering advice and rezone a Tallaght farm for housing and industrial use. The 190-acre farm at Ballycullen had been bought by the brothers about nineteen years earlier for £60,000.

The motion to rezone the land was proposed by Fianna Fáil TD Sean Walsh. Kevin O'Donnell, Dublin Chief Engineer, strongly advised councillors not to adopt it, due to concerns about sewage and road infrastructure. Dublin County Council voted by fifteen votes to four to rezone the land.

Gerry Jones had previously been a member of the Fianna Fáil National Executive and was a close personal friend of then ex-Taoiseach Charles J Haughey. Jones, who wore a distinctive eye patch, had been a prominent supporter of Haughey during the Arms Trial. Over 1,700 objections or 'representations' were made in relation to the rezoning. Dublin County Council's decision was a curious one.

Sixty-two-year-old Gerry Jones was recorded as stating at the time of the rezoning, 'We have a good track record and are not up for the fast buck … We did not enter into any conspiracy with any group to deny the County Council the land for houses for working class people.' Gerry noted his brother Chris was now going to be Managing Director of the Jones Group, 'now [that] I am going to sit back and take a bit of a rest'.

Many years later, it would be revealed at the Mahon Tribunal into planning irregularities that the Jones Group had later made cash payments to the disgraced Fianna Fáil TD Liam Lawlor, totalling over £15,900, for 'planning advice' in relation to further rezoning of lands at Ballycullen. The Company Secretary and a director of the Jones Group was Derry Hussey, husband of Government Minister Gemma Hussey. Derry was an advisor to Fine Gael and a confidante of Garret FitzGerald. Derry Hussey was later appointed Chair of VHI by a Fine Gael minister.

Carty's Castle casts its shadow over an ever-expanding Tallaght.

Houses, houses and more houses

Following Myles Wright's *The Dublin Region: Advisory Regional Plan and Final Report* of 1967, which proposed the establishment of planned new suburbs in Tallaght, Clondalkin, Lucan and Blanchardstown, the 1971 *Outline Development Plan for Tallaght* proposed that the town be developed as a 'super-satellite' of Dublin.

Wright's plan was never formally adopted by Government, but nor was it ignored. The 1972 Dublin County Development Plan, the local authority's first such plan, broadly reflected Wright's regional framework. However, a number of critical components of Wright's strategy were, at best, neglected. The model on which the 1967 *Regional Plan* was based had previously been successfully introduced in the UK, generally implemented by a single local authority or corporation. Those corporations in the UK had been empowered and resourced to coordinate and execute large-scale urban developments, involving multi-faceted public service delivery.

Myles Wright had incorporated a key warning in his final Regional Plan, concerning the difficulties in implementation of such plans, as experienced in Britain and in Europe. He noted: 'The successful carrying out of a Dublin Regional Plan will require guidance by a body specifically charged with that duty. Without such continued guidance a Regional Plan is likely to have little lasting influence. This has been proved many times in other countries.' No such agency in Dublin was appointed. While Dublin County Council had a mandate, it was neither empowered, resourced or equipped to effectively coordinate the implementation of such an ambitious strategy.

Under the 1971 *Outline Development Plan for Tallaght*, 5000 acres of land would be developed to become home, in time, to up to 136,000 inhabitants. 2151 acres would be for low-density residential development (ten houses per acre); 1410 for open space; 534 for industry; 120 for town centre; 455 for education and institutions; 100 for neighbourhood centres – shops, libraries, community centres and clinic – and 300 for major roads.

Coming out of the 1960s, the new model of suburbia, as had been developed in the UK and elsewhere, was predicated on the assumption that every household would have access to at least one motor car, if not two. It was, if not an optimistic assumption, at least a premature one.

The layout and street plans as they emerged in Tallaght were also predicated on the provision of 'shuttle bus' services to the main transport arteries, ultimately destined for the Town Centre. The 1967 Report, on which the *Outline Development Plan for Tallaght* was broadly based, could not have been more specific:

> We recommend that attention should be given to the introduction of small 10 or 12 seater buses that would serve a single district or two adjoining districts and start and end their journeys at points served by the express bus services. These points should be at shopping centres. They would be the destinations of many local bus passengers and the other passengers could fill in their time or at least wait under cover until their express bus arrived. The general proposal … shows in one case a loop service in a new town, and in the other a 'spine' service. Both begin and end at the principal shopping centre.

The planners of Tallaght New Town favoured the development of low-density residential estates over high-density or high-rise developments. This was, at least in part, a reaction to the overcrowding of the city's tenement slums and the more recent development of the 36 high-rise developments in Ballymun in the early 1960s, some of which reached fifteen storeys, and which had facilitated the clearance of city tenements.

Open space at Cushlawn, 1994.

Most of the planned residential schemes for Tallaght New Town were to be 'owner-occupied' and planners calculated that both banks and prospective buyers would favour low-density neighbourhoods. As noted by McCarron (1998), far higher residential densities had successfully been achieved in British new towns, but the products of the British new town development corporations were viewed as quasi-public housing. This was firmly avoided in Dublin.

Low-density developments, however, did not necessarily provide a critical mass of public transport passengers. Low housing densities, and the use of cul-de-sacs, also increased the cost of providing doorstep public services, such as refuse collection and postal deliveries.

Low-density developments also gave rise to vast tracts of essentially underutilised land, what MacLaren & Punch (2004) referred to as

> virtually functionless open spaces, the Dakota-like landscape presenting (a) striking example of 'prairie planning' … The non-urban appearance of the residential streets is reinforced by the ubiquitous grass strips between pavement and highway. Neither was the urban character enhanced by the regulations for carriageway width stipulated by local authority roads engineers to ensure that emergency services

vehicles could gain access to residential areas with ease and at speed. These have resulted in excessively wide tertiary-level roads and a residential environment that lacks any intimacy or visual complexity.

'Clean-sweep development' practices involved the removal of trees, hedges and old boundary walls, to maximise economy and profitability in the layout of estates, thus depriving the new neighbourhoods of mature greenery or any features predating the new development.

The lack of a single local authority or corporation with appropriate powers to coordinate the development of the town was a fundamental failing. The scramble for development land by large private-sector interests, often competing with two local authorities (Dublin Corporation and Dublin County Council) for the same land, who were themselves competing with each other, contributed to a lack of coordination and cohesion in the timely development of residential, industrial and commercial sites. It had been assumed that by the time a critical mass of residential units had been developed, industrial and commercial developments would have come to fruition to provide employment and economic opportunities to the emerging community. For many years, this synergy or cohesion eluded Tallaght New Town.

The defunding of local authorities through the abolition of residential rates in the late 1970s did little to enhance Dublin County Council's capacity for the development and delivery of critical infrastructure. The income it did receive from the exchequer failed to keep up with burgeoning inflation rates. The zoning of land for low-density residential housing had already diminished the viability and efficiency of essential public services.

As the new town of Tallaght emerged, it became apparent that some of the assumptions underpinning the planning and layout of the town had been flawed. The socio-economic profile of the emerging town failed to reflect the somewhat optimistic assumptions that the development plans were based on.

The economic slump in the early 1980s came at a critical time, contributing to a decline in employment and household income across all estates, and a rise in debt, in both local authority and private residential estates. Rising interest rates compounded an already dire economic outlook, impacting disproportionately on mortgage holders in the private estates. (The majority of residential development in Tallaght – over 60 per cent of the total by 1985 – was undertaken by private-sector developers building for owner occupation.) It is believed that some banks 'red circled' certain private estates in Tallaght at the time and were unwilling to lend to buy houses in those estates.

Assumptions around car ownership made in the late 1960s – an essential component in the design of many of the new estates – also proved to be false. As late as 1991, nearly 40 percent of households in Tallaght lacked access to a car. Car ownership rates in the large public-housing districts of west Tallaght amounted to barely twenty percent.

Cushlawn Park, 1994.

A Ramble About Tallaght

There was a prolonged lack, from 1972 to 1989, of any meaningful 'town centre', to provide a focal point in the community. The layout of estates and the location of those estates, predicated on the assumption of car ownership, mitigated against the efficient provision of public transport. The layout and use of cul-de-sacs in large outlying estates at a distance from primary transport routes essentially meant that only small, ten- or twelve-seater buses could access those areas.

Taking the above points together, not only was there nowhere to go, but even if there had been, many people had no real means of getting there. In 1971, the population of Tallaght was 6,174. Fifteen years earlier, in 1956, it had been 710. But by 1991, the population would top 60,000. This population growth was one of the few projections that had come to pass.

In 1987, a full twenty years after Myles Wright had noted the absolute necessity of a shuttle bus service for the new town, a 'Localink' hail-and-ride bus service was piloted in Tallaght. The success of the pilot scheme 'exceeded all expectations', according to the then-Minister for Transport. In the first two years of the scheme, over 11,000 people had regularly used the service. 'The Localink is designed to provide a proper and convenient public transport network for people in major suburbs,' the Minister stated. This appeared to be quite distinct from the traditional bus service that had served Tallaght during the previous two decades.

Only after The Square opened in 1990 did a meaningful 'town centre' emerge. The provision of the City Imp shuttle bus service, serving the dispersed estates of west Tallaght and the new town centre, transported not just customers to the new centre but, perhaps more importantly, workers to access new employment opportunities in the growing town centre.

Andrew MacLaran and Michael Punch of the Centre for Urban and Regional Studies, in their 2004 paper titled 'Tallaght: The planning and development of an Irish new town', gave a rigorous, academic and scathing assessment of the process through which the new town of Tallaght emerged:

> The development of Tallaght ... became primarily an experiment in the ability of a single local authority to facilitate private-sector residential, industrial and commercial development in specified localities ... Meanwhile, the provision of urban amenities depended upon the coordination of a variety of public bodies' expenditure plans in order to put in place a highly restricted range of public services which, all too frequently, were of indifferent quality ... Bereft of adequate powers to implement the development

plan and of the ability to control the most vital development resource, that of land, the local authority witnessed the emergence of a scramble for land between large-scale housing developers desperate to acquire large amounts of land zoned for development. Land dealing became a significant and profitable element in the development of the new residential areas, developers with large parcels subdividing their holdings and selling them on to smaller builders … Moreover, the acquisition of development land by a disparate array of private sector developers and small builders ensured that any public control of the phasing of development was rendered impossible, conditions prevailing within the private market becoming the sole determinant … The landscape which has emerged is profoundly monotonous and a visual testimony to developers' profitability criteria. Moreover, the inadequacy with which planning conditions were officially enforced saw developers often failing to provide adequate footpaths, public lighting and play spaces … the adoption of Radburn layout principles in the public housing development at Castle Park Estate, providing for vehicular access to the rear of dwellings, although this has become less than visually attractive with the subsequent development of a shanty-like township of garages in back gardens.

According to Radburn Theory, the design of a residential community should be focused on creating a central green space, surrounded by homes. All the homes would face inward toward the green space, while streets and alleys would be located on the periphery of the community.

In conclusion, Maclaren and Punch noted:

> The main beneficiaries of the entire process were the developers and landowners who were best positioned to take advantage of the local authority's reliance on private-sector activity to undertake much of the residential development. At the same time, significant costs were imposed on the prospective residents, who effectively had least input into the control and management of the new urban environment. The bankruptcy of imagination in design and landscaping, the clean-sweep approach to development and the imperatives of private-sector profit maximisation conspired to create a monotonous suburban landscape.

The outcomes of this process would have important long-term ramifications for those who moved to, or were born into, Tallaght New Town in the 1970s.

CHAPTER 13

The Coming of Age of Tallaght New Town

Let there be churches

In July 1974, before any new churches had been built in Tallaght and two years after the Dominican Order had been entrusted with the entirely new Parish of Tallaght by Archbishop Dr Dermot Ryan, three parochial houses were established in private houses in the newly built housing estates. These were 232 Balrothery Estate, 22 Millbrook Lawns and 39 Pineview in Oldbawn. Each house would accommodate two or three Dominican priests, living out in the community in which they would work, while new churches with adjoining accommodation were being built.

Church of St Dominic, Millbrook Lawns

On a balmy summer's day, 21 July 1975, the Church of St Dominic in Millbrook Lawns was blessed and opened. The £123,000 church, designed by architect Edward N Smith and built by Murphy Bros., could seat 800 parishioners. The Tallaght Youth Choir sang during the service, under the baton of a youthful Reverend Donal Sweeney OP.

Edward N Smith was familiar with the neighbourhood. He had designed a primary school in Oldbawn the previous year and would design a national school in Belgard Heights in 1976; a primary school in Woodlawn Park in Firhouse 1976; a national school in Fettercairn in1979; the extension of St Mark's Primary School in Springfield in 1982; and the primary school in Killinarden 1982.

An innovative feature of the building in Millbrook Lawns was the inclusion of a 'week-day chapel' – a smaller chapel for weekday mass goers under the curtilage of the main building, interconnected with the Parochial Office and Presbytery.

St Dominic's Church had residential accommodation onsite for three priests, who were tasked with serving all of the devout north of the River Dodder and east of Oldbawn Road, taking in Avonbeg, Bawnville, Bolbrook, Homelawns, Millbrook Lawns, Mountain Park and Seskin View. The building was built close to the site of the old Harlem House and Paper Mills, worked 100 years earlier by the Neill family.

The building was designed to save parishioners the embarrassment of being seen calling to a detached presbytery. Having priests in residence would also minimise the opportunity for vandalism to parochial property. The Church of St Dominic in Millbrook Lawns replaced a temporary prefabricated church that had served the area for the previous five years – the Church of Our Lady of Loreto, set down in Mountain Park on the Oldbawn Road.

Church of St Mark the Evangelist, Springfield

Only a week after St Dominic's was opened south of the village, a new church was opened in Springfield, to the west, replacing a small, temporary church that had served the area since December 1972. The Church of St Mark the Evangelist in Springfield was blessed on 27 July 1975. A more modest affair, the 800-seater cost a meagre £85,000 and took just six months to construct. Parish Priest Father Richard Sherry thanked all those in the diocese who contributed to the cost of the new building. Father Martin Noone was the Curate.

Church of St Aengus, Tymon North/Balrothery

Six months after St Dominic's and St Mark's were blessed, on 14 December 1975, the Church of St Aengus was opened in Tymon North by Archbishop Dr Dermot Ryan. Six hundred houses had been built in the locality in the preceding years and another 900 houses would be completed in the eighteen months following the blessing. Designed by Edward W Brady (who had designed the extension to St Mary's in 1969), it cost £80,000 and could seat 800 parishioners.

Few people in Tallaght knew that it would soon have a twin. Three months later, on 7 March 1976, an almost identical church, St Luke the Evangelist in Kilmore West, Coolock, was opened. Also designed by Edward W Brady, it cost £90,000 and could also seat 800 parishioners. It too was opened by Archbishop Ryan. Identical in design – modern, but Gothic-inspired – the churches had two sloping roofs, one higher and one lower, which meet in a high-level window running the entire length of the church, giving the interiors an unusually high degree of natural light. The design of the church wasn't to everyone's taste, and some of the parishioners humorously labelled it 'the Ball Alley'.

At the opening of St Aengus's Church, Archbishop Ryan was greeted by a young and committed Father Ben Moran OP. To this day, the community of St Aengus's remains well served by both. But only the church has a northside twin!

Church of St Martin de Porres, Oldbawn

The Church of St Martin de Porres was constructed close to the ancient site of Oldbawn House, on lands walked by Archdeacon Bulkeley back in the 1640s. Serving the Aylesbury, Oldbawn and Watergate estates, it was built in only eleven months at a cost of £121,000, and was blessed and officially opened in December 1976. The Dominicans Reverend Basil Turner OP, Curate, and Reverend Eugene Delahunt OP were assigned to the church, in the Parish of St Mary's. The Church of St Martin could seat 800 parishioners.

Following the death of Father Turner the following year, the former national school in Tallaght village, opened in 1930, was renamed St Basil's Training Centre in his memory, and he is remembered by a plaque on the wall there. The building is now a training centre for the Traveller community.

In March 1983, the three 'Dominican churches' of St Martin's, St Aengus's and St Dominic's became independent religious communities, no longer subject to the Prior of St Mary's (the Priory), and in July 1985, the three became independent parishes for the first time.

In 1999, the Parish of Oldbawn (St Martin's) was returned to the care of the Diocese, though the name 'St Martin De Porres' leaves the Dominican imprint on the church.

Church of St Kevin, Kilnamanagh

St Kevin's in Kilnamanagh, serving Greenhills, Ballymount and Kilnamanagh itself, was blessed in September 1978 and could seat 700 parishioners. It cost £140,000. The Very Reverend Donal O Scannaill PP and Reverend J O'Hanratty CC would minister to the faithful of Kilnamanagh. The area had a long association with St Kevin, and a holy well there retains his name.

Dominican archivist Father Hugh Fenning OP noted an unusual sequence of events in relation to the development of St Kevin's:

> Kilnamanagh was hived off as an independent parish in 1974. [*Prior to this the Dominicans of St Mary's had ministered to the new housing estates.*] When the first secular parish priest of Kilnamanagh was being inducted in 1974, the ceremony had to be held in St Mary's [Priory]. On formally giving him the key of his Parish church, the presiding prelate apologised for not being able to also give him a church door to open. Pending the building of Kilnamanagh Church, the Parish Priest used to say midday Sunday mass at St Mary's, after which he performed marriages and baptisms for his parishioners.

This continued until the Church of St Kevin was opened in 1978.

Church of St Killian, Belgard

Located between Tallaght and Clondalkin, the foundation stone of the Church of St Killian was laid by Most Reverend Dr Ryan in March 1982. It cost an eye-watering £280,000, arguably making it the most expensive church in Tallaght's long ecclesiastical history. It would also be one of the largest, capable of seating 1000 mass goers. It replaced a temporary church that had served the residents of the Castleview and Belgard areas. The Church of St Killian took just nine months to build.

The average cost of constructing a new church in 1974 was approximately £90,000. The cost of church construction in the Dublin Diocese tripled between the years 1974 and 1984, giving rise to a temporary embargo on the construction of new churches in 1983 and 1984.

A Ramble About Tallaght

Church of the Sacred Heart, Killinarden

A week before the official opening of the Church of the Sacred Heart in Killinarden in December 1989, something of a mystery emerged on the Father Michael Cleary Radio Show on 98FM. A female parishioner in Ballyfermot declared on live radio that the pews in her church in Ballyfermot had gone missing, and she demanded that Father Michael Cleary get to the bottom of the mystery.

A week later, at the opening ceremony in Killinarden, Father Sheehan MSC PP announced that there was no mystery. He informed the gathering that they were sitting on them!

December 1989 saw the Church of the Sacred Heart in Killinarden officially opened by Archbishop of Dublin the Most Reverend Dr Desmond Connell. Twenty years after the extension to St Mary's Priory in the village was opened, the opening of the Sacred Heart would perhaps mark a turning point in Tallaght's ecclesiastical history, at least for the time being. The Sacred Heart Missionary Congregation had taken over the parish five years earlier.

Before the opening ceremony, Archbishop Connell was entertained by the Sacred Heart Twirlettes, among them Natasha Dunne, Lisa Sheridan, Audrey Whitehall and Mandy Warner. Not to be outdone, Donna Gallagher and Pamela Byrne represented the Marie Carron School of Dancing, much to the amusement of His Grace.

The Church in Killinarden inherited Ballyfermot's well-worn pews. The Parish of the Sacred Heart was 'twinned' with Booterstown. Not quite identical!

Father Patrick Sheehan MSC would take over duties as Parish Priest, supported by curates Father John Maguire MSC and Father Kieran Burke MSC. Killinarden Parish had been established in 1977 and dedicated to the Sacred Heart. By 1989, Killinarden had a population of almost 3800 souls.

The Parish had previously been served by a prefabricated church building. After the opening of the new church, the prefab became home to A Community Together (ACT), a community group seeking to promote enterprise, trade and employment. The group, established with the support of the Society of Saint Vincent de Paul, had previously been based at 80 Killinarden Heights.

Traders and the temple

In 1994, it was announced that a bookmaker's in the four-year-old Square Town Centre, Early Bird Racing, was to be converted into a Catholic chapel. On 30 March the following year, the £60,000 Holy Family Oratory was opened on Level One of the complex. Jointly funded by ten neighbouring parishes, six noontime masses were scheduled a week, preceded by confessions. Mass on Sundays and holy days was not scheduled, as it would be in competition with the primary churches in the area.

The 70-seater Oratory was expected to service both staff and shoppers. In the previous December alone, 1.2 million shoppers had passed through the Town Centre. Father John Deasy, the Parish Priest of Springfield and driving force behind the initiative, explained the rationale behind the outreach: 'In an increasingly secular world, the idea was to branch out into the market place.'

The Stations of the Cross on the wall, of sparse design on burnt ash, were by Maria Wallace, an artist and writer originally from Catalonia (Wallace went on to win a Hennessy Literary Award, for Best Emerging Poetry). After mass or confession, the faithful could pop next door to the newly opened tanning parlour, where they could enjoy the new six-minute Honey-Tanning System – a one-stop shop for body and soul.

By 1999, the Oratory was struggling to remain financially afloat. Rent on the premises was £500 a week. Father Joe Cullen OP suggested The Square might gift the Oratory to the people of Tallaght as part of the impending Millenium celebration. It wasn't to be and in November 2005, after a significant rent hike, the Diocese was called in to support the ongoing rental of the unit. Extraordinarily, the Oratory continued on for another seventeen years, before finally closing its doors on 31 March 2022. Rising costs, dwindling numbers attending and the Covid-19 pandemic finally brought an end to the Holy Family Oratory of The Square, Tallaght.

The Square shopping centre, opened in 1990.

A Ramble About Tallaght

Unemployment in Tallaght

Between 1971 and 1984, the population of Tallaght skyrocketed, from 6000 to 60,000 people. Forty-two percent of the population was under fifteen years of age and in some of the newer neighbourhoods, 50% were under the age of ten years. By 1983, there were 4000 people queuing to sign on for unemployment benefit in Tallaght every week.

And it was about to get worse. By 1986, one in fourteen of all young unemployed people in the Republic of Ireland lived in Tallaght. The youth population had grown 213% in the previous five years, and 5000 school leavers in Tallaght were projected to enter the labour market over the following six years. The youth population had increased beyond the capacity of existing training facilities. The rate of unemployment had increased at three times the national average and the concentration of unemployment in certain neighbourhoods had a confounding effect – up to 70% in Killinarden, Jobstown, Brookfield and Fettercairn. Unemployment in west Tallaght was reported to be over 70% in 1985. Prospects were grim.

'Into the West', Cushlawn, 1994.

The Coming of Age of Tallaght New Town

Tallaght Youth at Avonbeg Flats.

To make matters worse, Tallaght did not yet have a labour exchange, or dole office. People had to sign on at the local Garda station and then go to the post office. The Garda station in question was no longer fit for purpose, so a caravan was brought onto the grounds to provide a temporary facility. In 1982, Tallaght Community Council sought assurances from public representatives that a temporary labour exchange would be secured, so that the unemployed of the area wouldn't need to queue at the Garda station. When the Garda station could no longer cope with the rising numbers, new claimants in Tallaght were required to sign on in Werburgh Street Employment Exchange in Dublin city.

Nor was there a 'jobs centre'. In 1983, the people of Tallaght picketed the Department of Social Welfare on Pearse Street in Dublin city, demanding a labour exchange and a jobs centre. By the mid-1980s, housing, schools and churches had come to Tallaght, but not much else.

In August 1985, a new 'Temporary Employment Exchange' was finally opened in West Park, Tallaght village. It was, initially, for woman only, designed to cater for 1000 claimants per week. There were 4000 people in Tallaght 'on the labour'. But now, at least the women of Tallaght no longer needed to go into Werburgh Street to sign on. It was progress of sorts.

A Ramble About Tallaght

Tallaght Institute of Technology

In 1979, a Higher Education Authority report recommended that a third-level Regional Technical College (RTC) should be built in Tallaght by 1985. Tallaght was one of the fastest-growing urban conurbations in Western Europe, and had one of the youngest population profiles in Ireland. In the following years, the Department of Education entered discussions with the Dominican Order in Tallaght around the possibility of acquiring a site in Tallaght on which to develop a third-level institution.

In 1984, Minister for Education Gemma Hussey stated that her department was actively engaged in the planning of RTCs in both Tallaght and Blanchardstown. The following year, she announced a major building project – a third-level college for Tallaght to provide 1200 student places at a capital cost of £13 million. Two years later, in May 1987, shortly before the general election, new Minister for Education Mary O'Rourke TD told Dáil Éireann that 'detailed architectural planning is being undertaken' for the new college for Tallaght.

Later that year – after the general election – the Department of Education revealed it had scrapped plans for a college in Tallaght. Minister O'Rourke announced that in examining the

Tallaght Regional Technical College, 1995.

estimates for Budget 1988, it was envisaged that additional capacity and college places in the third-level sector could be created nationally in existing colleges, by reducing the length of academic courses – four-year degree courses would be reduced to three years. In that context, a decision to proceed with the Tallaght College was 'deferred'. It was a blow for the town. A failure to proceed would leave Tallaght short not just of a third-level institution, but also of the prospect of two years of construction jobs on a significant capital project in the area.

In June 1989, a full ten years after the HEA recommendation and four years after it should have opened, the final go-ahead was approved by Minister for Education, Mary O'Rourke TD. The estimated cost of construction had risen from £13m in 1984 to £15m in 1989. Over 50% of the funding would now come from the European Community (EC). There were an estimated 17,000 pupils in 26 post-primary schools in the catchment area. European Social Fund grants would mean students of the new college wouldn't have to pay fees and those who lived more than fifteen miles away would get a maintenance allowance. Nobody in Tallaght lived fifteen miles away!

Minister O'Rourke promised that the college would open its doors for the first intake of students in September 1991. It was an ambitious timescale – 27 months to complete a £15m capital project, yet to be put out to tender; a project that only twelve months earlier had been scrapped.

The Dominican Order had agreed to sell a 25-acre site to the Department of Education, for below market value, back in 1981.

In September 1989, it was announced that Ireland would receive almost £2.82 billion in financial aid from the EU by the end of 1993. The funding was geared to help less prosperous countries prepare for the total opening of national frontiers in January 1993. The country would also benefit from a £1.3 billion reserve fund for special community projects. Altogether Ireland would receive approximately £4 billion over the following four years. Among the projects to benefit from the funding was Tallaght Regional Technical College. This commitment was enough to make the eventual development of a college in Tallaght a reality.

Later in 1989, when the Department was putting the final touches to a planning application for the college, the estimated cost of the project had risen to £17 million. Thirteen years after the HEA had first recommended it, and seven years later then the recommended timeframe, Tallaght Institute of Technology finally opened its doors in September 1992.

Patsy Walsh, fishmonger, trading beside the Charlie O'Toole Bridge.

Overground – the Charlie O'Toole Bridge

On 3 October 1978, a twelve-year-old boy from Maelruain's Park, Aidan Tully, was attempting to cross the Tallaght Bypass opposite the H Williams supermarket, when he was struck by a car and died. He had been involved in an accident only two weeks earlier, having been struck by a car close to his home. He had received several stitches to the head that day, but had luckily escaped without more serious injury.

This was the second tragedy to hit the family in a year. His mother had died of an illness the previous January. Eighteen months earlier, Local Fine Gael TD Larry Mc Mahon had highlighted the urgent need for a pedestrian bridge at the very spot the young boy had been struck.

Wooden planks had been laid by locals across the Whitestown stream, which ran along the Tallaght Bypass opposite the supermarket, between St Dominic's and the village. People could thus cross the stream to access the Bypass, but not cross the busy main road.

On 10 October, one week after the boy's death, Dublin County Council's Mid-west Committee was told that a pedestrian bridge over the Bypass was to be completed as a matter of urgency.

The Coming of Age of Tallaght New Town

Above: The recently constructed Civic Offices.
Below: Boyzone singing in front of an ecstatic crowd at Tallaght.

Seven months after the tragic and needless death of Aidan Tully, on 24 May 1979, a £90,000 pedestrian bridge was officially opened there. The following year, the bridge was named the Charlie O'Toole Bridge, after the first director of the Tallaght Welfare Society, who had died the previous June. (A wing of Tallaght University Hospital is now also called after Charlie O'Toole.)

The 200-metre bridge connected Tallaght village with St Dominic's, Avonbeg, Seskin View and Millbrook Lawns. The bridge has been replaced with a more accessible contemporary bridge in recent years. The commemorative stone monument to Charlie O'Toole, erected at the original bridge in 1980, appears to have been removed when the bridge was being replaced. It has not been reinstated, and must be unnecessarily taking up space in SDCC's Roads or Parks depot.

Underground – the underpass at Glenview

In the 1970s, a pedestrian underpass was planned and was partially constructed close to the junction of Avonmore Road and the Bypass, leading to Glenview. In 1983, the underpass was abandoned after local opposition, at considerable cost to the Council. Pedestrian traffic lights were installed there instead. For a couple of years in the early 1980s, the 'unofficial underpass' was still accessible and was frequently used by teenagers for social and anti-social behaviour! And BMX bandits! There may still be a substantial subterranean tunnel, long forgotten, under the Tallaght Bypass at Glenview.

Tallaght and District Credit Union

Tallaght and District Credit Union was founded in the autumn of 1968 by the Prior of the Dominican Fathers. Father Paul Hynes appointed Father Pius Doherty to get volunteers to set up a credit union for the Tallaght area. William Kennedy of Greenhills Cottages was the first Chairman.

Father Hynes was also instrumental in the establishment of Tallaght Welfare Society. A public park behind Bancroft estate, on land sold by the Dominicans to the County Council was officially named Father Paul Hynes Park. The name appears to have fallen out of use, either by design or administrative neglect. Father Hynes was remembered in the community as a charismatic, effective and committed community leader and organiser.

From a Settlement to a City – A Conclusion of Sorts

On New Year's Day in the year 2000, in the very early hours of the morning, I found myself walking home from Dublin city centre. I made my way towards Tallaght from Templeogue along the N81, the Tallaght Bypass. As the Tallaght of a new millennium stretched out west in the distance before me, it seemed an appropriate place in which to reflect on the development of my hometown.

The walk from the city to Templeogue had been a sobering one, a walk I had taken many times before. The skyline of Tallaght came into view as I passed the remains of Bella-Vista Mill and approached Glenview Roundabout. I could take a right turn to the old Balrothery road, following in the footsteps of the 'bold Fenian men' of 1867 for Tallaght Hill. Just like them, I was on shanks' mare.

I ruminated on the extraordinary: that 100 years earlier, when Tallaght had a population of 300 people, one could get a tram from Terenure to Blessington, but in the year 2000, when Tallaght had a population of almost 60,000, it was difficult even to get a taxi from Templeogue to Tallaght. It would be another five years before a tram would again visit the town. After 77 years of Irish independence, and 30 years after a plan for the development of Tallaght as a new town had been embraced, the town arguably had a less effective public transport infrastructure than that enjoyed by wheelwrights and blacksmiths, saddle makers and gravel men 100 years before.

A Ramble About Tallaght

Before and after: Aerial photographs from 1968 and more recently of development around Dodder Valley Park.

I kept to the 'new' road, the N81, and cast an eye over Bolbrook Lodge, the old Keating homestead – that young communist and TD, who had sold development land for £60,000 for housing in 1968. A good-quality new home then cost £4,000. The man did well, I thought – for a communist.

It is fair to say that the first generation born in Tallaght New Town were to some degree shortchanged. Unnecessary hardships were imposed on the community by poor planning and vested interests. Hardship was nothing new to Tallaght. If anyone was unsure of this, they simply had to talk to people who grew up here in the 1930s and 1940s. Poverty was nothing new. Unemployment was nothing new. A lack of facilities was nothing new. Families in Tallaght had, due to a shortage of housing in the 1940s, found temporary accommodation in Tin Town – old tram sheds and wagons set up on the banks of the Dodder in Bohernabreena. They had no electricity and no running water. Labourers in the sandpits and quarries around Tallaght routinely had their working lives, or indeed their lives entirely, cut short by occupational accidents. The tramline had come to Tallaght in 1888 at great expense – the lives of those who fell under its progress.

I thought now of the boys I had known that had never got to grow up, never got to see the Tallaght of a new millennium – boys of my own generation that had been struck down by 'progress'. Little David Lamb was only thirteen years old when he was mown down in a hit-and-run at the Oldbawn Crossroads in 1987. He had just finished his paper round. He had played football with Millmount United. Dave had previously made a remarkable recovery following an accident seven years earlier. The car that struck Dave was found burnt out in Old Court later that evening. It had no registration plate and no tax.

Edward Connors of Colbert's Fort was charged a week later with dangerous driving causing a death, leaving the scene of a crime and failing to report an accident to the Gardaí. He was disqualified from holding a driver's licence for ten years. Four years later, in September 1991, Connors was again charged with driving without a licence and insurance. He pleaded guilty. In the following years, he was charged with further offenses.

Every Sunday morning, for some years after David's death, I watched from afar as David's grief-stricken parents Gerry and Marie prayed at mass in St Dominic's Church, their faces a study of loss and bewilderment. I thought of David's mischievous grin and golden cheeks. We had played together on rope swings from one of the last great oak trees along the banks of the Dodder.

Eight weeks after David's death, another school pal, little Robbie Kelly from St Maelruain's Park, died when he was struck by a car at the junction of Oldbawn Road and the Bypass. He was fifteen years old, cycling home. I remembered his dark and furrowed brow, how he bit his bottom lip as he concentrated on a project in Mr Hughes's Tech-Drawing class. We had sat together in the recently opened Firhouse Community College.

For a young boy, Tallaght – a modern new town – had sometimes felt like the Wild West.

Anti-social behaviour, crime rates, drug use and joy riding all appeared to be significantly higher in Tallaght in the 1980s than the national average, as of course were unemployment and early school leaving. The medium-term prospects for young men and teenage boys in Tallaght appeared to be something of a concern for policy makers, economists and sociologists.

The overriding concern for most young men and teenage boys in Tallaght was how to get from A to B without being fleeced by modern-day highwaymen – older hoodlums, the 'giz ur odds' or 'giza smoke' boys that seemed to loiter in the shade of every laneway. Like the corner boys of the 1930s – the Firhouse Rowdies – they made difficult times even more challenging for the community. It turned out that the Rowdies had had grandkids.

A Ramble About Tallaght

But tonight, this night, there were no highwaymen. There were no corner boys. There were no rowdies. The roads were silent and the streets empty. An aeroplane flew overhead, silently tracing a distant arc – a shooting star in slow motion. Some had expected them to fall from the sky this night. The Y2K computer bug would end all of humanity, they said. Computers wouldn't recognise the year 2000, and nuclear reactors would melt down. The sky would fall in.

With every step as I advanced, I thought of the milestones in Tallaght's progress to get to this point, this end of an era: The arrival of St Maelruain about AD 774; the building of Tallaght Castle, the Archbishop's Palace; the rebuilding of St Maelruain's Church in 1829; the first tram arriving in 1888; the arrival of Urney Chocolates in 1924, Red Breast Preserves in 1949, Telectron in 1962; the building of housing estates – Newtown, Maelruain's or 'Mellors Park', Poynton's Estate, Bancroft – all before my time.

In my first eighteen years, from 1972, little seemed to have happened in Tallaght. The old Tallaght Town Centre had opened in 1977 and then swiftly declined. The Charlie O'Toole Bridge was a welcome development in 1979. We didn't need 'wellies' to get to the village. The Tallaght

Bypass, on which I now walked, had opened fully and finally without any great fanfare. A new Garda station had opened in 1987 at a cost of £900,000 – 'Southfork', we called it. That needed to be none of my concern – I should never see the inside of it, I had been forewarned by my parents. There were layoffs and strikes, redundancies and closures. Packard Electric was to pull out. Telectron had closed. Another young lad was struck by a car. No news was good news.

But then something extraordinary happened. As if eighteen years of possibility and potential burst forth, a great wave of development washed over Tallaght, transforming not so much its landscape as its social infrastructure. The opening of The Square in 1990, the Village Green in 1991, the Regional Technical College in 1992, the Civic Offices and new County Library in 1994, and Tallaght University Hospital in 1998 didn't just bring essential services to the community. Their development provided important capital building projects to the town throughout the 1990s. The opening of the new South Dublin County Council Civic Offices in 1994, symbolically at least, brought local government to where the citizens it serves could see it.

The opening of all of these services, public and private, created thousands of new jobs, full-time and part-time, permanent and temporary. Two new hotels were built – the Abberley Court (1995) and the Plaza (1998). We were told tourists from Iceland were coming to Tallaght to do their shopping in The Square! The Tour de France passed through Tallaght in 1998.

Unemployment figures gradually declined. School retention gradually increased. Third-level access gradually improved. Household income increased in line with local employment figures. People were spending locally, supporting local enterprise, creating a virtuous economic cycle. A sense of optimism and opportunity incrementally eroded what had for many years beset the town – a feeling of stasis, of squandered potential and, for some, hopelessness.

I reflected on the early 1980s, when virtually anything could be bought in Tallaght from the back of a van. Milk and coal were of course standard. But on any given week, we could buy eggs, bread, fruit and vegetables and meat from the half-dozen or so vans that did the rounds of the neighbourhood. Even dry cleaning could by deposited with the mobile laundry service. A mobile video library briefly rented Betamax tapes, door to door. Single cigarettes could be purchased from 'Pat the ice cream man'. He would oblige you with a safety match and a 'bit of brown' on which to strike it.

A Ramble About Tallaght

On the horizon now was a city about to awaken to a new millennium. Standing erect, its citizens moulding and shaping its form, working its clay into new shapes. Home to 60,000 souls, it struck me that there might just be 60,000 Tallaghts.

Mine had been born of legend and myth, a place of the Greek and a place of the Christian; a place writing its own questionable history, of pestilence and ritual, of hunger and plenty; a place of Lancelot Bulkeley, of palaces and baronets and knights. My Tallaght was home to archbishop and beggar and from its quill came a litany of saints and pagan lore.

The silhouette of Ballymorefin lay crisp in the moonlight – Tír na nÓg, a land of youth. At the end of the Bypass now stood Oz, El Dorado, Shangri-La, a mythical place of my own making, of our own making; a place in which we could all write our own histories and maybe, just maybe, unearth the unimaginable.

The sun setting over the pre-Norman cross known to locals as Moll Rooney's Loaf and Griddle.

Works Consulted and Bibliography

Bagnall, Sean, 2008, *Tallaght, 1835–50: A Rural Place*, Four Courts Press.

Ball, EF, 1906 (reprint 1979), *A History of the County Dublin*, 6 vols, Dublin: Gill and Macmillan.

Butler, Richard J, 2020, *Building the Irish Courthouse and Prison: A political history, 1750–1850*, Cork: Cork University Press.

Calamy, Edmund, 1830, *An Historical Account of My Own Life*, London: Henry Colburn and Richard Bentley.

Connolly, S, 'The "Blessed Turf": Cholera and Popular Panic in Ireland, June 1832', *Irish Historical Studies*, Vol. 23, No. 91 (May 1983), pp. 214–32, Cambridge University Press.

D'Alton, John, 1838, *History of the County of Dublin*, Hodges & Smith.

D'Alton, John, *Memoirs of the Archbishops of Dublin*, Hodges & Smith.

Davenport Hill, 'Journal of a third visit to the convict-gaols, refuges, and reformatories of Dublin and its neighbourhood', 1865: LSE Selected Pamphlets.

Domville Handcock, W, 1899, *The History and Antiquities of Tallaght in the County of Dublin*, Dublin: Hodges Figgis.

Fenning, Father Hugh, 2006. *The Dominicans in Tallaght* (privately published).

Fitzpatrick, William J, 1894, *The Life of the Very Rev. Fr. Thomas N. Burke OP* (Vols. I and II), London: Kegan Paul, Trench, Trubner & Co.

Harbison, Peter, 2005, *Cooper's Ireland*, O'Brien Press.

Head SJ, Michael, and Healy SJ, Gerard, 1999, *More Than a School: A History of St Patrick's College, East Melbourne 1854–1969*, Victoria, Australia: Eldon Hogan Trust and Jesuit Publications.

Healy, Patrick, 2004, *All Roads Lead to Tallaght*, South Dublin County Library.

Hennig, J, 'The Feast of the Blessed Virgin in the Ancient Irish Church', *The Irish Ecclesiastical Record 81* (1954) 161–71, p.162.

Herity MRIA, Michael (ed), 2001, *Ordnance Survey Letter Dublin*, Dublin: Four Masters Press.

Hone, Joseph, Craig, Maurice, Fewer and Michael, 2002, *The New Neighbourhood of Dublin*, A & A Farmer.

Hussey De Burgh, UH, 1878, 'The landowners of Ireland: An alphabetical list of the owners of estates of 500 acres or £500 valuation and upwards in Ireland, with the acreage and valuation in each county …'

Leask, HG, 'House at Oldbawn', 1913, *The Journal of the Royal Society of Antiquaries of Ireland*, sixth series, Vol. 3, No. 4, Dublin.

Leet, Ambrose, '*A directory to the market towns, villages, gentlemen's seats, and other noted places in Ireland ... to which is added a general index of persons names ... together with lists of the post towns and present rates of postage throughout the empire c.1*', 1814 (Kiltalown James Jackson).

Lentaigne, J, 'On Some Portions of a Skeleton, an Urn, and Fragment of Another, Found in the Townland of Kiltalown', *Proceedings of the Royal Irish Academy*, Vol. 4 (1847–50), RIA.

Little, Dr George, 1943, *Malachi Horan Remembers*, Old Dublin Society.

Local and Personal Laws 1864, Ch. 261/300 = 27/28 Vic, 1864: Great Britain.

Longfield, TH, 'Note on Some Cinerary Urns Found at Tallaght, County of Dublin', *Proceedings of the Royal Irish Academy, Vol. 2* (1891–93), pp. 400–1, RIA.

MacLaran, A, and Punch, M, 'Tallaght: The planning and development of an Irish new town', Centre for Urban and Regional Studies, Trinity College Dublin, and the Faculty of the Built Environment, Dublin Institute of Technology, Bolton Street, *Journal of Irish Urban Studies, Vol.3 (Issue 1)* (2004), pp. 17–39.

Maloney, Eamonn, 2010, Tallaght: *A Place With History* (self-published).

Martin, Violet & Liam, 1995, *Cameos of Tallaght & its Environs*, The Cobblestone Press.

McGrath, M, *Cinnlae Amhlaoibh Uí Shúileabháin* ('The Diary of Humphrey O'Sullivan'), ed. Irish Texts Society (4 vols., London, 1928–31), iii, 154.

McNally, Mary, 1999, *South County Scrapbook*, Tallaght Historical Society.

Mooney, Pearse, 1992, *Tallaght History and Legend – Illustrated* (self-published).

Murphy, É, *A Glorious Extravaganza: The History of Monkstown Parish Church* (2003), Wordwell, Bray, Co. Wicklow.

Ní Mharcaigh, M, 'The Medieval Parish Churches of South-West County Dublin', *Proceedings of the Royal Irish Academy: Archaeology, Culture, History, Literature, Vol. 97C, No. 5* (1997), pp. 245–96.

Nooij, Lars B, 'Made in Tallaght: An investigation of the origins of the early medieval Irish manuscript known as the Stowe Missal', online illustrated talk, Department of Early Irish Studies, Maynooth University. (youtube.com/watch?v=_V_P282xXQk&ab_channel=TheRoyalIrishAcademy)

Perris, Albert, 1999, *Since Adam Was a Boy*, Tallaght Welfare Society.

Plunkett, GT, 'On a Cist and Urns Found at Greenhills, Tallaght, County Dublin', *Proceedings of the Royal Irish Academy, Vol. 5* (1898–1900), pp. 338–47, RIA.

Royal Irish Academy, *Dictionary of Irish Biography*, www.dib.ie, RIA.

Royal Irish Academy, 1850, *Proceedings of the Royal Irish Academy v.4 1847–50*, RIA.

Shearman, John Francis, 'The Celtic Races of Great and Lesser Britain, or Armorica, Deduced from the Ancient Gael of Ireland. Illustrated by Pedigrees and Genealogies', *The Journal of the Royal Historical and Archaeological Association of Ireland, Fourth Series, Vol. 5, No. 46* (April 1881), pp. 460–81, Royal Society of Antiquaries of Ireland.

St John Joyce, W, 1912, *The Neighbourhood of Dublin*, MH Gill & Son.

Swan, L; Nolan, W; Hegarty, Father B; et al, 1982, Tallaght: A resource book for teachers, Blackrock Teachers' Centre.

Various contributors, 1992, *Knocklyon, Past and Present*, ICA.

Webb, Alfred, 1878, *A Compendium of Irish Biography*.

Wilde, William, *Memoir of Gabriel Berenger and his Labours in the Cause of Irish Art and Antiquities, from 1760 to 1780*.

For information on the Martyrology of Tallaght and the Martyrology of Óengus, I have drawn extensively on the numerous works and insights of Dr Pádraig Ó Riain.

TALLAGHT and District

COOKSTOWN

site of Tallaght Aerodrome and 'The Camp'

site of Urney Chocolates

WHITEHALL

FETTERCAIRN — Fettercairn House

JOBSTOWN

SPRINGFIELD

N81

Brookfield House

Jobstown Inn and tram office

WHITESTOWN

Kiltalown House

Killinarden House

KILTALOWN

KILLINARDEN

Tallaght Hill